Cover Illustrations
Front, Boeing P-12E at United States Air Force Museum
Back (upper), Saturn V at Lyndon B. Johnson Space Center
Back (center), U.S. Army Aviation Museum
Back (lower), Grumman F-14 Tomcat at National Museum of Naval Aviation

Photograph Acknowledgements
Front cover, courtesy United States Air Force Museum
Back cover (upper), courtesy National Aeronautics and Space Administration
Page 1, courtesy National Air and Space Museum
Page 81, courtesy National Air and Space Museum
Page 95, courtesy National Aeronautics and Space Administration
Page 192, courtesy National Park Service
Page 231, courtesy Confederate Air Force Museum
Page 244, courtesy National Aeronautics and Space Administration
Page 275, courtesy Museum of Flight

KITTY HAWK
TO NASA

A Guide To U.S. Air & Space Museums And Exhibits

Michael Morlan

From the **American Travel Themes** series

BON A TIRER
publishing

Kitty Hawk To NASA
A Guide To U.S. Air & Space
Museums And Exhibits

Copyright © 1991 Michael Morlan

All Photographs Copyright © 1991
Michael Morlan, unless noted in
Photograph Acknowledgements, page 2.

ISBN: 1-878446-04-5

Catalog number A&S-1
JE-SA-CM

Printed in the U.S.A.
Printed on acid-free paper

First Edition
10 9 8 7 6 5 4 3 2 1

From the **American Travel Themes** series

BON A TIRER
publishing

PO Box 3480
Shawnee, KS 66203
913-236-4828

Distributed to the book trade by:
Login Publishers Consortium/Chicago

Publisher: Joseph E. Zanatta

Technical Editor: Douglas Morlan
               U.S.A.F. (Ret.)

Acknowledgements

A book of this type is only successful if a
large group of people will contribute to
the project, and fortunately for me, the
expectations were exceeded. My thanks
to the museum curators, public relations
managers and other museum personnel
who responded to my questions and re-
quests for information with unreserved
help and cooperation.

My appreciation to Joe Zanatta for involv-
ing me in this book. My association with
Joe over the last few years has been interesting and productive. His initiative, hard
work and business acumen will serve him
well in future publishing endeavors.

A special thanks to my parents, who
have always provided encouragement and
help with anything I have undertaken.

Table of Contents

Introduction

A trip from Kitty Hawk to NASA is not a "geographical" trip, but one through time and history that permits the traveler to see aviation's evolutionary mileposts, from balloon ascents through winged flight to space exploration.

KITTY HAWK TO NASA is not the usual road map pulled from the glove compartment or desk. And it's not the typical guide book focusing on a geographical area. It's quite specific: *A Guide to U.S. Air & Space Museums and Exhibits.* But for those who enjoy a glimpse of a historically significant airplane, an exotic prototype or an icon of the space race, this guide is hopefully the roadmap to many successful sidetrips and vacations.

CONTENTS

Many museums are miles from towns, shops and other facilities that provide the normal conveniences for travelers. And an appropriate tour may take hours, if not the better portion of a day. This guide attempts to anticipate questions the visitor might have concerning the logistics of a visit. The guide lists museums and exhibits alphabetically by state. The information in each entry provides the following information:

- Mail address; phone number.
- General information about the museum or military installation. This will vary according to the identity of the museum, primarily if it is affiliated with a military base. If the museum is located on or near a military base, information may be provided on the history, current operations and types of aircraft flying from the base.
- Information concerning unique or significant aircraft or spacecraft on display.
- Directions to the museum, generally from the major highways near the museum.
- Admission cost.

- Hours of operation — subject to change for special events and holidays.
- Museum notes — whether aircraft are indoors or outdoors (nice to know if it's cool and rainy outside); whether there is a gift shop and if film can be purchased; whether there is a restaurant nearby; brochure availability.
- List of aircraft and spacecraft — listed by manufacturer, model and popular name. Where applicable, the original manufacturer is listed with the actual manufacturer in parentheses, for instance, Boeing originated the B-17, but they were also built by Douglas and Vega. Popular names are generally those established by the manufacturers and the military and may not agree with the colorful nicknames created by aircrew and maintenance personnel. Italics denote the name of a specific aircraft or spacecraft, i.e. *Enola Gay.* Quotes indicate a code name, such as "Val," or an unofficial, popular name, such as "Huey."

Throughout the book are snippets of facts included in the museum listings as well as in the photograph captions. These are provided as entertaining and educational sidebars for the reader interested in aviation history.

In the back of the book is the Aircraft Locator section that cross-references by page number the aircraft and spacecraft listed in the museum entries. This special index should provide the reader interested in locating specific aircraft or spacecraft with a practical reference tool.

Anyone visiting an aviation museum will likely want to attend an air show. The flying aircraft found in museums are usually flown in air shows, along with aerobatic performers and military demonstration planes. An air show is an entertaining way to spend the day looking at aircraft up close and in action. Following the museum listings is information concerning the Air Force Thunderbirds and Navy Blue Angels, the premier military demonstration teams, and where to write or look for air show schedules.

The information is as accurate as possible at time of publication, but as in other museums, certain pieces may be removed for restoration or returned to a private owner. And some museums will cease operation for various reasons, including a couple that are located on soon-to-be-closed military bases, which are noted when known. If a particular plane or item is of interest, call the museum.

ACCESS FOR THE HANDICAPPED

Efforts to provide detailed information concerning the accommodation of handicapped persons proved impossible to include in useable form. While most museums and exhibits accommodate the handicapped, exactly what constitutes "handicap accessible" remains ill-defined and troublesome for unique facilities such as aviation museums. While accomodations may be made at entrances and restrooms, access to some exhibits and aircraft could prove difficult, if not impossible. For detailed information, contact the museum.

VISITING MILITARY BASES

The operator of a vehicle entering a military base should possess three documents: a driver's license, proof of automobile insurance and the vehicle's registration (all must be current). Virtually all military bases will require that a visitor obtain a pass before entering the base. There may be signs at the gate that direct visitors to park at a visitor's center before proceeding, otherwise, visitors must ask for directions from the military police manning the gate.

Do not hesitate to visit a military base, but keep a couple of things in mind. Most

passes limit a visitor to driving the roads that lead to the museum; a sightseeing tour of the base is generally unauthorized unless approved by proper authority; inquire at visitors center or gate. While on the base vehicles are subject to search. The military police must be notified of any firearms or other weapons before entering the base. Some bases are training facilities and formations of marching troops may be encountered. These formations always have the right-of-way and visitors must heed directions from military personnel.

MUSEUM ETIQUETTE

Here are a few notes for the inexperienced museum visitor. Just as in museums of fine art, the watchword for all visitors is DON'T TOUCH, unless invited. Aircraft look massive and eternal, but the touch of fingers leaves acid on metal surfaces that must be cleaned off, or laboriously polished out if left to corrode. Aircraft are enticing "Jungle Gyms" for youngsters, but they can be a dangerous place to play, with possible injury to children as well as damage to the aircraft. Some museums may restrict smoking because museum hangers may contain aircraft in flying condition with oil and fuel onboard.

AIR SHOW NOTES

For those who have never attended an air show, here are a couple of thoughts for consideration. Large air shows take place on acres of concrete or asphalt that can reach scorching temperatures on a clear, summer day. Don't forget the sunscreen, dress appropriately and drink lots of liquids. Dispose of trash in designated trash receptacles. Wrappers, cups and other debris can be blown long distances at an airfield, and possibly ingested by a jet engine, which may cause expensive internal damage. Pay attention to children and don't allow them to climb or play on the aircraft.

Southern Museum of Flight

4343 73rd Street North, Birmingham, Alabama 35206
(205) 833-8226

Located adjacent to Birmingham Municipal Airport, the Southern Museum of Flight features a variety of unique aircraft. There are several antique airplanes as well as more modern airplanes such as a Rutan VariEze. The VariEze is a homebuilt airplane constructed of composite materials. There is also a Mini-Mac homebuilt powered by a four-cylinder, air-cooled engine derived from the Volkswagen Beetle.

The museum contains an extensive collection of aircraft engines. An early example of aircraft powerplants is the Gnome nine-cylinder engine dating from 1916. Massive engines that powered the huge four-engine transports of the middle 1950s are represented by the Pratt & Whitney 18- and 24-cylinder engines. An 18-cylinder Wright radial engine is cutaway to show the inner workings of the engine.

DIRECTIONS TO MUSEUM: From I-20/59 take exit 129 onto Airport Blvd. and follow signs.

ADMISSION COST: Adults $2.00; children 1st grade through college age $1.00; preschool age free. Closed major holidays.

HOURS OF OPERATION: Open Tuesday-Saturday 9am-5pm; Sunday 1-5pm.

MUSEUM NOTES: Display aircraft are inside except for a F4 Phantom on a pedestal outside. There is a restaurant nearby. Film is not available at the museum.

A brochure is available.

Built to fill a market that never materialized, Republic constructed over 1,000 Seabees after World War II in hopes that returning GIs were eager future pilots. After two years production, construction of the amphibians ceased.

The Alexander Eaglerock was built in 1928 and cost $2,475. Maximum speed was 100 mph while cruise speed was 85 mph. The plane could fly 395 miles before refueling and reach a maximum altitude of 10,200 feet.

Display Aircraft

MANUFACTURER	MODEL	POPULAR NAME
Aeronca	11AC	Chief
Alexander	Eaglerock	
Bushby	Mustang II	
Curtiss Pusher (replica)	D-5	
Fairchild	PT-19	Cornell
Forney	F-1	Ercoupe
Great Lakes	2-T-1	
Huff-Daland		
McDonnell	F-4	Phantom II
Mini-Mac		
Mitchell	Wing	
Monerai		
Mooney	M-18	Mite
North American	AT-6	Texan
Pitts	S-1	
Republic	RC3	Seabee
Rotec	Ralley	
Rutan	VariEze	
Stinson	10A	
Stinson	SR-5	

U.S. Army Aviation Museum

P.O. Box 610, Fort Rucker, Alabama 36362
(205) 255-4507

Fort Rucker, Alabama, is home for Army aviation. Originally based at Fort Sill, Oklahoma, the Army Aviation Center moved to Fort Rucker in 1955 to accomodate the greater role of aviation in Army operations. The initial experimental use of airplanes and helicopters gradually changed to multipurpose use during World War II and the Korean War. As the capabilities of airplanes and helicopters increased and Army commanders understood and used aviation to their advantage, Army aviation expanded into a separate and distinct branch of the Army. Army aviators fly missions for observation, artillery spotting, transport, medical evacuation, aerial photography and aerial fire support.

The museum collection comprises both helicopters and fixed-wing aircraft. Here is one of the finest collections of helicopters in the world. With a collection as extensive as this, it's possible to trace the evolution of the helicopter. An example of a Sikorsky R4-B (the first military production helicopter) appears benignly simple when compared with

The Hughes AH-64 Apache is the Army's large, anti-tank attack helicopter. Although Hughes won the contract in 1976, continuous development deferred authorization for production until 1982. Included among the sophisticated equipment onboard the Apache is a 30 mm chain gun under the fuselage nose. The gun is electronically linked to the gunner's helmet. Using an aiming device attached to his helmet, the gunner points the gun by turning his head and looking at the object he wants to shoot.

In the center of the museum's main display area is an exhibit depicting troops disembarking from a "Huey." The Bell UH-1 was the Army's first turbine-powered aircraft. Later variations remain in service with the Army and National Guard. Maximum speed is 138 mph and maximum operating ceiling is 17,700 feet. The UH-1 has proven successful in the export market with the helicopter operating in approximately 40 countries.

the museum's Hughes AH-64 Apache, one of the most sophisticated and lethal aircraft in the world.

DIRECTIONS TO MUSEUM: The musem is located just inside the south entrance of Fort Rucker. Stay to the left when entering Fort Rucker from Daleville (there is no gate) and the museum will be on the left. Fort Rucker is adjacent to Daleville which is approximately 25 miles west of Dothan. Fort Rucker can also be entered from the north on Hwy. 249 at Ozark.

ADMISSION COST: Free.

HOURS OF OPERATION: Open daily 9am-4pm. Closed New Year's Eve, New Year's Day, Thanksgiving, Christmas Eve and Christmas Day.

MUSEUM NOTES: Display aircraft are located inside and outside. There are restau-

The H-13 entered the Army inventory in 1946 and was noteworthy for its use during the Korean War as a medevac and observation helicopter. The helicopter was highly visible in the popular MASH television series. The civilian version model 47 was the first helicopter to gain certification for general use and performed jobs ranging from police surveillance to agricultural spraying. Over 5,000 were produced collectively in the United States, Japan and Italy.

rants located near Fort Rucker. Film can be purchased at the gift shop.

A brochure is available.

Display Aircraft

MANUFACTURER	MODEL	POPULAR NAME
Aeronca	L-16A	Champ
American	XH-26A	Jet Jeep
Beech	U-8	Seminole
Bell	207	Sioux Scout
Bell	AH-1G	Cobra
Bell	OH-13	Sioux
Bell	OH-58A	Kiowa
Bell	UH-1	Iroquois "Huey"
Boeing-Vertol	CH-47A	Chinook
Boeing-Vertol	XCH-62	HLH

The Sikorsky H-19 was the first helicopter to prove the multi-faceted capabilities of the military helicopter. The H-19 first saw service during the Korean War and entered service in all U.S. military branches. The helicopter was the first to be used for moving large bodies of troops for air assault, a manuever latered refined in Vietnam. The Navy pioneered submarine detection from helicopters using the Navy version, and the Air Force flew H-19s extensively for many years to rescue downed pilots. Over 1,200 were produced, with some updated later by replacing the original piston engine with a turbine engine.

Cessna	LC-126	
Curtiss-Wright	VZ-7AP	Aerial Jeep
de Havilland	U-1A	Otter
de Havilland	U-6A	Beaver
de Havilland	YC-7A	Caribou
Del Mar	DH-1A	Whirlymite
Grumman	OV-1	Mohawk
Hiller	H-23	Raven
Hiller	OH-23	Raven
Hiller	ROE-1	Rotocycle
Hiller	YH-32	Hornet
Hughes	OH-6A	Cayuse
Hughes	TH-55A	Osage
Hughes	YAH-64A	Apache

Lockheed	AH-56A	Cheyenne
Lockheed	YO-3A	Silent One
North American	L-17A	Navion
Piasecki	CH-21C	Shawnee
Piasecki	H-25A	Army Mule
Sikorsky	CH-34A	Chocktaw
Sikorsky	CH-37B	Mojave
Sikorsky	H-4B	Hoverfly
Sikorsky	H-19C	Chickasaw
Stinson	L-5	Sentinel

U.S.S. Alabama Battleship Memorial Park

P.O. Box 65, Mobile, Alabama 36601
(205) 433-2703

Moored in Mobile Bay, the World War II battleship U.S.S. *Alabama* and submarine U.S.S. *Drum* are open for self-guided tours. The visitor may tour the many decks of the *Alabama*, one of the largest type of war machines ever constructed. Equally interesting, unless the visitor is claustrophobic, is the cramped confines of the small, but deadly *Drum*. In the park adjacent to the ships is the collection of thirteen military aircraft.

To tour the *Alabama* extensively, several stairways must be negotiated. Appropriate footwear is recommended.

DIRECTIONS TO MUSEUM: From I-10 take either exit 27 or 30 onto Battleship Parkway and follow signs.

ADMISSION COST: Adults $5.00; children (6-11 yrs.) $2.50.

The advantages of having aircraft available to ships resulted in the development of seaplanes that could be launched from a catapult. Seaplanes like the Kingfisher in the photograph were launched from battleships and cruisers for gun spotting, scouting and observation. A crane would lift the seaplane out of the water after its flight and reposition it on the catapult. Helicopters have taken over most of the jobs previously performed by these ship-borne airplanes.

HOURS OF OPERATION: Open daily 8am-sunset. Closed Christmas.

MUSEUM NOTES: Display aircraft are out-doors. There is a gift shop, but film is not available. There is a snack bar onsite and there are restaurants nearby.

A brochure is available.

Display Aircraft

MANUFACTURER	MODEL	POPULAR NAME
Bell	UH-1B	Iroquois "Huey"
Boeing	B-52	Stratofortress
Douglas	C-47	Skytrain
Grumman	F6F	Hellcat
Grumman	HU-16E	Albatross
North American	B-25J	Mitchell
North American	F-86L	Sabre
North American	P-51D	Mustang
Piasecki	CH-21B	Workhorse
Republic	F-105B	Thunderchief
Sikorsky	HH-52A	Sea Guard
Vought	F4U-7	Corsair
Vought	OS2U	Kingfisher

U.S. Space & Rocket Center

One Tranquility Base, Huntsville, Alabama 35807
(205) 837-3400

Huntsville became a part of the rocket age when in 1950 the Army moved its Missile Command to the Redstone Arsenal just outside Huntsville. The Army enlisted the services of a group of German rocket scientists (among them noted scientist Wernher von Braun) at the end of World War II and their work at Redstone Arsenal contributed significantly to the U.S. rocket and space programs. Redstone continues as an important facility for the research, development and testing of rockets for the Army.

In 1960 the National Aeronautics and Space Administration (NASA) created the Marshall Space Flight Center adjacent to Redstone Arsenal. Marshall Center, the main propulsion system center for NASA, was responsible for development of the Saturn V rocket system that carried the Apollo missions into space and to the moon. Recent projects assigned to Marshall include the Hubble Space Telescope and space station development.

The Space and Rocket Center opened in 1970 as a facility to educate and entertain visitors interested in the roles and accomplishments of the Missile Command at Redstone

A group of rockets that were instrumental in the U.S. space program occupy a portion of the outdoor display area. From left to right are a Jupiter, Juno II, Redstone, Mercury/Redstone and Jupiter-C.

Adjacent to the main building is the Space Shuttle Pathfinder *sitting atop a rust-colored external tank. The* Pathfinder *was a full-scale mockup used by NASA to test equipment and procedures. The external tank was used for ten years during engine test firings. On early Space Shuttle flights, external tanks were painted white, but changing to a rust-colored primer saved approximately 1,000 pounds per tank. The external tank is the only major component not reused on Space Shuttle flights. After emptying, it drops into the ocean.*

Arsenal and Marshall Space Flight Center, as well as the nation's involvement in space. The vast number and variety of exhibits results in an attraction for all ages and interest levels. A typical visit may encompass four to six hours. Here is an opportunity to see in person what has been seen on television by millions. As one official stated, "Here, everyone can be an astronaut for the day."

The manned-flight artifacts are the centerpiece of the Space and Rocket Center. In the museum are found Mercury, Gemini and Apollo spacecraft, as well as a Lunar Module. There are a multitude of rocket and space artifacts, with over 1,500 pieces of rocket and space hardware in the collection. Interactive exhibits include a spinning gyro chair, a moon lander, a manned manuevering unit and a rocket engine. Adjacent to the museum is the Spacedome where the audience views breathtaking space panoramas on a 67-foot hemispherical screen.

The outdoor display areas are dominated by the Space Shuttle *Pathfinder* and the Saturn V rocket. Both were originally used for ground testing at the Marshall Space Flight Center. The Space Shuttle on display is the only full-scale Shuttle on exhibit. Adjacent to the Saturn rocket is an accurately-reproduced Lunar surface area. Elsewhere on the grounds is the Shuttle Liner, which depicts a futuristic voyage aboard a space transport to a space station. Near the Rocket Park is the Centrifuge, which allows the audience to experience the 3-G force (three times normal body weight) felt by Space Shuttle crews.

A bus tour of Marshall Flight Center (included in the package admission cost) leaves and returns at the museum entrance. The tour includes viewing the facility and demonstrations related to the current work performed at Marshall.

Sponsored by the Space and Rocket Center are the Space Camp and Space Academy programs for young people. Five- to eight-day programs for fourth- through eleventh-grade students offer training in areas such as rocketry, propulsion, space science and history of space exploration. Advanced classes address the study of aerospace, technology and engineering. Simulators add realism and emphasis to the subject matter. For more information on these programs, contact the Space and Rocket Center.

DIRECTIONS TO MUSEUM: From I-65 exit onto US 72-Alternate (exit 340) and travel east towards Huntsville. Space Center is approximately fifteen miles from I-65.

ADMISSION COST: Adults $11.95; senior citizen $7.95; children (3-12 yrs.) $7.95. Price includes Spacedome and tour of Marshall Space Flight Center. Museum only, or other single attractions: all ages $6.95.

HOURS OF OPERATION: Open 9am-6pm daily. Closed Christmas.

MUSEUM NOTES: Display spacecraft are indoors and outdoors. Film can be purchased in the gift shop and a one-hour film processing facility is in the main lobby. A cafeteria and a snack bar are on-site. There is a RV campground. A pet kennel is situated adjacent to the entrance walkway.

A brochure is available.

Display Rockets

MANUFACTURER	MODEL	POPULAR NAME
McDonnell Douglas	Saturn V	
Bell/Western Electric	Spartan	
Bell/Western Electric	Sprint	
Boeing	LGM-30	Minuteman
Chrysler	Mercury Redstone	
Chrysler	Saturn I	
Douglas	Little John	
Douglas/Emerson	Honest John	
Firestone	Corporal	
Ford Aerospace	Chaparral	
General Dynamics	Atlas	
Germany	V-1	
Germany	V-2	

JPL/Sperry	Sergeant	
Martin Marietta	Pershing I	
Martin Marietta	Pershing II	
North American	X-15	
Raytheon	Hawk	
Rockwell	Hound Dog	
Rockwell	Quail	
Rockwell	Space Shuttle	*Pathfinder*
Vought	Lance	
Western Electric	Nike Ajax	
Western Electric	Nike Hercules	

Museum of Alaska Transportation & Industry

P.O. Box 909, Palmer, Alaska 99645
(907) 745-4493

Alaska presents formidable barriers to any traveler with its imposing terrain and fearful weather. Growth in Alaska is directly related to the capability of the transportation system. The Museum of Alaska Transportation & Industry documents the story of transportation through artifacts and displays.

Aviation has been an important segment of life in Alaska. Early aviators expanded the capabilities of the airplane to serve the needs of Alaska's small and widespread populace resulting in today's multipurpose role of aircraft as cargo hauler, air ambulance, fish spotter, firefighter, bus and observor. As the northernmost part of the United States, Alaska is important militarily. Since World War II, Alaskan air bases have served defense and transport Air Force units. The museum addresses both the civilian and military facets of aviation in Alaska.

DIRECTIONS TO MUSEUM: The museum is located at the State Fairgrounds situated near milepost 40.2 on Glenn Highway.

ADMISSION COST: Adults $3.00; children 6-12 yrs. $1.50; under 6 yrs. free.

HOURS OF OPERATION: Open Tuesday-Saturday 8am-4pm.

MUSEUM NOTES: Display aircraft are indoors and outdoors. There is a gift shop, but film is not available. A restaurant is nearby.

A brochure is available.

Display Aircraft

MANUFACTURER	MODEL	POPULAR NAME
Boeing	CIM-10	Bomarc
Bowers	Fly Baby	
Convair	F-102	Delta Dagger
Douglas	C-47A	Skytrain
Fairchild	C-123	Provider
Lockheed	10A	Electra
Piasecki	H-21	Workhorse
Sikorsky	H-5H	Dragonfly
Stinson	Junior	Reliant
Travel Air	6000	
Waco	UIC	

Champlin Fighter Museum
4636 Fighter Aces Drive, Mesa, Arizona 85205
(602) 830-4540

The Champlin Fighter Museum is devoted exclusively to the preservation of noteworthy fighter airplanes constructed from 1914 to 1970. Two wings of the museum contain restored fighters and replicas of fighters from World War I, World War II, the Korean War and the Vietnam War.

An extensive collection of World War I airplanes is presented in one of the wings. With fifteen wood and fabric flying machines on display, you can trace the evolutionary changes in World War I fighters from flimsy, unarmed, multipurpose airplanes to stout, single-purpose, lethal, flying weapons.

The Sopwith F.1 was the first British World War I fighter to carry twin Vickers machine guns. The guns were just forward of the pilot. A panel protruded up from the fuselage and over the gun breeches creating a hump, hence the airplane's name, "Camel." The plane was highly manueverable, but could enter a fatal spin if the pilot was inattentive to the plane's traits.

The Rumpler Taube was constructed prior to World War I. Taube means pigeon or dove in German, aptly reflecting the plane's bird-like wings and tail.

In the second wing are found planes from more modern times, among them are several interesting planes not often found elsewhere. Of the World War II airplanes, the Messerschmitt Bf 109E, Focke-Wulf Fw 190D, Supermarine Spitfire and Republic P-47 are rarely seen. Most of the WWII planes flying or displayed today were obtained by private collectors from foreign air forces, crash sites or post-war surplus. At the close of the War, all Axis fighters were destroyed. Production of piston-engined fighters in Allied countries virtually ceased with the emergence of the jet age. Thousands of combat aircraft were scrapped as inventories were slashed. Ironically, the German Messerschmitt Bf 109 outlasted all of its contemporaries. Originally produced in 1935, the last 109 was built in Spain in 1956 (some were also manufactured in Czechoslovakia). Approximately 35,000 were built.

Noteworthy in the collection from the jet era are two MiGs, a MiG-15 and a MiG-17. Both aircraft were designed by the Soviet aircraft company Mikoyan-Gurevich and built in the U.S.S.R., as well as other communist countries. MiG-15s were the predominate fighter flown by China and North Korea during the Korean War, while MiG-17s served with the North Vietnamese Air Force during the Vietnam War.

A portion of the museum contains artifacts and memorabilia from personal collections of the American Fighter Aces Association. A sizeable collection of aviation art is displayed. There is also a collection of automatic weapons dating from 1895.

DIRECTIONS TO MUSEUM: The museum is located adjacent to Falcon Field Airport. From McKellips Rd. turn onto Falcon Rd. and follow to Fighter Aces Dr.

ADMISSION COST: Adults $5.00; children (5-14 yrs.) $2.50.

HOURS OF OPERATION: Open daily 10am-5pm. Closed Easter, Thanksgiving and Christmas.

MUSEUM NOTES: Display aircraft are indoors. Film is available in the gift shop. There is a restaurant nearby.

A brochure is available.

Display Aircraft

MANUFACTURER	MODEL	POPULAR NAME
Albatros	D-Va	
Avatik	D-II	
Curtiss	P-40N	Warhawk
Focke-Wulf	Fw 190D	
Fokker	D.VII	
Fokker	D.VIII	
Fokker	Dr.I	
Fokker	E.III	
Grumman	F6F-3	Hellcat
Grumman (General Motors)	FM-2	Wildcat
Lockheed	P-38L	Lightning
McDonnell	F-4	Phantom II
Messerschmitt	Bf 109E	
Mikoyan-Gurevich	MiG-15	"Fagot"
Mikoyan-Gurevich	MiG-17	"Fresco"
Nieuport	27	
North American	F-86	Sabre
North American	P-51D	Mustang
Pfalz	D-XII	
Republic	P-47D-2	Thunderbolt
Royal Aircraft Factory	S.E.5a	
Rumpler	Taube	
Sopwith	F.1	Camel
Sopwith	Pup	
Sopwith	7F.1	Snipe
Sopwith	Triplane	
SPAD	XIII	
Supermarine	Mk IX	Spitfire
Vought (Goodyear)	F2G-1	Corsair

na

Pima Air Museum

6000 E. Valencia Road, Tucson, Arizona 85706
(602) 574-9658

A hot, dry climate is ideal for preserving machinery, and that's exactly the reason the Air Force and Pima Air Museum can park aircraft outdoors with minimal deterioration. Fortunately for the visitor to the Pima Air Museum, several restored aircraft are exhibited indoors, out of the hot Arizona sun. Nearby is Davis-Monthan Air Force Base and the graveyard or temporary storage area for hundreds of military aircraft.

The museum possesses several unique aircraft. Among the notable aircraft are the Boeing YC-14 medium transport prototype, a Douglas B-18A Bolo, a Douglas B-23, the Douglas VC-118A used to transport Presidents Kennedy and Johnson, the Lockheed C-121A Constellation used by General Eisenhower, a Martin PBM-5A Mariner seaplane and a North American F-107 prototype.

The F-107 was not ordered into production by the Air Force. Instead, the Republic F-105 was chosen as the Tactical Air Command's fighter/bomber for the 1960s. The F-107 prototype exceeded Mach 2 and proved to be a very capable airplane, resulting in surprise when the contract was cancelled. North American, later Rockwell, the company that built two classic fighters in the Mustang and Sabre, has not produced fighters since.

DIRECTIONS TO MUSEUM: The museum is southeast of Tucson. From I-10 exit onto Valencia and travel east.

ADMISSION COST: Adults $5.00; senior citizens $4.00; children (10-17 yrs.) $3.00.

HOURS OF OPERATION: Open daily 9am-5pm. No admittance after 4pm. Closed Christmas.

MUSEUM NOTES: Display aircraft are indoors and outdoors. Film is available in the gift shop. A snack bar is located on-site.

A brochure is available.

Display Aircraft

MANUFACTURER	MODEL	POPULAR NAME
Beech	AT-7	Navigator
Beech	AT-11	Kansas
Beech	D18S	Twin Beech
Beech	N35	Bonanza
Beech	U-8D	Seminole
Beech	UC-45J	Expeditor
Bell	P-63E	Kingcobra
Bell	UH-1F	Iroquois "Huey"

Bellanca	14-13-2	Cruisair
Boeing	B-17G	Flying Fortress
Boeing	B-29	Superfortress
Boeing	B-52D	Stratofortress
Boeing	C-97G	Stratofreighter
Boeing	EB-47E	Stratojet
Boeing	KB-50J	Superfortress
Boeing	KC-97G	Stratofreighter
Boeing	NB-52A	Stratofortress
Boeing	S-307	Stratoliner
Boeing	YC-14	
Bowers	Fly Baby	
Budd	RB-1	Conestoga
Bushby	MM-II	Midget Mustang
Cessna	120	
Cessna	C-150L	
Cessna	O-2A	Skymaster
Cessna	UC-78B	Bobcat
Columbia	XJL-1	
Consolidated	B-24J	Liberator
Convair	B-58A	Hustler
Convair	F-102A	Delta Dagger
Convair	F-106A	Delta Dart
Convair	TF-102A	Delta Dagger
Convair	VT-29B	Flying Classroom
Culver	PQ-14	Cadet
Curtiss	C-46D	Commando
de Havilland	DHC-1	Chipmunk
de Havilland	U-6A	Beaver
Douglas	A4D-2	Skyhawk
Douglas	A-4C	Skyhawk
Douglas	A-26C	Invader
Douglas	AIR-21	Genie
Douglas	B-18B	Bolo
Douglas	B-23	Dragon
Douglas	B-26K	Invader
Douglas	C-47	Skytrain
Douglas	C-54D	Skymaster
Douglas	C-117D	Super Gooneybird
Douglas	C-124C	Globemaster II
Douglas	C-133B	Cargomaster
Douglas	EA-1F	Skyraider
Douglas	F-6A	Skyray
Douglas	TF-10B	Skynight
Douglas	VC-118A	Liftmaster

Douglas	WB-66D	Destroyer
Douglas	YEA-3A	Skywarrior
Evans	VP-1	Volksplane
Fairchild	C-82A	Packet
Fairchild	C-119C	Flying Boxcar
Fairchild	C-123B	Provider
Fairchild	PT-19A	Cornell
Fairchild	PT-26	Cornell
Flagler	Sky Scooter	
Focke-Wulf	FW 44-J	Stieglitz
Globe	KD6G-2	
Grumman	E-1B	Tracer
Grumman	F6F-3	Hellcat
Grumman	F9F-8	Cougar
Grumman	F-11A	Tiger
Grumman	HU-16A	Albatross
Grumman	OV-1C	Mohawk
Grumman	RF-9J	Cougar
Grumman	S2F-1	Tracker
Grumman	TF-9J	Cougar
Grumman	US-2A	Tracker
Grumman (General Motors)	TBM-3	Avenger
Gyrodyne	QH-50	Dash
Hiller	UH-12C	
Hughes	AIM-4	Falcon
Hughes	TH-55A	Osage
Kaman	H-43F	Huskie
Kaman	OH-43D	Huskie
Lockheed	AP-2H	Neptune
Lockheed	C-69	Constellation
Lockheed	C-121A	Constellation
Lockheed	C-130D	Hercules
Lockheed	EC-121T	Constellation
Lockheed	EC-121T	Constellation
Lockheed	P-80B	Shooting Star
Lockheed	T-1A	Seastar
Lockheed	T-33A	Shooting Star
Lockheed	TF-104D	Starfighter
Lockheed	TV-2	Shooting Star
Lockheed	UC-36	Electra
Lockheed	VC-140B	Jetstar
Lockheed	YO-3A	Quiet Star
Martin	AGM-12	Bull Pup
Martin	B-57E	Canberra
Martin	PBM-5A	Mariner

Martin Marietta	LGM-25C	Titan II
Martin Marietta	SM-68	Titan I
Martin/General Dynamics	EB-57D	Canberra
Martin/General Dynamics	WB-57F	Canberra
McCulloch	HUM-1	
McCulloch	J-2	Gyrocopter
McDonnell	ADM-20C	Quail
McDonnell	F-3B	Demon
McDonnell	F-4C	Phantom II
McDonnell	F-101B	Voodoo
McDonnell	RF-101C	Voodoo
McDonnell	RF-101H	Voodoo
McDonnell	YF-4J	Phantom
McDonnell Douglas	YC-15	
North American	AF-1E	Fury
North American	AT-6B	Texan
North American	B-25J	Mitchell
North American	CT-39A	Sabreliner
North American	F-86H	Sabre
North American	F-86L	Sabre
North American	F-100C	Super Sabre
North American	F-107A	
North American	RA-5C	Vigilante
North American	T-28C	Trojan
North American	X-15A-2	
Northrop	F-89J	Scorpion
Northrop	MQM-33	
Northrop	MQM-57	
Northrop	T-38A	Talon
Northrop	YC-125A	Raider
Pereira	Osprey 2	
Piasecki	CH-21C	Shawnee
Piasecki	HUP-3	Army Mule
Piper	U-11A	Aztec
Pitts	S-1	Special
Radioplane/Frankfort	OQ-3	
Republic	F-84F	Thunderstreak
Republic	F-105D	Thunderchief
Republic	F-105G	Thunderchief
Republic	RF-84F	Thunderflash
Rockwell	AGM-28A	Hound Dog
Rutan	Long-EZ	
Rutan	Quickie	
Ryan	PT-22	Recruit
Ryan	ST-A	

Scheibe	III-B	Zugvogel
Schweizer	TG-3A	
Sikorsky	CH-37B	Mojave
Sikorsky	HH-52A	Sea Guard
Sikorsky	UH-19B	Chickasaw
Sikorsky	VH-34C	Chocktaw
Squadron Aviation	SPAD XIII (replica)	
Stearman	PT-17	Kaydet
Taylorcraft	BC-12D	
Teledyne Ryan	AQM-34	Compass Dawn
Teledyne Ryan	AQM-34L	Compass Bin
Teledyne Ryan	YQM-98A	Compass Cope
Temco	D-16	Twin Navion
Vought	DF-8F	Crusader
Vought	F4U-4	Corsair
Vultee	BT-13A	Valiant
Wright Flyer (replica)		

Titan Missile Museum

Duval Mine Road, Green Valley, Arizona 85614
(602) 791-2929

During the 1960s, 1970s and early 1980s the Air Force maintained numerous Titan-series Intercontinental Ballistic Missiles in silos in western states. With safety a major concern, the liquid-fueled Titan was phased out of service as a strategic weapon in 1987. Capable of delivering a nuclear warhead to a target over 6,000 miles away, the Titan missile was the keystone of the nation's nuclear missile deterent. The Minuteman and Peacekeeper solid-fueled missiles now comprise the nation's land-based strategic missile force.

The Titan Missile Museum provides the only opportunity for the general public to inspect what once was an operating Titan missile silo. On display is a Titan missile and the equipment that supported the missile and the silo. While the Titan may have been hazardous when operational, the Titan on display has been rendered benign (all hazardous material has been removed).

DIRECTIONS TO MUSEUM: The museum is approximately 20 miles south of Tucson. From I-19 take exit 69 and follow signs.

ADMISSION COST: Adults $5.00; senior citizens $4.00; children (10-17 yrs.) $3.00.

HOURS OF OPERATION: November-April open daily 9am-5pm, last tour 4pm; May-October open Wednesday-Sunday 9am-5pm, last tour 4pm.

MUSEUM NOTES: Guided tours only. The gift shop stocks film. A restaurant is nearby. Wearing high-heeled shoes not permitted on tour.

A brochure is available.

Arkansas Air Museum
P.O. Box 1911, Fayetteville, Arkansas 72702
(501) 521-4947

The Arkansas Air Museum consists primarily of airplanes dating from the era between the World Wars. During this "Golden Era," aviation was in transition from military and exhibition uses to commercial and recreational transportation. Powerplant and aircraft designs were rapidly evolving to provide the practicality and reliability necessary to entice businesses and individuals into owning airplanes. This was also the heyday of air racing and the museum has two examples of race planes on display.

Representative of the 1920s and 1930s airplanes are the museum's Travel Air airplanes including a replica of the Travel Air R *Mystery Ship* racer. The museum also has on dis-

The DGA-11 was built in 1937 by Ben Howard's aircraft company. Before manufacturing planes, Howard built and piloted air racers while serving as an airline captain. The DGA model prefix stood for "damned good airplane," a comment from an early buyer. The DGA-11 was a commercial version of Howard's successful racer Mr. Mulligan. *With a maximum speed of 200 mph, the DGA-11 was one of the fastest personal planes of its era. Most were built for the wealthy at an approximate cost of $16,000.*

Compared to the other air racers of its day, Ben Howard's Mister Mulligan *looked bulky and ungainly. But* Mister Mulligan *was the only plane to ever win both the Bendix and Thompson air races in the same year, 1935. It was also the only air racer to evolve into a successful commercial airplane.*

play a replica of the Howard racer *Mr. Mulligan* (winner of both the Bendix and Thompson air races). A variety of aircraft engines are also exhibited, with the Curtiss OX-5 World War I engine particularly noteworthy.

DIRECTIONS TO MUSEUM: The museum is located on the east side of US 71 at Fayetteville Airport (Drake Field).

ADMISSION COST: Free (donation requested).

HOURS OF OPERATION: Open 9:30am-4:30pm daily except major holidays.

MUSEUM NOTES: Display aircraft are indoors. The gift shop does not stock film. There are vending machines onsite and restaurants nearby.

A brochure is available.

Display Aircraft

MANUFACTURER	MODEL	POPULAR NAME
Beech	T-34B	Mentor
Travel Air	4000	

Travel Air	A6000	
Travel Air (replica)	R1000	*Mystery Ship*
Howard (replica)	DGA-6	*Mr. Mulligan*
Howard	DGA-11	
Great Lakes		
Meyers	OTW	
Stearman		
Stinson	Jr. SM8	

Air Force Flight Test Center Museum

6500 ABW/CCM, Edwards Air Force Base, California 93523
(805) 277-8050

One of aviation's historic locations, Edwards Air Force Base originated as a pre-World War II bombing and gunnery range. Previously named Muroc Army Air Field, the Army needed a secluded field with good flying weather to test new aircraft. The California desert suited the Army's needs. With over 60 square miles of suitable landing area, a test pilot's chances of safely landing in a dangerous situation are greatly improved.

Since World War II, virtually all Air Force aircraft have undergone some flight testing at Muroc/Edwards. Edwards also hosts the Air Force Test Pilot School and other agencies utilizing Edwards special facilities, including the Army and NASA.

Edwards has been the site of a multitude of aviation records and achievements, but the most important was the breaking of the sound barrier. Accomplished by Captain Charles "Chuck" Yeager on October 14, 1947, the world was not told for another eight months due to the perceived need for military secrecy. A series of "X" (for experimental) planes increased the available knowledge concerning manned flight culminating in the X-15, which set a speed record of Mach 6.72 (4,520 mph) and an altitude record of 354,200 feet. The work performed at Edwards has resulted in better-performing, safer aircraft for both military and civilian pilots.

The broad expanse of Edwards also provides a desirable landing strip for the Space Shuttle. The runway at Kennedy Space Center was built as the primary destination with Edwards intended as an auxiliary field. However, due to operational considerations Edwards has greeted most returning Space Shuttles.

If you are flying into or out of the Los Angeles area, some flights fly over the desert area north of Los Angeles within viewing distance of Edwards. Close observation will pick out the runways marked on the hard, dry lake-bed of the desert.

At the time of this book's publication, the museum was undergoing remodeling. Expected opening is September 1991. Aircraft available for viewing are situated in an air park along Lancaster Blvd.

DIRECTIONS TO MUSEUM: Edwards Air Force Base is approximately 90 miles north of Los Angeles on Hwy. 14. At Rosamond, turn east on Rosamond Blvd. to main gate. Obtain visitor's pass at main gate and ask for directions to air park.

ADMISSION COST: Free.

HOURS OF OPERATION: Sunrise to dusk (air park only).

MUSEUM NOTES: Display aircraft are outdoors. There is a restaurant nearby.

A brochure is available.

Display Aircraft

MANUFACTURER	MODEL	POPULAR NAME
Boeing	B-52D	Stratofortress
General Dynamics	F-111A	
Lockheed	F-104A	Starfighter
North American	CT-39A	Sabreliner
North American	T-28B	Trojan

The Air Museum "Planes of Fame"
7000 Merrill Avenue, Box 17, Chino, California 91710
(714) 597-3722

Begun in 1957, The Air Museum was created in an effort to preserve, preferably in flying condition, at least one example of as many aircraft types as possible. The museum has succeeded in acquiring approximately seventy aircraft, which are now on display, undergoing restoration or stored.

The restoration facility and museum occupy the same location, and for those who are curious from a "nuts-and-bolts" perspective, airframes, engines and various pieces of planes undergoing restoration are sometimes visible.

Besides its fine collection of U.S. aircraft, the museum also possesses some rare examples of Axis aircraft. Noteworthy planes include the only Japanese "Zero" fighter in flying condition, two Japanese rocket planes, a Fuji Ohka 11 and a Mitsubishi J8M1, and two German jet fighters, a Messerschmitt Me 262 and a Heinkel He 162A.

Among the U.S. aircraft are the only Boeing P-26 and Seversky AT-12 in flying condition. The museum's Boeing B-17 is displayed outdoors, and weather permitting, visitors can look around inside.

At time of this book's publication, the museum was nearing completion on its restoration of the only surviving Northrop N-9M Flying Wing. Northrop built four, twin-engined N-9M airplanes before producing the larger multi-engined prototypes after World War II. The Flying Wing project died in controversy in 1949 when the government canceled its

A hanger houses most of the museum's flying World War II era fighters. The museum's Douglas RA-26 Invader, like many planes in the museum, is flyable and participates in airshows.

The museum's B-17 Flying Fortress is parked near the entrance to the museum. The plane is open for viewing, weather permitting. It's a great opportunity to look inside one of the legendary planes of World War II.

funding. Revived with modern materials and engineering as the B-2 stealth bomber, the flying wing continues to generate controversy.

In 1990 the museum moved the bulk of its jet airplanes from an outdoor display area into a nearby hanger. Be sure to see all of the collection.

A couple of times each year, an airshow is sponsored by the museum at the Chino Airport. Call the museum for information.

DIRECTIONS TO MUSEUM: The museum is located at Chino Airport which is southeast of Chino on Hwy. 83 (Euclid Ave.). At airport turn east on Merrill Ave. and follow signs.

ADMISSION COST: Adults $4.95; children $1.95.

HOURS OF OPERATION: Open daily 9am-5pm.

MUSEUM NOTES: Display aircraft are located indoors and outdoors. Film is available at the gift shop. There are vending machines onsite and a restaurant is nearby.

A brochure is available.

Display Aircraft

MANUFACTURER	MODEL	POPULAR NAME
Aichi	D3A	"Val"
Bell	P-39N	Airacobra
Bell	YP-59A	Airacomet
Benson		Gyrocopter

The museum's Japanese Zero was captured at Saipan during World War II and is the only Zero in flying condition. The Zero was the first carrier-based fighter capable of besting land-based fighters. Fast and highly maneuverable, the Zero was flown by pilots who had sharpened their dogfighting skills in combat over China. An inability to replace experienced pilots and slow engine development placed Zeros increasingly at a disadvantage as World War II progressed. Modest horsepower increases occurred, but the airplane's weight also increased resulting in little gain in performance.

Boeing	B-17G	Flying Fortress
Boeing	P-12E	
Boeing	P-26A	Peashooter
Chanute glider		
Convair	F-102A	Delta Dagger
Cosmic Wing racer		
Culver drone	PQ-14	
Curtiss	P-40N	Warhawk
Douglas	D-558-U	Skyrocket
Douglas	RA-26C	Invader
Douglas	SBD-5	Dauntless
Fieseler	Fi 103(V-1)	
Fuji	Ohka 11	
Grumman	F6F-5	Hellcat
Grumman	F9F-5P	Panther
Grumman	F11F-1	Tiger
Grumman (General Motors)	FM-2	Wildcat
Grumman (General Motors)	TBM-3	Avenger
Hanriot	HD-1	Scout
Heinkel	He 162A-1	Volksjager
Lockheed	P-38J	Lightning

The Boeing P-26 was the first all-metal monoplane fighter in the Army Air Corps. Entering service in 1934, P-26s were front-line fighters for approximately five years, but obsolete at the advent of World War II. Nicknamed "Pea Shooter," several of the fighters saw service with foreign air forces. The P-26 on display formerly flew in the air forces of Panama and Guatemala.

Lockheed	P-80A	Shooting Star
Lockheed	Q-5	
Lockheed	T-33A	Shooting Star
Lockheed	X-7	
Martin	TM-61	Matador
Messerschmitt	Bf 109G-10	Gustav
Messerschmitt	Me 262A-1a	Schwalbe
Mitsubishi	A6M5	Zero "Zeke"
Mitsubishi	J2M3	Raiden "Jack"
Mitsubishi	J8M1	Shushui
North American	AT-6	Texan
North American	B-25J	Mitchell
North American	F-86A	Sabre
North American	P-51A	Mustang
North American	P-51D	Mustang

North American	QF-86H	Sabre
North American Rockwell	Apollo Command Module (mock-up)	
Republic	F-84C	Thunderjet
Republic	F-84E	Thunderjet
Republic	P-47G	Thunderbolt
Republic	RF-84K	Thunderflash
Rick Jet	RJ-1	
Ryan	FR-1	Fireball
Seversky	AT-12	Guardsman
Stinson	L-5G	Sentinel
Vought	F4U-1	Corsair

California Museum of Science and Industry

700 State Drive, Los Angeles, California 90037
(213) 744-7400

The California Museum of Science and Industry comprises several buildings near the University of Southern California campus and the Coliseum. A wide spectrum of subjects is presented in the various rooms with several "hands-on" exhibits. A full day is needed to go through the whole museum and to watch a show at the IMAX movie theater.

The Aerospace Museum of the California Museum of Science and Industry presents its contents in a truly unique fashion. This is first apparent when seeing the F-104 Starfighter attached to the side of the building. Inside the museum are multiple floors from which to view aircraft and satellites suspended as if in flight. One museum section explains the principles of flight and propulsion while another section is devoted to the specific missions and uses of spacecraft and satellites. The award-winning *Windows of the Universe* depicts the universe from birth to future exploration using a 21-projector system.

The IMAX theater is adjacent but separate from the museum building. The theater encompasses a screen five stories high and seventy feet wide with a surround-sound system utilizing six channels. Call (213) 744-2014 for show information.

DIRECTIONS TO MUSEUM: From I-110 (Harbor Fwy.) exit onto Exposition Blvd. Go west on Exposition. Museum is located at intersection with Figueroa. NOTE: Parking may be expensive and hard to find if there is a sporting event at the Coliseum. This is usually noted on the recorded message of the museum's telephone.

ADMISSION COST: Free except IMAX.

HOURS OF OPERATION: Open daily 10am-5pm. Closed New Year's Day, Thanksgiving and Christmas.

MUSEUM NOTES: Aircraft are located inside and outside. The gift shop stocks film. There is a McDonald's restaurant on-site and other restaurants are located nearby.

A brochure is available.

Display Aircraft

MANUFACTURER	MODEL	POPULAR NAME
Douglas	DC-3	
Douglas	DC-8	
Lockheed	F-104	Starfighter
North American	P-51	Mustang
Northrop	T-38	Talon
Wright		Flyer

Castle Air Museum

P.O. Box 488, Atwater, California 95301
(209) 723-2178

The museum is adjacent to Castle Air Force Base. The primary mission for aircraft based at Castle AFB has been bombardment and the museum reflects that heritage by displaying a large collection of Air Force bombers.

Most of the significant bombers in the Air Force inventory from World War II to the present are exhibited. The list includes the A-26, B-17, B-24, B-25, B-29, B-36, B-47, B-52 and WB-50. Of the bombers in the collection, the B-36 is one of the rarest. Very few of these huge airplanes are on display, and none are flying. Some versions of the B-36 carried a crew of 22 men and were capable of flying 10,000 miles without refueling. The B-36 served as an intercontinental bomber at the beginning of the nuclear age and never in combat. Using both piston and jet engines, it was an intermediate step until replaced by the all-jet B-52. The museum is restoring the B-36 with completion targeted for 1994. Portions of the plane are visible.

Also on display is a SR-71 Blackbird, the famous strategic reconnaissance airplane (spyplane). In February 1990 a similar airplane set a coast-to-coast record of 68 minutes at a speed in excess of 2,100 miles-per-hour.

The Air Force placed over 3,000 Curtiss C-46s in service during World War II. The C-46 was larger and capable of carrying more cargo than its contemporary, the C-47. Gross weight for the C-47 was 33,000 pounds, while gross weight for the C-46 was 51,000 pounds. This increased capacity was particularly useful for the flight across the inhospitable Himalayas, the "Hump." Due to Japanese occupation of most of Southeast Asia, virtually all supplies to Allied forces in China were flown in by a constant stream of C-46s and C-47s.

The B-36 was one of the largest airplanes ever built. The tail height is 46 feet and the wing span is 230 feet. Originally designed for World War II use, the bomber's role changed to a nuclear bomb delivery system with the advent of the atomic bomb and the Cold War. The long-range bomber was capable of dropping a nuclear bomb on any U.S. enemy in the world. This photo was shot at Chanute AFB before the plane's shipment to Castle.

DIRECTIONS TO MUSEUM: From Hwy. 99 exit on Buhach. Follow Buhach and turn left onto Sante Fe Dr. Museum entrance is 200 yards north of Castle AFB main gate.

ADMISSION COST: Free.

HOURS OF OPERATION: Open daily 10am-4pm. Closed New Year's Day, Easter, July 4, Christmas.

MUSEUM NOTES: Display aircraft are indoors and outdoors. Film is available in the gift shop. There is a restaurant onsite.

A brochure is available.

Display Aircraft

MANUFACTURER	MODEL	POPULAR NAME
Avro	CF-100	Canuck
Beech	AT-11	Kansas
Beech	C-45	Expeditor
Beech	T-34	Mentor
Boeing	B-17	Flying Fortress
Boeing	B-29	Superfortress
Boeing	B-47	Stratojet
Boeing	B-52	Stratofortress
Boeing	KC-97	Stratofreighter

In the late 1930s, military policy dictated an emphasis on inexpensive, twin-engine bombers. Douglas developed the B-18 Bolo, on display at Castle, and its successor, the B-23 Dragon, shown above. Douglas reduced costs by using components from the DC-3. The B-23 was the first U.S. bomber equipped with a tail gun, but the plane was outmoded by the beginning of World War II. Only 38 were produced.

Boeing	WB-50	Superfortress
Cessna	O-2A	
Cessna	U-3A	
Convair	B-36	Peacemaker
Curtiss	C-46	Commando
de Havilland	L-20	Beaver
Douglas	A-26	Invader
Douglas	B-18	Bolo
Douglas	B-23	Dragon
Douglas	C-47	Skytrain
Fairchild	C-123K	Provider
Hawker Siddeley	MkII	Vulcan
Kaman	HH-43	Huskie
Lockheed	C-60	Lodestar
Lockheed	F-104	Starfighter
Lockheed	T-33	Shooting Star
McDonnell	F-101	Voodoo
North American	B-25	Mitchell
North American	B-45	Tornado
North American	F-86	Sabre
North American	T-6	Texan
Northrop	A-9A	
Republic	F-105	Thunderchief
Vultee	BT-13	Valiant

Edward F. Beale Museum

9 SRW/CCX, Building 2471, Beale Air Force Base, California 95903
(916) 634-2038

Contrary to the practice of naming air bases after aviators, Beale Air Force Base was named for early Californian Edward F. Beale. Beale is best known for the ill-fated attempt to introduce camels into the southwest. Beale AFB is presently home base for the 9th Strategic Reconnaissance Wing, which flies U-2 and TR-1 airplanes. Beale was home for the SR-71 Blackbirds before their phase out in 1990. The SR-71 was the world's most complex reconnaissance aircraft and still holds the speed record for the fastest production aircraft ever built. The sophisticated surveillance system of the Blackbird was capable of covering 100,000 square miles in one hour.

Some display items are related to the SR-71 Blackbird. Hanging on the wall of a display room are pictures of all pilots and "backseaters" qualified to fly in Blackbirds. In the airplane's 25-year lifespan there were only 235 flying crewmembers. The selection process and training were nearly as demanding as that for astronaut.

Note that the BT-13, KC-97 and U-2 are displayed at locations other than at the museum. The sites are shown on maps available at the museum.

The Lockheed U-2 was a purpose-built, high-altitude surveillance airplane. U-2s entered service in 1956, but were not known publicly until Gary Powers was downed in the Soviet Union in 1960. Looking like a jet-powered sailplane, U-2s were also flown on non-military missions such as atmospheric research and land survey. An updated design, the Lockheed TR-1, entered service in 1981 and is capable of flying at altitudes greater than 70,000 feet. Pilots of the U-2 and TR-1 must alter their normal high speed, jet-airplane landing techniques and adapt more to the landing approach of a sailplane.

The English Electric Company in Britain originally designed and built the Canberra, which first flew in 1949. The Air Force realized during the Korean War that it lacked a tactical jet bomber, and rather than suffer a long development period, selected the Canberra for domestic production. The Martin Company was contracted to build the plane, designated the B-57, under license from English Electric. Production began in 1953 and ceased in 1959 with over 400 built. The last versions were converted to electronic countermeasures EB-57Bs, which remained in service with the Air Guard until the later 1980s.

DIRECTIONS TO MUSEUM: Beale AFB is east of Marysville. From Hwy 70 exit onto N. Beale Rd. or Feather River Rd. Follow N. Beale Rd. and signs to Beale AFB. The base is approximately 14 miles from freeway. Inquire at gate for directions.

ADMISSION COST: Free.

HOURS OF OPERATION: Open 10am-4pm Tuesday-Saturday; noon-4pm Sunday; closed Monday. Closed major holidays.

MUSEUM NOTES: Display aircraft are outdoors. The gift shop does not stock film. There is a restaurant near the museum.

A brochure is available.

Display Aircraft

MANUFACTURER	MODEL	POPULAR NAME
Beech	AT-11	Kansas
Boeing	KC-97	Stratofreighter
Douglas	B-26	Invader
Douglas	C-47	Skytrain
Lockheed	U-2	
Martin	B-57	Canberra
North American	B-25	Mitchell
Stinson	L-5	Sentinel
Vultee	BT-13	Valiant

Jet Propulsion Laboratory

Visitor Center, 4800 Oak Grove Drive, Pasadena, California 91109
(818) 354-2337

The Jet Propulsion Laboratory (JPL) is a part of the California Institute of Technology, but is operated under contract by the National Aeronautics and Space Administration. JPL directs its efforts towards scientific study of the solar system and exploration of the planets using automated spacecraft.

JPL was largely responsible for the spacecraft sent into space during the 1960s and 1970s, including the Ranger and Surveyor series that photographed the lunar surface in the mid-1960s, the Viking spacecraft that landed on Mars, and the Voyager spacecraft that explored the solar system.

Several spacecraft are on display at the facility, including a version of Explorer I, the first U.S. satellite to orbit in space. There are also mockups of the Viking, Mariner and Surveyor spacecraft.

Admittance is available only for guided tours that are scheduled for one day in each month. Length of the tour is approximately two hours. Special group tour reservations are also accepted. Visitors must be at least 10 years old. Inquire for additional information and reservations by calling JPL.

DIRECTIONS TO MUSEUM: From I-210 exit onto Berkshire then travel north (towards mountains) on Oak Grove Drive.

ADMISSION COST: Free.

HOURS OF OPERATION: No set time for tour.

MUSEUM NOTES: Spacecraft are indoors. There are restaurants nearby. No film available.

A brochure is available.

March Field Museum
22 AREFW/CVM, March Air Force Base, California 92518
(714) 655-3725

March Air Force Base originally began service in 1918 as March Field and is the oldest Air Force base on the west coast. For much of its existence, March has been home for bomber units. It is currently headquarters for the 15th Air Force of the Strategic Air Command. Presently, the resident aircraft are the huge tankers used to refuel inflight aircraft, as well as cargo planes of the Air Force Reserve and fighter planes of the Air National Guard.

The museum contains artifacts that reflect the history of March Field. Chronicling March's long history also outlines a considerable portion of U.S. military aviation history. Particularly interesting among the displays is the cutaway fuselage of a B-47 that was used during the filming of the movie *Strategic Air Command* starring Jimmy Stewart. The cutaway provides a rare exposed view of the equipment and crew positions in the B-47.

The bulk of the display aircraft are parked on the flightline. Buses carry visitors to the ramp. The bus ride provides an interesting view of an active Air Force flightline, its broad expanse and the huge tankers parked on the ramp. Among the display planes on the flightline is one of the SR-71 Blackbirds recently retired from service.

DIRECTIONS TO MUSEUM: March Air Force Base is located southeast of River-side off of I-215S. From I-215S exit at March Air Force Base offramp. Stop at

The MiG-19 was the world's first supersonic production fighter. The "MiG" model prefix is derived from the names of noted Soviet designers Artem Mikoyan and Mikhail Gurevich. The code name "Farmer" was attached to the plane by Allied air forces. MiG-19s were manufactured in Czechoslovakia as well as the Soviet Union. China copied the design and produced several thousand copies of their version designated the Shenyang J-6. Production ceased in 1984.

The Northrop A-9 prototype was built to compete with the Fairchild A-10 prototype for a contract to build airplanes to fly close air-support missions. Criteria for the planes included two fuel-efficient engines, ability to carry mixed ordnance, ability to fly out of short airfields, high survivability from enemy fire, and cost-effectiveness. The A-10 was judged winner and the two A-9 prototypes are now in museums (the other A-9 resides at Castle Air Museum).

visitors center at base entrance for directions to museum.

ADMISSION COST: Free.

HOURS OF OPERATION: Open Monday-Friday 10am-4pm; Saturday & Sunday noon-4pm. Closed New Year's Day, Thanksgiving and Christmas.

MUSEUM NOTES: Display aircraft are indoors and outdoors. There is a gift shop, but film is not available. A restaurant is near base entrance.

A brochure is available.

Display Aircraft

MANUFACTURER	MODEL	POPULAR NAME
Aichi (replica)	D3A	Val
Beech	C-45	Expeditor
Bell	P-39	Airacobra
Bell	P-59	Airacomet
Bell	UH-1F	Iroquois "Huey"
Boeing	B-17G	Flying Fortress
Boeing	B-29	Superfortress
Boeing	B-47	Stratojet
Boeing	B-52	Stratofortress
Boeing	KC-97	Stratofreighter
Cessna	O-2B	Skymaster
Convair	C-131	Samaritan
Douglas	A-1E	Skyraider

Serving primarily in the air forces of Finland and India, the British Folland FO 141 Gnat was a lightweight fighter that first flew in 1955. The Royal Air Force wasn't interested in the little fighter, but did purchase a significant number as trainers.

Douglas	B-26	Invader
Fairchild	C-119	Flying Boxcar
Fairchild	C-123	Provider
Fairchild	PT-19	Cornell
Folland	FO-141	Gnat
Grumman	SA-16	Albatross
Lockheed	C-60	Lodestar
Lockheed	SR-71	Blackbird
Lockheed	T-33	Shooting Star
Lockheed	U-2	
Martin	EB-57	Canberra
Martin Marietta	SM-68	Titan I
McDonnell	F-4	Phantom II
McDonnell	F-101B	Voodoo
Mikoyan-Gurevich	MiG-19	"Farmer"
North American	AT-6	Texan
North American	B-25	Mitchell
North American	F-86	Sabre
North American	F-100	Super Sabre
North American	T-39	Sabreliner
Northrop	A-9	
Northrop	F-89	Scorpion
Piasecki	HU-21	Workhorse
Republic	F-84C	Thunderjet
Republic	F-84F	Thunderstreak
Republic	F-105D	Thunderchief
Stearman	PT-13	Kaydet
Stinson	L-5	Sentinel
Vultee	BT-13	Valiant

McClellan Aviation Museum

P.O. Box 553, North Highlands, California 95660
(916) 643-3192

The museum is situated on McClellan Air Force Base, which is a component of the Air Force Logistics Command. The base was originally named the Sacramento Air Depot and during World War II the B-25s of the Doolittle Raid were modified here. McClellan AFB is currently responsible for the support and repair of a variety of aircraft.

The museum opened in 1986 and is growing rapidly with several aircraft undergoing restoration for eventual display. Particularly interesting among the aircraft on display is the Russian MiG-21F. The MiG-21 was designed and built by Mikoyan-Gurevich. Capable of twice the speed of sound, MiG-21s were produced for over thirty years and served in several air forces. Also on display are simulators that give the visitor a look at an airplane's cockpit.

DIRECTIONS TO MUSEUM: McClellan AFB is northeast of Sacramento. From I-80 exit onto Watt Ave. and travel north to the air base. Enter base at Gate 3 for a pass and directions.

ADMISSION COST: Free.

The North American F-86L was an upgrade from the earlier D model. The F-86L flew under the direction of the Semiautomatic Ground Environment (SAGE) air defense system. The pilot was vectored to intruding aircraft, then the computerized fire control system automatically fired the plane's rockets. Twenty-four rockets were carried in a movable pod that extended beneath the fuselage. The Convair F-102 replaced the F-86L during the late 1950s.

During World War II the Navy sought an upgraded version of the Grumman JRF Goose then in service. The result was the Grumman Albatross, designated UF-1 in the Navy or SA-16 in the Air Force (later redesignated HU-16 in all services). The primary mission of the amphibian was air-sea rescue. During the Korean War, Albatrosses were credited with rescuing over 1,000 downed aviators from the sea. The planes remained in service until the mid-1970s.

HOURS OF OPERATION: Open Monday-Saturday 9am-3pm; closed Sunday and holidays.

MUSEUM NOTES: Display aircraft are indoors and outdoors. The gift shop does not stock film. There is a restaurant nearby.

A brochure is available.

Display Aircraft

MANUFACTURER	MODEL	POPULAR NAME
Convair	F-102A	Delta Dagger
Convair	VC-131D	Samaritan
Douglas	A-1E	Skyraider
Douglas	C-53D	Skytrooper
Douglas	C-54D	Skymaster
Fairchild	C-119G	Flying Boxcar
Grumman	HU-16	Albatross
Lockheed	EC-121D	Warning Star
Lockheed	F-104B	Starfighter
Lockheed	P-80B	Shooting Star
Lockheed	T-33A	Shooting Star
McDonnell	F-4C	Phantom II
McDonnell	F-101B	Voodoo
Mikoyan-Gurevich	MiG-21F	"Fishbed"
North American	F-86L	Sabre

The Soviet Union has produced one of its greatest exports in the MiG-21. Approximately 34 countries have flown the plane. Although lacking some of the sophisticated systems found in more advanced fighters, the MiG-21 has proven itself to be an inexpensive and highly functional fighter for over thirty years.

North American	T-28B	Trojan
North American	T-39A	Sabreliner
Piasecki	H-21C	Shawnee
Republic	F-84F	Thunderstreak
Republic	F-105D	Thunderchief
Taylorcraft	L-2M	Grasshopper
Vought	A-7D	Corsair II

NASA Ames Research Center

Visitor Center, Ames Research Center, Moffett Field, California 94035
(415) 604-6274

The Ames Research Center began operation in 1939 as an aircraft research laboratory under the direction of the National Advisory Committee for Aeronautics, the forerunner of the National Aeronautics and Space Administration (NASA). Research at Ames focuses on aerodynamics, guidance systems, human factors and life sciences. Found at Ames are the world's most advanced supercomputers and the largest wind tunnel.

Ames is adjacent to Moffett Field Naval Air Station. Located on Moffett Field and visible for miles is Hanger One, the South Bay area's most prominent structure. Originally constructed in the 1930s to house the airship U.S.S. *Macon*, the hanger stands 198 feet high and encompasses eight acres. The structure is a Naval Historical Monument.

The highlight of a visit to Ames is a tour of the facility. The exact tour route will depend on status of projects when the tour is conducted. Possible stops along the tour include the largest wind tunnel in the world, research aircraft, centrifuge and flight operations facility. The tours are conducted by guides versed in science and technology, as well as particular Ames' projects.

The Visitor Center presents exhibits that outline past, present and future projects conducted at the Ames Research Center. On display is a Lockheed U-2 high-altitude airplane, a Mercury capsule, wind tunnel models of future military aircraft and models of spacecraft.

DIRECTIONS TO MUSEUM: Ames is near Mountain View. From US Highway 101 take the Moffett Field exit. Follow signs to Moffett Field. In front of main gate for Moffett Field turn left and follow signs to NASA Ames Visitor Center.

ADMISSION COST: Free.

HOURS OF OPERATION: Open Monday-Friday 9am-4:30pm. See above for tour hours. Closed federal holidays.

MUSEUM NOTES: Displays are indoors. Film is available at the gift shop. Restaurants are nearby.

TOUR NOTES: Tours are conducted at 9:30am and 1:30pm Monday through Friday. Call tour office (415-604-6497) at least two weeks in advance to reserve a position (two months notice is required for large groups). Participants must be at least nine years old. Tour lasts approximately two hours. A large portion of the tour is outdoors, so tour may be canceled if it rains.

A brochure is available.

NASA Ames-Dryden Flight Research Facility

P.O. Box 273, Edwards, California 93523
(805) 258-3446

The Dryden Flight Research Facility is located at Edwards Air Force Base (see also page 35), the site of a multitude of aviation records and achievements including breaking the sound barrier by Captain Charles "Chuck" Yeager on October 14, 1947. As a facility of the National Aeronautics and Space Administration (NASA), Dryden is responsible for flight testing of advanced aeronautical technologies.

Since the late 1940s, Dryden has been the controlling facility for non-military flight research at Edwards. The most important program under Dryden's auspices was the X-15 series of flights. Three rocket-powered, experimental X-15s were constructed by North American, collectively flying 199 missions. Speed and altitude records were set, then broken by another flight of an X-15. When the program ended in 1968, the X-15 held the speed record of Mach 6.72 (4,520 mph) and the altitude record of 354,200 feet. Data from the X-15 flights, as well as research in lifting body technology, formed the basis for Dryden's contribution to the space program.

Current research at Dryden involves testing the Grumman X-29, an airplane with a forward-swept wing, and a General Dynamics F-111 that is capable of altering its wing curvature. Dryden also supports the landing phase of the Space Shuttle, whose original concept was proven by research performed at Dryden.

Daily tours of the hanger facility are conducted Monday through Friday at 10:15 am and 1:15 pm. Aircraft available for viewing are listed under DISPLAY AIRCRAFT, but some aircraft may not be present due to flight scheduling. The tour lasts approximately 90 minutes. Groups larger than ten must call for reservations.

DIRECTIONS TO MUSEUM: Dryden is located on Edwards Air Force Base which is near Rosamond. Enter Edwards Air Force Base from either Hwy 14 or Hwy 58. Ask for directions at gate.

ADMISSION COST: Free.

HOURS OF OPERATION: Open Monday-Friday 7:45am-3:30pm. Closed federal holidays.

MUSEUM NOTES: Display aircraft are indoors and outdoors. The gift shop has film. A cafeteria is in the Visitor Center.

A brochure describing the museum is available if requested.

Display Aircraft

MANUFACTURER	MODEL	POPULAR NAME
Bell	X-1E	
Boeing	B-52	Superfortress

Convair	990	
General Dynamics	F-16XL	Fighting Falcon
General Dynamics	F-111	
Grumman	X-29	
McDonnell Douglas	F-15	Eagle
McDonnell Douglas	F-18	Hornet

San Diego Aerospace Museum

2001 Pan American Plaza, Balboa Park, San Diego, California 92101
(619) 234-8291

With over sixty aircraft on exhibit, the San Diego Aerospace Museum provides the opportunity to view aircraft from several decades of flight. The majority of the aircraft on display predate World War II and include replicas of early gliders, several World War I aircraft and a Ford Trimotor.

Interesting modern aircraft include a Douglas SBD-5 Dauntless, Consolidated PBY-5A Catalina and a Convair YF2Y-1 Sea Dart.

The Seadart outside the museum is a jet-powered seaplane that was not purchased by the Navy. Interested in investigating a seaplane design without the restriction of propellers, the Navy awarded Convair a contract for development of a fighter seaplane. The plane was fitted with skis that retracted into the fuselage and two jet engines. One prototype exceeded the speed of sound, but disintegrated in a later flight. The Navy lost interest in the concept and evaluation ceased in 1957.

Visitors may also be interested in the International Aerospace Hall of Fame and the presentations at the Reuben H. Fleet Space Center and Science Center, also within the Balboa Park Complex.

The McDonnell F-4S was the last variation produced of the famous Phantom II series. The F-4S models were upgraded F-4J models. During the late 1960s and early 1970s, the Phantom II was the front-line fighter for the Air Force, Navy and Marine Corps, a rare occurrence of the last fifty years. When the F-14 and F-15 entered service the F-4s were relegated to Guard and Reserve units.

DIRECTIONS TO MUSEUM: The museum is located off of Park Blvd. in the museum area of Balboa Park. Facilities throughout the park provide maps.

ADMISSION COST: Adults $4.00; children (6-17 yrs.) $1.00. Ticket packages are available in the gift shops throughout Balboa Park that offer savings on multi-museum tickets.

HOURS OF OPERATION: Open daily 10am-4:30pm. Closed New Year's Day, Thanksgiving and Christmas.

MUSEUM NOTES: Display aircraft are inside and outside. Film can be purchased in the gift shop. A restaurant is onsite and other restaurants are nearby.

A brochure is available.

Display Aircraft

MANUFACTURER	MODEL	POPULAR NAME
Aeronca	C-3	Duplex
Albatros	D.Va	
American Eagle	A-1	
Bleriot	XI	
Boeing	F4B-4	
Cayley Glider		
Chanute Glider		
Consolidated	PBY-5A	Catalina
Consolidated	PT-1	
Convair	YF2Y-1	Sea Dart
Curtiss		*Little Looper*
Curtiss	A-1	Triad
Curtiss	B-1	Robin
Curtiss	JN-4D	"Jenny"
Curtiss	P-40E	Warhawk
Curtiss-Wright	CW-1	Junior
de Havilland	60-GM	Moth
de Havilland	DH-4	
Deperdussin	C	
Douglas	A-4B	Skyhawk
Douglas	SBD-5	Dauntless
Fleet	2	
Fokker	D.VII	
Fokker	Dr.I	
General Dynamics	BGM-109 Tomahawk	
Glasflugel		Libelle
Grumman	F6F-3	Hellcat
Grumman	J2F-6	Duck
Jungster	VI	
Junkers	Ju 87	Stuka
Leonardo di Vinci Ornithopter		

Lilienthal Glider		
McDonnell	F-4S	Phantom II
McDonnell	Gemini Capsule	
McDonnell	Mercury Capsule	
Mercury Air		Shoestring
Messerschmitt	Bf 109G-14	Gustav
Mikoyan-Gurevich	MiG-15	"Fagot"
Mikoyan-Gurevich	MiG-17F	"Fresco"
Mitsubishi	A6M7	Zero "Zeke"
Montgolfier Ballon		
Montgomery Glider		
Nieuport	28	
Nieuport	XI	
North American	F-86	Sabre
North American Rockwell	Apollo Command/	
		Service Module
Piper	J-3	Cub
Pitts	S-1-S	Special
Radioplane	OQ-2	
Ryan	B-5	Brougham
Ryan	Firebee II	
Ryan	M-1	
Ryan (replica)	NYP	*Spirit of St. Louis*
Ryan	PT-22	Recruit
Ryan	S-T	
Ryan	X-13	
SPAD	VII	
Standard	J-1	
Stearman	N2S-3	Kaydet
Sundancer		
Supermarine	Mk XVI	Spitfire
Thomas-Morse	S-4C	
Waco	YKS-7	
Wee Bee		
Wright (replica)	EX	*Vin Fiz*
Wright Flyer		

Silver Wings Aviation Museum
Mather Air Force Base, California 95655
(916) 364-2177

The Silver Wings Aviation Museum is situated on Mather Air Force Base. Mather was established in June 1918 making it one of the older airbases in the United States. Originally used for pilot training, Mather is now the primary training facility for all US military navigators, as well as those from many foreign countries. However, Mather is scheduled for closure in 1993 due to an armed forces reduction.

The museum presents a set of exhibits that reflects over eight decades of aviation history pertaining to Mather AFB, the local area, general aviation and military aviation. Particularly interesting are the exhibits and artifacts related to navigation.

Cross-country flight during flying's infancy was advisable only on clear days over land. Maritime navigational techniques and implements were used at first, but military and commercial demands for safe flying in inclement conditions forced improvements. Radio, radar and electronic navigational aids gradually evolved. In today's most sophisticated systems, computers direct and fly the aircraft with no more input from the pilot than pushing buttons to identify the destination.

DIRECTIONS TO MUSEUM: Mather Air Force Base is southeast of Sacramento. From US 50 take Mather AFB exit and follow signs. Stop at Visitor Center for pass and directions.

Known as the Beech Model 18, Beech produced over 4,000 of the plane in a number of variants including AT-7 Navigator, AT-11 Kansas, C-45 Expeditor and F-2. The AT-11s similar to the one shown here were the standard bombing trainer for the Air Force during World War II. Over 40,000 bombardiers received training in the AT-11 Kansas.

ADMISSION COST: Free.

HOURS OF OPERATION: Open Monday-Friday 10am-4pm; Saturday and Sunday noon-4pm. Closed major holidays.

MUSEUM NOTES: Display aircraft are indoors and outdoors. Film is not available at the gift shop. A restaurant is located offbase.

A brochure is available.

Display Aircraft

MANUFACTURER	MODEL	POPULAR NAME
Beech	AT-11	Kansas
Convair	T-29	Flying Classroom
Corben	Super Ace	
McDonnell	F-4	Phantom II
Republic	F-105	Thunderchief

Spruce Goose

P.O. Box 8, Long Beach, California 90801
(213) 435-3511

Mammoth and unique aptly describe the one-of-a-kind *Spruce Goose*. The airplane's creator was the eccentric tycoon Howard Hughes. Hughes, in collaboration with industrialist Henry Kaiser, built the *Spruce Goose* during World War II to fulfill a government contract for a troop-carrying flying boat. The war ended before completion of the plane and the contract expired. Hughes bankrolled construction until the plane was finished. On November 2, 1947, during planned taxi tests, the plane lifted off the water and flew for about a mile, to the consternation of the press reporters on board and to the delight of the pilot, Howard Hughes. The *Spruce Goose* was relegated to a hanger and never flew again. The $28 million paid by the government for the plane was considered excessive by some members of Congress, and a boondoggle by others.

The *Spruce Goose* is the largest airplane ever flown, although the Lockheed C-5 and Russian Antonov An-124 exceed it in length. The wing span exceeds the length of a football field and supports eight engines. Officially designated the HK-1, but dubbed the *Spruce Goose*, the plane was built of birch. Wood was chosen to lessen the demand for aluminum needed for other aircraft.

Also on display is a replica of the Hughes H-1 Special. Built during the heyday of air racing and record setting, the specially built H-1 was piloted by Howard Hughes to the landplane record of 352 mph in 1935. Hughes also set the transcontinental record in the H-1 at 7 hours 28 minutes in 1937. The plane was retired the same year. The original H-1 is a part of the Paul E. Garber Facility collection (see also page 137).

The *Spruce Goose* and other aviation exhibits are a part of the Queen Mary Entertainment Center. Admission is for the whole complex and separate admission just to the *Spruce Goose* is not offered.

DIRECTIONS TO MUSEUM: The complex is located in the bay area of Long Beach. Follow Long Beach Fwy. to Long Beach area then follow signs to Queen Mary.

ADMISSION COST: Adults $17.50; children $9.50.

HOURS OF OPERATION: Open daily 10am-6pm; open until 9pm during summer months.

MUSEUM NOTES: Display aircraft are indoors. Film can be purchased in the gift shop. There are restaurants in the complex.

A brochure is available.

Travis Air Force Museum
Travis Air Force Base, California 94535
(707) 424-5605

Serving as the exit or entry point for thousands of military personnel traveling to or from points west of the United States, Travis Air Force Base is known as the "Gateway to the Pacific" to the military. The base was created in 1943 and originally named Fairfield-Suisun Army Air Field. Navy and Marine pilots took advantage of the strong prevailing winds and used the base for landing practice in its early years. First assigned to the Air Transport Command, the base came under the command of the Strategic Air Command during the fifties, but reverted to the Air Transport Service (later Military Airlift Command) in 1958.

Now home for the huge C-5 and C-141 transports, a variety of aircraft have been stationed at Travis. Several of the aircraft on display are transport category airplanes, although fighters and bombers are also exhibited. Included among the display aircraft is a Douglas C-124 Globemaster II. Known as "Old Shakey" to aircrew, C-124s provided air transport for bulky cargo such as tanks, trucks and field vehicles. Globemasters flew to all continents performing military and humanitarian missions from their introduction into service in 1950 until 1974.

Known as the Beech Model 18, Beech produced over 4,000 of the planes in a number of variants including AT-7 Navigator, AT-11 Kansas, C-45 Expeditor and F-2. C-45s like that shown above were used for transport and utility flying. Several hundred were rebuilt during the 1950s and continued in service until 1963.

The Douglas C-124 Globemaster II evolved from the C-74 Globemaster, a less than desireable design that resulted in only 14 C-74s entering service. But with the modification to a much larger fuselage and resulting capacity increase, the plane satisfied Air Force requirements and 448 Globemaster IIs were purchased. The large size of the fuselage permitted the use of clam-shell doors at the front. Heavy equipment such as tanks and trucks could be driven up a ramp into the airplane. C-124s entered service in 1950 and were flown until the mid-1970s.

DIRECTIONS TO MUSEUM: Travis Air Force Base is located off of I-80 near Fairfield. Exit I-80 at Fairfield and follow Air Base Parkway to Travis Air Force Base main gate. Stop at Visitor Registration Building to right of gate entrance for directions and a pass.

ADMISSION COST: Free.

HOURS OF OPERATION: Open Monday-Friday 9am-4pm; Saturday-Sunday 9am-5pm. Closed New Year's Day, Thanksgiving and Christmas.

MUSEUM NOTES: Display aircraft are indoors and outdoors. There is a gift shop. A restaurant is located nearby.

A brochure is available.

Display Aircraft

MANUFACTURER	MODEL	POPULAR NAME
Beech	AT-11	Kansas
Beech	C-45	Expeditor
Boeing	B-52	Stratofortress
Cessna	AT-17	Bobcat
Cessna	LC-126	
Cessna	O-2A	
Cessna	U-3A	

The LC-126 was a militarized version of the Cessna 195. Powered by a Jacobs radial engine, LC-126s were used as instrument trainers for pilot training, as well as flying missions for liason and arctic rescue. The civilian 195 was produced from 1947 to 1954 as a four-place luxury plane.

Convair	C-131	Samaritan
Convair	F-102	Delta Dagger
Douglas	A-26K	Counter-Invader
Douglas	C-54	Skymaster
Douglas	C-118	Liftmaster
Douglas	C-124	Globemaster II
Fairchild	C-119	Flying Boxcar
Fairchild	C-123	Provider
Fairchild	PT-19	Cornell
Gonzales	1912 biplane	
Grumman	HU-16	Albatross
Kaman	HH-43	Huskie
Lockheed	C-56	Lodestar
Lockheed	F-104	Starfighter
McDonnell	F-4C	Phantom II
McDonnell	F-101B	Voodoo
North American	F-86L	Sabre
North American	T-39A	Sabreliner
Piasecki	H-21	Workhorse
Piper	L-4	Grasshopper
Republic	F-105D	Thunderchief
Sikorsky	CH-34	Choctaw
Stinson	L-5	Sentinel
Vultee	BT-13	Valiant

Western Aerospace Museum

P.O. Box 14264, Airport Station, Oakland, California 94614
(415) 638-7100

The museum is located in Hanger 5 at Oakland's North Field, site of the original Oakland airport. The hanger was constructed in 1929 for United Airlines and Boeing School of Aeronuatics. North Field had the first paved runway in the world and was the airport of choice during the 1920s and 1930s when flying in the Bay Area, overshadowing the San Francisco airport. World class events such as the Dole races, the flight of *Southern Cross*, and Amelia Earhart's Pacific flights began at North Field. North Field remains as a major general aviation airport while commercial aviation uses the adjacent Oakland International Airport. An interesting film of North Field's history is shown at the museum.

A Lockheed 10A Electra is in the museum's collection. The airplane was developed during the 1930s to compete with the Boeing 247 and Douglas DC-3 in the airline market. The model 10A Electra was marginally successful. However, a variant of the model 10A, the model 14, was produced in large numbers as the Hudson during World War II.

The Lockheed 10 Electra was originally designed with a single vertical stabilizer in the tail. The tail was unable to provide sufficient control with only one engine operating, so Clarence "Kelly" Johnson, a recently-hired fledgling engineer, was given the task to solve the problem. The tail was modified to a twin-stabilizer arrangement. The Electra became a successful endeavor for Lockheed, and Johnson went on to organize and lead the renowned "Skunk Works" design group for Lockheed.

The Short Solent was one of the last large flying boats. Derived from a World War II design, the Solents were built shortly after the war, but there was insufficient interest to continue production. Large flying boats were no longer desirable due to the development of large land-based airplanes during the war, and the construction of airfields around the world.

Amelia Earhart was flying a model 10A Electra during her mysterious around-the-world attempt.

Also on display is the Short Solent flying boat used in the movie Raiders of the Lost Ark. There is also the Chezh-Zlin, a world championship aerobatic airplane during the 1960s and 1970s.

DIRECTIONS TO MUSEUM: The museum is located at Oakland International Airport at 8260 Boeing St., Building 621. From I-880 exit onto Hegenberger and follow signs to airport. Turn right at Earhart Rd. (North Field), then turn right at Cooke St. (museum sign). Museum is visible straight ahead.

ADMISSION COST: Free (donation requested).

HOURS OF OPERATION: Open Tuesday-Sunday 10am-4pm. Closed major holidays.

MUSEUM NOTES: Display aircraft are indoors and outdoors. There is a gift shop, but film is not available. There are vending machines onsite and a restaurant is nearby.

A brochure is available.

Display Aircraft

MANUFACTURER	MODEL	POPULAR NAME
Chezh-Zlin	526F	
Grumman (General Motors)	TBM	Avenger
Lockheed	10A	Electra
Short	Mk III	Solent

Edward J. Peterson Space Command Museum
3 SSW/PAH (Stop 15), Peterson AFB, Colorado 80914
(719) 554-4915

The museum is located on Peterson Air Force Base, home for the Air Force Space Command. With the military aspects of space becoming more critical for national defense, the Space Command was created in 1982 to serve as a focal point for Air Force missions involved with space. Missions are predominately concerned with satellites, communications, missile tracking and warning, and monitoring of all the nation's satellites.

The original terminal building, built in 1941, for Colorado Springs airport now houses the museum. Inside the museum you will find artifacts and memorabilia reflecting the history of civilian and military flying in the Pikes Peak region. One area is set aside to display equipment, including a satellite, that characterize Air Force efforts in space.

The aircraft exhibit consists primarily of fighter airplanes. Two examples of early interceptors are the Lockheed F-94C Starfire and Northrop F-89J Scorpion. Both airplanes were designed to intercept Russian intercontinental bombers, the primary threat to national defense in the 1950s. These "nearly automatic" interceptors utilized what were then sophisticated fire-control systems and air-to-air missiles. The F-89 was the first airplane capable of firing an air-to-air missile with a nuclear warhead. Both airplanes were replaced by supersonic F-101s and F-102s, versions of which are also on display.

DIRECTIONS TO MUSEUM: Peterson AFB is adjacent to Colorado Springs airport which is located on east side of Colorado Springs off of US 24. Follow signs to main gate of base. Stop at Visitors Center to obtain pass and directions.

ADMISSION COST: Free.

HOURS OF OPERATION: Open Tuesday-Friday 8:30am-4:30pm; Saturday 9:30am-4:30pm. Closed Sunday, Monday and holidays.

MUSEUM NOTES: Display aircraft are outdoors. A gift shop is in the museum. There are no restaurants nearby.

A brochure is available.

Display Aircraft

MANUFACTURER	MODEL	POPULAR NAME
Avro	CF-100	Canuck
Boeing	CIM-10	Bomarc
Convair	F-102A	Delta Dagger
Curtiss	P-40N	Warhawk
Lockheed	EC-121T	Constellation
Lockheed	F-94C	Starfire
Lockheed	F-104A	Starfighter
Lockheed	T-33A	Shooting Star

Martin	EB-57E	Canberra
McDonnell	CF-101B	Voodoo
McDonnell	F-101B	Voodoo
North American	F-86L	Sabre
Northrop	F-89J	Scorpion
Republic	P-47	Thunderbolt
Western Electric	Nike	
Western Electric	Nike Hawk	
Western Electric	Nike Hercules	

Lowry Heritage Museum

LTTC/LHM, Lowry AFB, Colorado 80230
(303) 676-3028/3230

Lowry Air Force Base is situated on the eastern perimeter of Denver just south of Stapleton International Airport. No longer possessing an active flying unit, Lowry serves as a training and support base. From 1955 to 1958 the base was the temporary location for the Air Force Academy (see also page 73).

Although no longer serving as host base for an active flying unit, Lowry AFB has been a base for a wide variety of aircraft. The museum exhibits some of the aircraft based at Lowry. Here you'll find a collection of the "Century Series" fighters that were the backbone of the Air Force's fighter force during the 1950s and 1960s.

DIRECTIONS TO MUSEUM: From I-225 exit onto 6th Ave., travel west and enter base gate at Dayton and 6th Ave. From Colfax Ave. travel south on Havana to 6th Ave. then west to gate at Dayton. Directions to museum will be provided at gate.

ADMISSION COST: Free

HOURS OF OPERATION: Open Monday-Friday 9am-4:30pm; Saturday 10am-4pm; closed Sunday.

MUSEUM NOTES: Display aircraft are located inside and outside. Film is not available at gift shop. Vending machines are onsite and restaurants are nearby.

A brochure is available.

Display Aircraft

MANUFACTURER	MODEL	POPULAR NAME
Beech	C-45H	Expeditor
Boeing	B-29	Superfortress
Boeing	B-52B	Stratofortress
Cessna	U-3A	Blue Canoe
Convair	F-102A	Delta Dagger
Convair	F-106A	Delta Dart
Convair	VC-131E	
Douglas	B-18	Bolo
Lockheed	F-104A	Starfighter
Martin	EB-57E	Intruder
McDonnell	F-4C	Phantom II
McDonnell	F-101B	Voodoo
North American	F-86H	Sabre
North American	F-100D	Super Sabre
Piasecki	H-21	Workhorse
Republic	F-105	Thunderchief
Republic	RF-84K	Thunderflash

United States Air Force Academy

Public Affairs, USAF Academy, Colorado 80840
(719) 472-4050

The mission of the United States Air Force Academy is to provide instruction and experience for the cadets who are the future career officers of the Air Force. Approximately 4,400 cadets comprise the student population, of which 10-12 per cent are women. Graduating cadets earn bachelor degrees in science and receive a commission as a second lieutenant in the regular Air Force. Graduates who do not attend flying training must serve five years on active duty. Graduates accepted for flight training must serve eight years after training if a pilot, or five years if a navigator.

The Academy encompasses 18,000 scenic acres along the Rampart Range just north of Colorado Springs. Until the present campus site could be completed, the Academy was located for three years at Lowry Air Force Base near Denver. In the fall of 1958 the first wing of cadets occupied the Colorado Springs campus. In the main campus area is the often photographed and impressive Cadet Chapel. Visitors can visit the Chapel and view the Cadet area after walking the trail from the Visitor Center.

One of the better times to visit the Academy is prior to lunchtime. During the academic year (mid-August to first week in June), there is a noon formation, then the Cadet Wing marches to the dining hall. The best viewing location is at the wall that surrounds the Chapel and overlooks the Cadet area. Prior to the noon formation, observe the "doolies" (freshman) as they walk the quadrangle in straight lines and square corners.

The Visitor Center provides exhibits, displays and movies related to the Air Force and the Academy. One of the displays is a replica of a typical cadet room. Maps of self-guided tours are available at the Visitor Center. Along the entrance road is a Boeing B-52 Stratofortress. Airplanes are on display in the Cadet area but cannot be viewed up close as the area is normally closed to the general public.

Just south of exit to Academy on west side of I-25 is a turnout that allows viewing the Academy airfield. Flight operations at the airfield focus on cadet flight training in light planes and sailplanes.

DIRECTIONS TO ACADEMY: The Academy is approximately 12 miles north of Colorado Springs. From I-25 take exit 156-B and follow signs to Visitor Center.

ADMISSION COST: Free.

HOURS OF OPERATION: Open daily 9am-5pm. Closed New Year's Day and Christmas Day.

ACADEMY NOTES: There is a gift shop at the Visitor Center and film is available. A snack bar is located in the Visitor Center. If visiting Academy in fall, check football schedule to miss traffic congestion.

A brochure is available.

New England Air Museum

Bradley International Airport, Windsor Locks, Connecticut 06096
(203) 623-3305

The New England Air Museum proclaims it is the "Largest Aviation Museum in the Northeast." Based on the number of aircraft exhibited, the statement may be correct. The aircraft collection ranges from homebuilts to a commercial airliner. There is also an extensive collection of engines including several which predate 1911. Igor Sikorsky's contributions to aviation are commemorated in a special exhibit along with two Sikorsky helicopters.

A number of interesting airplanes are on display. Four racers from the heyday of air races in the 1930s are exhibited: a Gee Bee R-1, Gee Bee Z, Laird *Solution* and Marcoux Bromberg. Easily identified by their characteristic "engine with an airplane attached" shape, the Gee Bees were equally well known by their pilots for their evil handling characteristics. Once asked how he flew the Gee Bee, Jimmy Doolittle replied, "Very carefully." Gee Bees were winners of the Thompson Trophy in 1931 and 1932. Fast, but dangerous, a pilot was killed flying a Gee Bee in 1931, 1933, 1934 and 1935. Faster, better designed planes overtook the Gee Bees and the famous racers eventually faded from air racing.

The engine collection spans the period from the turn-of-the-century internal combustion engine to the modern jet. Of interest is a cutaway of one of the earliest jets, a German Junkers Jumo developed during World War II.

DIRECTIONS TO MUSEUM: The museum is located north of Bradley International Airport. From I-91 take Exit 40 onto Rt. 20. Go west to Rt. 75. Turn right on Rt. 75 and watch for museum sign.

ADMISSION COST: Adults $5.50; senior citizens $4.50; children (6-11 yrs.) $2.00.

HOURS OF OPERATION: Open daily 10am-5pm. Closed Thanksgiving and Christmas.

MUSEUM NOTES: Display aircraft are located indoors and outdoors. Film can be purchased at the gift shop. There are vending machines and a restaurant is nearby.

A brochure is available.

Display Aircraft

MANUFACTURER	MODEL	POPULAR NAME
Bell	UH-1B	"Huey"
Bleriot	XI	
Boeing	B-29A	Superfortress
Boeing	B-47E	Stratojet
Chanute Glider		

Corben	Jr. Ace	
Curtiss	XF 15C-1	
de Havilland	U-6A	Beaver
Douglas	A-3B	Skywarrior
Douglas	A-4A	Skyhawk
Douglas	A-26C	Invader
Douglas	F4D-1	Skyray
Dyndiuk Sport		
Fairey Gannet	AEW3	
Fokker	Dr.I	Triplane
Gee Bee	A	
Gee Bee (replica)	R-1	
Gee Bee (replica)	Z	
Grumman (General Motors)	FM-2	Wildcat
Goodyear	ZNP-K	
Grumman	E-1B	Tracer
Grumman	F6F-5K	Hellcat
Grumman	HU-16E	Albatross
Gyrodyne	QH-50C	Dash
Heath	Parasol	
Hiller	OH-23G	Raven
Kaman	HH-43F	Huskie
Kaman	K-225	
Laird	*Solution*	
Lockheed	F-94C	Starfire
Marcoux Bromberg		
Martin	RB-57A	Canberra
Mead Rhone	Ranger	
Monerai	S	
Nixon Special		
North American	F-100A	Super Sabre
North American	T-28C	Trojan
Piper	J-3	Cub
Rearwin	Cloudster	
Republic	F-105B	Thunderchief
Republic	P-47D	Thunderbolt
Rutan	Quickie	
Rutan	VariEze	
Sikorsky	LH-34D	Seabat
Sikorsky	R-4B	Hoverfly
Stinson	Detroiter	
Sud	VI-R	Caravelle
Vought	F-8K	Crusader
Vought	XF4U-4	Corsair

Dover AFB Historical Center

P.O. Box 02050, Dover Air Force Base, Delaware 19902
(302) 677-5938

Established in 1941, Dover Air Force Base is a part of the Military Airlift Command and home base for a wing of the huge C-5A/B Galaxy transport airplanes. Capable of carrying over 145 tons of cargo, the C-5 is the largest aircraft flying in the Western world.

The museum possesses military artifacts and memorabilia as well as several display airplanes. Among the airplanes is a Boeing B-17 Flying Fortress. Leading the strategic bombing campaign against Germany in World War II, over 12,000 B-17s were manufactured in several variations. Most were scrapped after the war, but a considerable number operated in foreign air forces, some into the 1960s. A few served as chemical bombers for forest fire fighting. A very small number continue flying on the warbird circuit.

DIRECTIONS TO MUSEUM: Follow US 113 south of Dover to main gate of Dover Air Force Base. Obtain pass and directions at main gate.

ADMISSION COST: Free.

HOURS OF OPERATION: Open Monday-Friday 10am-noon; Saturday 10am-2pm. Closed Sunday and holidays.

MUSEUM NOTES: Display aircraft are indoors and outdoors. Film is not available in the gift shop. A restaurant is nearby.

A brochure is available.

Display Aircraft

MANUFACTURER	MODEL	POPULAR NAME
Beech	C-45	Expeditor
Boeing	B-17	Flying Fortress
Cessna	O-2	Skymaster
Convair	C-131	Samaritan
Douglas	C-47	Skytrain
Douglas	C-54	Skymaster
McDonnell	F-101	Voodoo

National Air and Space Museum

6th St. & Independence Ave., S.W., Washington, D.C. 20560
(202) 357-2700

To use an overworked phrase, "the National Air and Space Museum has something for everyone." The museum caters to everyone from school-age children to knowledgeable enthusiasts. Each year approximately nine million people view the nation's aircraft treasures, and although the museum is spacious and well laid out, it can be crowded.

The museum is primarily arranged in a series of galleries, each depicting an era or segment of aviation. Some of the aircraft and spacecraft exhibited in the galleries are historically significant. In the Milestones of Flight gallery are found the sound breaking Bell

Hanging in the Air and Space Museum is the Ryan NYP Spirit of St. Louis *flown solo by Charles Lindbergh in 1927 across the Atlantic. With meticulous attention, Lindbergh contributed to the design and construction of the plane. Anything not absolutely required was left out—no radio—to obtain the lightest weight possible. Lindbergh computed fuel consumption rather than install heavy fuel gauges. No sextant was carried since Lindbergh couldn't fly and use the instrument simultaneously. Lindbergh's flight and that of other long-distance flyers helped prove to the public that air travel was safe and reliable.*

The Albatros D.Va was one of the best fighters of World War I. German ace von Richtofen scored many of his victories in an earlier model of the Albatros.

X-1 *Glamorous Glennis* flown by Captain Charles "Chuck" Yeager, Major John Glenn's Mercury capsule and the Ryan *Spirit of St. Louis* flown by Charles Lindberg across the Atlantic.

In other galleries are exhibited types of aircraft and spacecraft that were significant for their advancement of flight capabilities. Among these are a Messerschmitt ME-262A German jet fighter, a Wright 1909 Military Flyer (the world's first military airplane), Lockheed XP-80 Shooting Star, Douglas DC-3 and North American X-15A-1.

An extensive collection of space related items ranges from rockets constructed by early rocket pioneer Robert Goddard to present-day spacesuits. Several satellites are on display, including an example of the first man-made satellite, Sputnik. Among the rockets on display are a German World War II V-1, an Air Force Jupiter C, and a Soviet SS-20. Included among the spacecraft are the Gemini 7 capsule and Skylab 4 Command Module, as well as a variety of Lunar equipment, such as a Lunar Rover.

In addition to aircraft and spacecraft, the Air and Space Museum presents artifacts and memorabilia to enlighten, explain and inform the museum visitor of the history, technol-

Boeing built the F4B for the Navy and Marine Corps. The F4B and the Army's P-12 version were a result of Boeing developing the fighter in 1928 with its own money. The project proved successful with the military purchasing over 500 of the planes, a significant number considering the small size of the country's military air branches at that time.

ogy and feeling of flight. Aviation and space related programs are shown in the theater and planetarium. Whether its a one-hour side trip or a day-long excursion, visiting the National Air and Space Museum is a "must do" for anyone interested in aviation.

DIRECTIONS TO MUSEUM: Located on Independence Ave. between 4th and 7th Sts., S.W., the best means of transportation is the subway system. The museum is situated on the National Mall adjacent to other Smithsonian museums. The museums are marked on most Smithsonian literature, on map markers on the Mall, and on detailed maps of Washington, D.C.

ADMISSION COST: Free

HOURS OF OPERATION: Open daily 10am-5:30pm except Christmas. Hours may be extended during summer.

MUSEUM NOTES: All display aircraft are indoors. There are three gift shops and film is available. An 800-seat cafeteria and a 200-seat restaurant are within the museum.

A brochure is available.

Display Aircraft

MANUFACTURER	MODEL	POPULAR NAME
Double Eagle gondola		
Explorer II gondola		
Albatros	D.Va	
Beech	C17L	Staggerwing
Bell	206L	LongRanger
Bell	X-1	*Glamorous Glennis*
Bell	XP-59A	Airacomet
Bensen	B-6	Gyroglider
Bensen	B-8M	Gyrocopter
Bleriot	XI	
Boeing	247D	
Boeing	F4B-4	
Boeing	P-26A	Peashooter
Boeing	Minuteman	
Chrysler	Jupiter C	
Curtiss	D	Headless Pusher
Curtiss	F9C-2	Sparrowhawk
Curtiss	J-1	Robin *Ole Miss*
Curtiss	P-40E	Warhawk
Curtiss	R3C-2	
de Havilland	DH-4	
Douglas	A4D-2N	Skyhawk
Douglas	D-558-2	
Douglas	DC-3	
Douglas	DC-7	
Douglas	DWC	World Cruiser *Chicago*
Douglas	M-2	
Douglas	SBD-6	Dauntless
Ecker	Flying Boat	
Fairchild	FC-2	
Firestone	WAC Corporal	
Focke-Achgelis	Fa 330	Rotor Kite
Fokker	D.VII	
Fokker	T-2	
Ford	5-AT	Trimotor
Gallaudet	Hydro-Bike	
Germany	V-1	
Goodyear "Pilgram" gondola		
Grumman	F4F-4	Wildcat
Grumman	G-22	Gulfhawk II
Grumman	X-29	
Hawker Siddeley	Kestrel	

Hiller	XH-44	Hiller-Copter
Kellett	XO-60	
Langley	Aerodrome	
Lilienthal 1894 Glider		
Lockheed	5	Vega (Earhart)
Lockheed	5-C	Vega *Winnie Mae*

Standing together are examples of intermediate-range nuclear missiles of the United States and the Soviet Union. On the right is a U.S. Army Pershing II and on the left a Soviet SS-20. Their brethren are to be dismantled and destroyed according to the Intermediate Range Nuclear Forces Treaty.

Lockheed	8	Sirius (Lindbergh)
Lockheed	F-104A	Starfighter
Lockheed	U-2C	
Lockheed	XP-80	Shooting Star
Macchi	MC 202	Folgore
MacCready	Gossamer Condor	
Martin	B-26B	Marauder Flak Bait
Martin	Vanguard	
Martin	Viking	
McDonnell	FH-1	Phantom I
McDonnell	Gemini Capsule	
McDonnell	Mercury Capsule Friendship 7	
Messerschmitt	Bf 109G-6	Gustav
Messerschmitt	Me 262A	Schwalbe
Mitsubishi	A6M5	Zero "Zeke"
North American	P-51D	Mustang
North American	X-15A	
North American Rockwell	Apollo 11 Command Module	
Northrop	Alpha	
Northrop	Gamma	Polar Star
Northrop	M2-F3	Lifting Body
Pentecose	E III	Hoppicopter
Piasecki	PV-2	
Pitcairn	PA-5	Mailwing
Rockwell	HiMAT	
Ryan	NYP	Spirit of St. Louis
Sikorsky	UH-34D	Seahorse
Sikorsky	XR-4	
SPAD	XIII	
Supermarine	Mk VII	Spitfire
Voyager		
Wittman		Buster
Wright	Flyer	
Wright 1909 Military Flyer		
Wright	EX	Vin Fiz

Air Force Armament Museum

100 Museum Drive, Eglin Air Force Base, Florida 32542
(904) 882-4062

Encompassing over 460,000 acres, Eglin Air Force Base is the largest air force base in the Western world. Originally named Valpraiso Bombing and Gunnery Base, the site became a major missile test center in the 1950s. Much of the munitions and missiles found in past or present Air Force inventory was developed or tested at Eglin.

The museum reflects the history and development of the armament systems tested at Eglin. On display are examples ranging from early unguided bombs to the later sophisticated laser-guided bombs. Missiles on display range from the early Mace to the later cruise missiles. One museum room houses an extensive collection of automatic weapons, rifles and handguns dating from the flintlock era.

The Mace was a subsonic surface-to-surface missile, popularly known as a "cruise missile." They were deployed and launched from a trailer. The Mace possessed an inertial navigation guidance system and a terrain-following radar system that made it less vulnerable to enemy countermeasures than earlier systems. Deployed from 1959 until the early 1970s, Mace was capable of delivering a nuclear warhead up to 1,200 miles away.

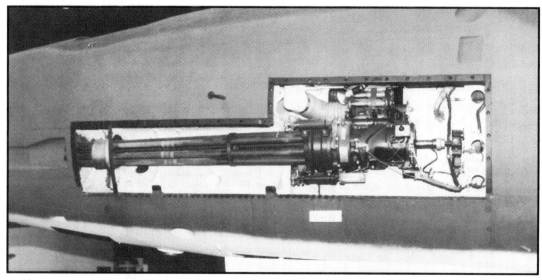

Early in the 1950s General Electric developed a rapid-firing, multiple-barrel cannon. The barrel cluster rotates similar to the 1800s Gatling gun, but at very high speed. Typical machine gun rate-of-fire is 800-1,200 rounds-per-minute. Rate-of-fire for the "minigun" of the F-105 in the photograph is 6,000 rounds-per-minute. Most current U.S. fighters are equipped with a version of the minigun.

Among the display aircraft is a Lockheed SR-71 Blackbird. Deactivated in 1990, the SR-71 airplanes were used extensively to gather intelligence at speeds in excess of 2,000 miles per hour and at altitudes exceeding 80,000 feet. Complexities in flight required that the two-man crew wear flight suits similar to those of astronauts and undergo similar training.

DIRECTIONS TO MUSEUM: The museum is located on Hwy. 85 just outside the main gate to Eglin AFB.

ADMISSION COST: Free.

HOURS OF OPERATION: Open daily 9:30am-4:30pm. Closed New Year's Day, Thanksgiving and Christmas.

MUSEUM NOTES: Display aircraft are located indoors and outdoors. There is a gift shop. Restaurants are located nearby.

A brochure is available.

Display Aircraft

MANUFACTURER	MODEL	POPULAR NAME
Boeing	B-17	Flying Fortress
Boeing	CIM-10	Bomarc
Boeing	RB-47	Stratojet

Douglas	C-47	Skytrain
Lockheed	F-80	Shooting Star
Lockheed	F-104	Starfighter
Lockheed	SR-71	Blackbird
Lockheed	T-33	Shooting Star
Martin	CGM-13	Mace
McDonnell	F-4	Phantom II
McDonnell	F-101	Voodoo
North American	B-25	Mitchell
North American	F-86	Sabre
North American	P-51	Mustang
Republic	F-84	Thunderjet
Republic	F-105	Thunderchief
Republic	P-47	Thunderbolt
Rockwell	AGM-28	Hound Dog

Florida Military Aviation Museum

P.O. Box 17332, 16055 Fairchild Drive, Clearwater, Florida 34622
(813) 535-9007

The Florida Military Aviation Museum is primarily oriented towards the collection and preservation of military aircraft based at some time in Florida. The task appears considerable when you consider the important air bases in Florida, namely Eglin, Homestead, MacDill, Patrick and Tyndall Air Force Bases, and Cecil, Jacksonville, Key West, Pensacola and Whiting Naval Air Stations. A wide variety of military aircraft have flown from the runways of those bases.

The aircraft in the museum range from the simple T-41 trainer, a variant of the popular civilian Cessna 172 Skyhawk, to the fast-moving McDonnell F-4A Phantom II fighter (the plane displayed is the third production Phantom II built). All of the aircraft were important members of Air Force, Navy, Army and Coast Guard inventories.

DIRECTIONS TO MUSEUM: The museum is located on the northwest corner of Tampa-St. Petersburg International Airport at 16055 Fairchild Dr.

ADMISSION COST: Adults $2.00; children 75¢.

HOURS OF OPERATION: Open Tuesday, Thursday & Saturday 10am-4pm; Sunday 1-5pm. Closed major holidays.

MUSEUM NOTES: Display aircraft are indoors and outdoors. There is a gift shop, but film is not available. Vending machines are onsite and a restaurant is nearby.

A brochure is available.

Display Aircraft

MANUFACTURER	MODEL	POPULAR NAME
Beech	AT-11	Kansas
Cessna	T-41	Mescalero
Convair	F-102D	Delta Dagger
de Havilland	L-20	Beaver
Douglas	A-4	Skyhawk
Douglas	C-47	Skytrain
Grumman	OV-1	Mohawk
Lockheed	P2V-3	Neptune
Lockheed	T-33	Shooting Star
North American	F-86D	Sabre
Republic	F-105B	Thunderchief
Sikorsky	H-34	Seahorse

Flying Tigers Warbird Air Museum
231 N. Hoagland Boulevard., Kissimmee, Florida 34741
(407) 933-1942

The focus of Flying Tigers Warbird Air Museum is displaying World War II era airplanes that have been restored to flying condition. The museum is an outgrowth of Tom Reilly's restoration company. After more than a decade of resurrecting tired, often unflyable warbirds, Reilly created the museum in 1988 so the public could view the craftsmanship of the artisans of the Warbird Air Museum.

Although not on display, but significant as an example of the work performed by the museum's staff, is the Consolidated B-24J Liberator *All American* now flying due to the work performed at the Warbird Air Museum. *All American* is the only fully restored B-24 flying in the world. The project required over 97,000 hours of labor, often entailing fabrication of new components. Several restorations are usually underway and within view.

The museum sponsors an airshow during the last week of December. Contact the museum for dates and times.

DIRECTIONS TO MUSEUM: The museum is located on the west side of Kissimmee Airport. From Hwy. 192 travel south on Hoagland Blvd. to museum.

ADMISSION COST: Adults $5.00; children $4.00.

HOURS OF OPERATION: Open all week 9am-5pm including holidays.

MUSEUM NOTES: Display airplanes are inside and outside. Film can be purchased in the gift shop. There are vending machines onsite and a restaurant is nearby.

A brochure is available.

Display Aircraft

MANUFACTURER	MODEL	POPULAR NAME
Aeronca	C-3	
Consolidated	PB4Y-2	Privateer (fuselage)
Curtiss	P-40E	Warhawk
de Havilland	D.H.82	Tiger Moth
Douglas	A-4	Skyhawk
Fairchild	KR-21	
Fleet	2	
Funk		
Grumman	TBM	Avenger
Kreider Reisner	KR-34	
North American	P-51D	Mustang
North American	SNJ-5	Texan

North American	TB-25N	Mitchell
Piper	J-3	Cub
Piper	PA-11	Cub Special
Pitts	Special	
Ryan	PT-22	
Stinson	JRS-8	Junior
Taylor Young		
Taylorcraft	L-2	Grasshopper
Vought	F4U-5	Corsair
Waco	UPF-7	

National Museum of Naval Aviation
P.O. Box 33104, NAS Pensacola, Florida 32508
(904) 452-3604

The museum is located on the grounds of Pensacola Naval Air Station, the "Cradle of Naval Aviation." The Navy's presence in Pensacola predates the Civil War and in 1913 the base was selected to be the first Naval Aeronautic Station. Pensacola NAS remains the training hub for naval aviators and in 1944 there were 12,000 aviators trained. The U.S.S. *Lexington*, the only aircraft carrier used exclusively for flight training, is stationed at Pensacola.

To some moviegoers, the star of the movie Top Gun *was not Tom Cruise, but the Grumman F-14 Tomcat. The museum's F-14 is the only one on public display. The most noticeable identifying feature of the F-14 is its pivoting wing. The wing automatically swings through an arc of 48 degrees. The wing extends to the forward position during slow-speed flight such as takeoff and landing. As airspeed increases the wings swing rearward to minimize air resistance. Tomcats entered service with the Navy in 1972, but through updating they remain among the best fighters in the world today.*

A mock-up of a flight deck from a typical World War II aircraft carrier occupies a portion of the museum's floor. Most flight decks were 148 feet wide during that period. Seemingly spacious when vacant, a flight deck turns into a dangerous environment when crammed with twenty or thirty planes and their spinning propellers.

The museum presents aircraft, artifacts, memorabilia and exhibits that depict the aviation history of the Navy, Marines and Coast Guard from first flight to space exploration. The displayed aircraft range from biplanes and blimps to present day jet airplanes, as well as spacecraft.

The museum was expanded in the fall of 1990 thereby doubling the museum's floor space. As part of the expansion, a replica of an aircraft carrier island and deck occupies a portion of the museum floor, and a four-plane diamond formation of Blue Angel Skyhawks is suspended in the Blue Angel Atrium.

Over 120 aircraft are on display. Many are one-of-a-kind with unique properties. Outside is the only F-14 Tomcat on public display in the world, while inside is a replica of the Navy's first airplane, an A-1 Triad. In 1919 the Curtiss NC-4 on display was the first airplane to cross the Atlantic. McDonnell Douglas F-18 Hornets now in service were derived from the museum's YF-17 prototype. Aircraft representative of the vast inventory of Naval World War II aircraft are present, as well as Korean War and Vietnam era aircraft. Among the space-related artifacts is a Skylab Command Module, a Mercury capsule and a replica of the space suit worn by astronaut Eugene Cernan, USN, the last man to walk on the moon.

The mezzanine provides an interesting view of the airplanes below, the carrier deck on the lower floor and the Blue Angels diamond formation in the atrium. Several rooms adjoining the mezzanine contain artifacts related to naval aviation.

DIRECTIONS TO MUSEUM: From US 98 southwest of Pensacola turn south on Navy Blvd. and follow to Pensacola Naval Air Station. Directions to museum will be provided at gate entrance.

ADMISSION COST: Free.

HOURS OF OPERATION: Open daily 9am-5pm. Closed New Year's Day, Thanksgiving and Christmas.

MUSEUM NOTES: Display aircraft are indoors and outdoors. Film is available in the gift shop. A cafe is onsite.

A brochure is available.

Display Aircraft

Prior to September 18, 1962, the Navy used a model designation system for aircraft that was exclusive to the Navy. On September 18, 1962, all U.S. military aircraft were redesignated where necessary to conform to a uniform model designation system. Where applicable, the old model designation appears in parenthesis.

MANUFACTURER	MODEL	POPULAR NAME
Beech	GB-2	Traveler
Beech	RC-45J(SNB)	Expeditor
Beech	T-34	Mentor
Bell	HUH-57A(TH-57)	JetRanger
Bell	TH-13M(HTL-4/6)	Sioux
Bell	UH-1	Iroquois "Huey"
Cessna	JRC	
Cessna	O-1	Bird Dog
Consolidated	N2Y-1	
Consolidated	PB4Y-2	Privateer
Consolidated	PBY2Y	Coronado
Consolidated	PBY	Catalina
Convair	C-131(R4Y)	
Convair	OY-1	Sentinel
Culver	TDC	
Curtiss	F6C-1	Hawk
Curtiss	JN-4	"Jenny"
Curtiss	MF	
Curtiss	N2C-2	Fledgling
Curtiss	NC-4	
Curtiss	R5C	Commando
Curtiss	SB2C	Helldiver
Curtiss	SNC-1	
Curtiss (replica)	A-1	Triad
Douglas	A-1(AD)	Skyraider
Douglas	A-3(A3D)	Skywarrior
Douglas	A-4(A4D)	Skyhawk
Douglas	C-47(R4D)	Skytrain
Douglas	C-118B(R6D-1)	Liftmaster
Douglas	D-558	Skystreak
Douglas	F3D	Skynight
Douglas	F-6A(F4D)	Skyray
Douglas	SBD	Dauntless
Fairchild	GK-1	
Fokker	D.VII	
Ford	RR-5	Trimotor
Grumman	AF	Guardian
Grumman	F6F	Hellcat
Grumman	F7F	Tigercat
Grumman	F8F	Bearcat
Grumman	F9F	Panther
Grumman	F9F-6/8	Cougar
Grumman	F-11A(F11F-1)	Tiger
Grumman	FF-1	Fifi

Grumman	HU-16(UF)	Albatross
Grumman	J2F-6	Duck
Grumman	J4F-1	Widgeon
Grumman	JRF	Goose
Grumman	S-2(S2F)	Tracker
Grumman (General Motors)	FM	Wildcat
Grumman (General Motors)	TBM	Avenger
Gyrodyne	QH-50C	Dash
Hanriot-Dupont	HD-1	
Hiller	HTE-1	
Howard	GH-3	Nightingale
Interstate	TDR-1	
Kaman	OH-43D(HOK-1)	
Lockheed	EC-121K(WV)	Warning Star
Lockheed	P2	Neptune
Lockheed	PV-2D	Harpoon
Lockheed	SP-2H(P2V-7)	Neptune
Lockheed	T-33(TV-2)	Shooting Star
Lockheed	TV-1	Shooting Star
Martin	AM	Mauler
Martin	SP-5B	Marlin
McDonnell	F2H	Banshee
McDonnell	F-4(F4H)	Phantom II
McDonnell	FH-1	Phantom
McDonnell	Mercury Capsule	
Naval Aircraft Factory	N3N	
Naval Aircraft Factory	TS-1	
New Standard	NT-1	
Nieuport	28	
North American	A2(AJ-2)	Savage
North American	F-1E(FJ-4)	Fury
North American	FJ-1	Fury
North American	FJ-2/3	Fury
North American	RA-5(A3J)	Vigilante
North American	SNJ	Texan
North American	T-28	Trojan
North American	T-39	Sabreliner
Northrop	YF-17	Hornet
Piasecki	HRP	Flying Banana
Piasecki	UH-25(HUP)	Retriever
Piper	J-3	Cub
Piper	NE-1	Grasshopper
Ryan	NR-1	Recruit
Sikorsky	CH-19(HRS-3)	Chickasaw
Sikorsky	CH-37C(HR2S-1)	

Sikorsky	CH-53A	Sea Stallion
Sikorsky	HH-52	
Sikorsky	HNS-1	Hoverfly
Sikorsky	HO3S	
Sikorsky	HO5S	
Sikorsky	HOS-1	
Sikorsky	UH-34D(HUS-1)	Seahorse
Skylab Command Module		
Stearman	N2S	Kaydet
Thomas-Morse	S-4C	Scout
Timm	N2T-1	Tutor
Vought	F4U	Corsair
Vought	F-8(F8U)	Crusader
Vought	OS2U	Kingfisher
Vultee	SNV-1	Valiant

Spaceport USA - Kennedy Space Center

Visitor Center-TWRS, Kennedy Space Center, Florida 32899
(407) 452-2121

Kennedy Space Center sits on Florida's Cape Canaveral. The Cape has been utilized by the Air Force for the past forty years as a launch site for military and civilian rockets. Generally known only to the military prior to the 1960s, the "space race" focused the world's attention on the Cape and Kennedy Space Center. Through the era of space-flight, the Cape has been the starting point for some of man's greatest space adventures,

Currently, U.S. manned space flight is flown in the Space Shuttle. Officially designated the Space Transportation System (STS), the Shuttle is a reusable space vehicle capable of transporting astronauts and hardware into space, then returning to Earth to be refurbished and relaunched.

As the influx of visitors (over 3 million in 1989) increased, the original visitor center was expanded into Spaceport USA. Exhibited at Spaceport are rockets, memorabilia, artifacts and equipment from the U.S. space program. There are also movies, demonstrations and "hands-on" exhibits. Note that the aforementioned are free.

Viewing the launch of a Space Shuttle can be the highlight of a trip to Spaceport USA, if a lot of variables work in your favor.

There are also tours and a movie that require a ticket purchase. The tours pass through Kennedy Space Center or Cape Canaveral Air Force Station and last approximately two hours. Tours include visits to launch pads, support facilities and equipment that are currently used or have been a part of the space program. The movie is presented at the IMAX theater on a five-story-tall screen. Outlining various facets of space missions, the movie includes spectacular views shot in space by NASA astronauts.

Rocket launches at Kennedy and Cape Canaveral Air Force Station occur sporadically. Space Shuttle launch information is available in Florida by calling 1-800-432-2153, or by calling 1-900-321-LIFT OFF (75¢ per call). During Shuttle launches Kennedy Space Center is closed to the public. Good viewing locations are along US 1, along State Rd. 528 (Bennett Causeway), and along the ocean off State Rd. A1A. Motels may be full.

DIRECTIONS TO MUSEUM: Kennedy Space Center is on the Atlantic Coast between Cocoa and Titusville.

From I-95 take exit 78 to State Rd. 407 eastbound then to State Rd. 405 (NASA Parkway) eastbound, or take exit 79 to State Rd. 405 (NASA Parkway) eastbound and follow signs to Kennedy Space Center or Spaceport USA.

From State Rd. 50 turn onto State Rd. 405 (NASA Parkway) eastbound and follow signs.

From State Rd. 528 (Beeline Expressway) turn onto State Rd. 407 eastbound and follow to State Rd. 405 (NASA Parkway) eastbound. Follow signs.

ADMISSION COST: Free except for tours (adults $6.00; children $3.00) and IMAX (adults $2.75; children $1.75).

HOURS OF OPERATION: Open daily from 9am to dusk. Closed Christmas Day. NOTE: Facility is closed during Space Shuttle launches.

MUSEUM NOTES: Displays are indoors and outdoors. There is a gift shop. Cameras and film are available. A restaurant is onsite. A free pet kennel is provided (bring a water dish).

A brochure is available.

Display Rockets

MANUFACTURER	MODEL
Chrysler	Juno I
Chrysler	Juno II
Chrysler	Redstone
Chrysler	Saturn IB
General Dynamics	Atlas
General Dynamics	Atlas-Agena
Martin Marietta	Titan II
McDonnell	Delta

Sun 'n Fun Aviation Museum
P.O. Box 6750, Lakeland, Florida 33807
(813) 644-2431

The Sun 'n Fun Aviation Museum is the culmination of efforts by a group of people who enjoy all phases of flying. The diversity of the collection outlines the wide range of design and construction techniques that have evolved in commercial and general aviation. The visitor can inspect examples of manufactured as well as homebuilt airplanes.

The museum is affiliated with the Experimental Aircraft Association (EAA) and each year a Sun 'n Fun EAA Fly-In is held. Usually scheduled for the spring, the fly-in attracts the second largest group of show planes in the nation. Seminars covering safety, construction and flying are conducted for attendees. Contact the museum for dates.

Two significant airplanes are a part of the museum's collection. A Convair Sea Dart is on outside display and an Auster Mark 9 is displayed indoors. The Sea Dart was a jet-powered seaplane that existed only as a prototype and research vehicle and never reached production. The Auster Mark 9 is the only example in the United States.

DIRECTIONS TO MUSEUM: From I-4 exit onto Medulla Rd. (exit 15) and turn left to museum at Lakeland Airport.

ADMISSION COST: Free.

HOURS OF OPERATION: Open 9am-5pm all week from February to April; open weekdays 9am-5pm remainder of year. Call ahead for holiday schedule.

MUSEUM NOTES: Display aircraft are indoors and outdoors. Film is available in the gift shop. A restaurant is located at the airport.

A brochure is available.

Display Aircraft

MANUFACTURER	MODEL	POPULAR NAME
Aero Sport	Scamp	
Aeronca	C-3	
American	Eagle	
Auster	Mark 9	
Convair	XF2Y-1	Sea Dart
Corben	Baby Ace	
Curtiss-Wright	CW-1	
Eaglet		
Grumman	HU-16	Albatross
McDonnell	F-101	Voodoo
Neismith	Cougar	
Royal Aircraft Factory (replica)	S.E.5A	
Rutan	Quickie I	

Tyndall Air Park

Tyndall Air Force Base, Florida

Like many other air bases, Tyndall Air Force Base began operations during World War II. The mission at Tyndall was to train gunnery officers and among the hundreds trained was Clark Gable. Through its history Tyndall has been utilized as a facility for pilot training and weapons testing and evaluation. Since 1958 Tyndall has been the site for the biennial William Tell weapons meet. Air and ground crews from throughout the Air Force compete in this prestigious event that tests the proficiency of fighter units in a combat environment.

Four of the planes in the park area served as interceptors: the North American F-86D, the Northrop F-89, the Convair F-102 and the McDonnell F-101. The F-86D and F-89 represent the early 1950s subsonic period while the F-101 and F-102 could attain supersonic flight. Variants of the F-89 and F-101 were capable of carrying the Genie air-to-air nuclear missile. The task of the Genie missile was to destroy large groups of enemy airplanes with a nuclear blast.

DIRECTIONS TO AIR PARK: Tyndall AFB is located along US 98 approximately 10 miles southeast of Panama City. The air park is situated along US 98. Parking adjacent to the air park is not available, but a parking lot is located at the traffic light just east of the park. The air park and parking lot are outside the base gate.

ADMISSION COST: Free.

Characterized as a "missile with a man in it," the Lockheed F-104 Starfighter was, and appears, fast. Lockheed gave the Air Force what it wanted, a fast fighter capable of high altitudes (F-104s set records of 1,404 mph and 103,389 feet). But the Air Force reevaluated the parameters for its fighters and relegated the few F-104s in the inventory to the Air Guard. Lockheed offered the fighter to foreign air forces where it served capably from the 1960s into the 1980s.

VIEWING HOURS : Sunrise to sunset.

AIR PARK NOTES: Display aircraft are outdoors. There are restaurants nearby.

Display Aircraft

MANUFACTURER	MODEL	POPULAR NAME
Convair	F-102	Delta Dagger
Lockheed	F-104	Starfighter
Lockheed	T-33	Shooting Star
McDonnell	F-101	Voodoo
North American	F-86D	Sabre
Northrop	F-89	Scorpion

Valiant Air Command Museum

6600 Tico Road, Titusville, Florida 32780
(407) 268-1941

At the time of this book's publication, the Valiant Air Command was working to complete their museum. The organization anticipates opening the museum during the summer of 1991. The Valiant Air Command has existed for a number of years as an association dedicated to preserving and flying military aircraft, and the museum will reflect the Air Command's efforts.

The Valiant Air Command operates a restoration facility. Museum visitors may view work underway in the shop.

DIRECTIONS TO MUSEUM: The museum is located at Space Center Executive Airport in Titusville. The airport is situated off of Hwy. 405 and US 1.

ADMISSION COST: Undetermined at press time.

HOURS OF OPERATION: Undetermined at press time.

MUSEUM NOTES: Display aircraft are indoors and outdoors. Film is available in the gift shop. There are restaurants nearby.

A brochure is available.

Display Aircraft

NOTE: The following list was compiled prior to the museum's opening and may change. Several airplanes participate in air shows and may be gone. Call the museum to determine if a specific airplane is on display.

MANUFACTURER	MODEL	POPULAR NAME
Cessna	L-19	Bird Dog
Curtiss	P-40	Warhawk
de Havilland	D.H.114	Vampire
Douglas	A-26	Invader
Douglas	AD-4	Skyraider
Douglas	C-47	Skytrain
Grumman	F9F	Panther
Grumman (General Motors)	TBM	Avenger
North American	P-51	Mustang
North American	T-28	Trojan
Ryan	PT-22	Recruit
Stearman	PT-17	Kaydet

Weeks Air Museum
14710 S.W. 128th Street, Miami, Florida 33186
(305) 233-5197

The Weeks Air Museum opened in 1987 and contains over 35 aircraft with the bulk of the collection made up of World War II era airplanes. The majority of the airplanes are in flying condition.

There are several airplanes exhibited that are rarely found elsewhere. Of note are the B-29 Superfortress, de Havilland Mosquito, Seversky P-35, Kawasaki Ki-61 "Tony," Tupelov TU-2 and Yakolef YAK-11. A look at the following list of display aircraft indicates the quality of the collection. There is also a wide variety of engines and other artifacts exhibited.

DIRECTIONS TO MUSEUM: Located on west end of Kendall-Tamiami Executive Airport, which is southwest of Miami.

ADMISSION COST: Adults $5.00; senior citizens $4.00; children (12 & under) $3.00.

HOURS OF OPERATION: Open daily 10am-5pm. Closed Thanksgiving and Christmas.

MUSEUM NOTES: Display aircraft are indoors and outdoors. Film is available in the gift shop. There is a restaurant nearby.

A brochure is available.

Display Aircraft

MANUFACTURER	MODEL	POPULAR NAME
Abernathy		Streaker
Avro	504K	
Beech	D19	Staggerwing
Beech	SNB-1	
Boeing	100	
Boeing	B-17	Flying Fortress
Boeing	B-29	Superfortress
Curtiss	P-40E	Kittyhawk
de Havilland		Mosquito
DeWoitine	D-27	
Douglas	A-26	Invader
Douglas	B-23	Dragon
Grumman	F6F-3	Hellcat
Grumman	F7F-3	Tigercat
Grumman	J2F-6	Duck
Grumman (General Motors)	FM-2	Wildcat
Grumman (General Motors)	TBM-3	Avenger
Kawasaki	KI-61	"Tony"

Lockheed	P-38L	Lightning
Morane-Saulnier	230	
North American	AT-6D	Texan
North American	P-51D	Mustang
Piper	L-4	Grasshopper
Pitts	S-1-S	Special
Seversky	P-35	
Sopwith		Pup
Sopwith		Triplane
SPAD	S-7	
Stephens	Akro	
Stinson	L-1	
Thomas-Morse	T-M4	Scout
Tupelov	TU-2	
Weeks	Solution	
Weeks	Special	
Yakovlev	Yak-11	"Moose"

Museum of Aviation
P.O. Box 2469, Warner Robins, Georgia 31099
(912) 923-6600

The museum is located adjacent to Robins Air Force Base. The Air Force Logistics Command oversees operation of the base which provides support for a variety of aircraft and avionics systems. Robins employs over 21,000 military and civilian personnel making it the largest industrial complex in Georgia.

The Museum of Aviation characterizes itself as the "fastest growing military aviation museum in the Southeastern United States." Situated on a 43-acre site, the museum has ambitious expansion plans and completed phase one of their program in 1984. The exhibits highlight Air Force history and Georgian's contributions to aviation.

The aircraft collection is comprised of military aircraft dating from World War II. The collection is extensive with over 55 aircraft on display, including a Lockheed SR-71 Blackbird. Blackbirds last flew in 1990 after over twenty years service flying strategic reconnaissance missions. There is also a large collection of artifacts including items from prisoners of war, the Black Eagles, German Luftwaffe and General Robert L. Scott (author of *God is my Co-pilot*).

DIRECTIONS TO MUSEUM: The museum entrance is off Hwy. 247 just south of Russell Pkwy.

ADMISSION COST: Free.

HOURS OF OPERATION: Open Tuesday-Sunday 10am-5pm. Closed Monday and major holidays.

MUSEUM NOTES: Display aircraft are outdoors. Film is available at gift shop. There

The Lockheed SR-71A Blackbird displayed at the Museum of Aviation was the ninth built. In July 1976 the plane set the world's absolute speed record of 2,193 mph, as well as setting the speed record over a 1,000 kilometer long course at a speed of 2,092 mph. The records still stand. All the Blackbirds have been retired from military service. A couple remain available for non-military research.

The Lockheed F-80C Shooting Star was the Air Force's first operational jet fighter. The plane was developed during World War II and was originally designated P-80, in keeping with the early system that used "P" for pursuit. Early flights were plagued with engine problems and resulting crashes killed six pilots, among them respected test pilot Milo Burcham and the top American World War II ace, Major Richard Bong. Initially used as a fighter at the outset of the Korean War, the F-86 Sabre took over as the premier Air Force fighter and F-80s served as fighter-bombers. The T-33 trainer version outlived the F-80 in service life.

is a snack bar onsite and restaurants are nearby.　　　**A brochure is available.**

Display Aircraft

MANUFACTURER	MODEL	POPULAR NAME
Beech	AT-11	Kansas
Beech	C-45G	Expeditor
Beech	T-34A	Mentor
Bell	TH-13M	Sioux
Bell	UH-1F	Iroquois "Huey"
Bell	UH-13P	Sioux
Benson	X-25A	Gyrocopter
Boeing	B-29B	Superfortress
Boeing	B-52D	Stratofortress
Boeing	CIM-10A	Bomarc
Boeing	KC-97L	Stratofreighter
Cessna	L-19A/O-1	Bird Dog
Cessna	O-2A	Super Skymaster
Cessna	U-3B	Blue Canoe
Convair	F-102A	Delta Dagger
Convair	T-29A	Flying Classroom

The Lockheed Jetstar was purchased in small numbers by the Air Force and designated the C-140. The plane is easily identified by the four engines attached to the rear of the fuselage, and by the pod-like fuel tanks located at midpoint on each wing. The C-140 was used to transport personnel and to check the operation of navigational devices. Civilian Jetstars are still flying as business jets.

de Havilland	C-7A	Caribou
de Havilland	U-6A	Beaver
Douglas	A-26C	Invader
Douglas	C-47B	Skytrain
Douglas	C-54G	Skymaster
Douglas	C-124C	Globemaster II
Douglas	WB-66D	Destroyer
Fairchild	C-119C	Flying Boxcar
Fairchild	C-123K	Provider
Fairchild	PT-19A	Cornell
Grumman	HU-16B	Albatross
Gyrodyne	QH-50C	Dash
Helio	U-10D	Super Courier
Hiller	OH-23C	Raven
Kaman	HH-43A	Huskie
Kaman	HH-43B	Huskie
Laister-Kauffman	TG-4A	
Lockheed	C-140B	Jetstar
Lockheed	EC-121K	Constellation
Lockheed	F-80C	Shooting Star
Lockheed	F-104A	Starfighter
Lockheed	RB-69A	Neptune
Lockheed	T-33A	Shooting Star
Lockheed	U-2C	Dragon Lady

Lockheed	YMC-130H	Hercules
Martin	MGM-13A	Mace
Martin	RB-57A	Canberra
Martin	TM-61C	Matador
McDonnell	F-4C	Phantom II
McDonnell	F-101F	Voodoo
North American	B-25J	Mitchell
North American	F-86H	Sabre
North American	F-100C	Super Sabre
North American	T-6G	Texan
North American	T-28C	Trojan
North American	T-39A	Sabreliner
Northrop	F-89J	Scorpion
Northrop	SM-62	Snark
Piasecki	CH-21B	Workhorse
Republic	F-84E	Thunderjet
Republic	F-105G	Thunderchief
Republic	RF-84F	Thunderflash
Ryan	AQM-34A	Firebee
Ryan	BQM-34F	Firebee
Ryan	PT-22	Recruit
Sikorsky	H-19D	Chickasaw
Sikorsky	HH-34J	Chocktaw
Stearman	PT-17	Kaydet

Norton Aero Museum

Silverwood Theme Park, N. 26225 Highway 95, Athol, Idaho 83801
(208) 772-0515

The Norton Aero Museum is a segment of the Silverwood Theme Park. Access to the museum is possible only after paying admission to the park.

The museum's airplane collection is very diverse and possesses aircraft that are note-worthy both for historical and technological significance. The Stinson Trimotor and Ford Trimotor are examples of early commercial aircraft built during the 1920s. Fledg-ling airlines in the '20s were enticing first-time flyers and attempting to provide sched-uled service for business flyers. The Ford Trimotor was the popular plane of the day, but its slow speed and noisy, cold interior did not draw sufficient travelers and many airlines folded.

From the same era as the Trimotor is the Pietenpol. Using wood and a Ford Model A en-gine, the Pietenpol is a 1920s design for homebuilt construction that has survived to to-day. Pietenpols are still built and may be powered by more modern engines. Appearing archaic next to later designed homebuilts, the Pietenpol caters to the low, slow flyer.

DIRECTIONS TO MUSEUM: Silverwood Theme Park is located approximately 15 miles north of Coeur d'Alene on US 95.

ADMISSION COST (to Silverwood Park): Adults (8-64 yrs.) $13.50; senior citizens $10.00; children (3-7 yrs.) $7.00.

HOURS OF OPERATION: Open daily noon-8pm from Memorial Day to Labor Day.

MUSEUM NOTES: Display aircraft are in-doors. There is a gift shop and film is available. A restaurant is onsite.

A brochure is available.

Display Aircraft

MANUFACTURER	MODEL	POPULAR NAME
Aerocar		
Aeronca	7AC	Champ
Aeronca	C3	
Aeronca	K	
Bücker	Bu 133	
Cessna	421	Golden Eagle
Curtiss	Robin	
Curtiss Jr. Pusher		
de Havilland	DH-2	
de Havilland	DH-4	
Fleet		
Fokker	Dr.I	Triplane
Ford	Trimotor	

Great Lakes-Redfern		
Laister-Kauffman	BA100	Bowlus
Monocoupe		
North American	P-51D	Mustang
Pietenpol		
Piper	PA-25	Pawnee
Pitcairn	PA8	
Royal Aircraft Factory	S.E.5a	
Schweizer	232	
Schweizer	233	
Sopwith	F.1	Camel
Stearman		
Stinson	Trimotor	
Travel Air	4000	
Waco	9	
Waco	YKS-6	

Chanute Display Center

Office of Public Affairs, Chanute Technical Training Center
Chanute Air Force Base, Illinois 61868

Originally opened in 1917 as a training facility for pilots, Chanute Field trained over 200,000 personnel in a variety of specialties during World War II. Chanute Air Force Base presently serves as a training center for the Air Force, although current military re-organization plans call for closing the base in September 1993. When driving on the base adhere to speed limits and instructions from military personnel commanding marching units.

The bulk of the collection is situated in an air park. Four airplanes are parked in a ramp area and several planes are on display along Eagle Drive, the main road bisecting the base. The North Gate to the base leads directly to Eagle Drive. A map is available at the Visitors Center adjacent to the North Gate.

Disposition of the collection after the base closes was not known at time of publication.

DIRECTIONS TO AIR PARK: Chanute AFB is near Rantoul. From I-57 take exit 250 onto US 136 eastbound. At Century Blvd. turn right and follow Century to Chanute AFB North Gate. You must stop at the Visitors Center where directions to the air park are available.

ADMISSION COST: Free.

HOURS OF OPERATION: Daylight hours.

AIR PARK NOTES: Display aircraft are outdoors. Restaurants are nearby offbase.

The Republic F-105 Thunderchief in Chanute's Air Park is painted in the colors of the Thunderbirds, the Air Force's aerobatic demonstration team. The Thunderbirds flew the F-105 during 1964, but for only six shows before returning to the F-100.

Display Aircraft

MANUFACTURER	MODEL	POPULAR NAME
Bell	UH-1B	Iroquois "Huey"
Boeing	B-29	Superfortress
Boeing	B-52B	Stratofortress
Boeing	C-97G	Stratofreighter
Boeing	LM-99A	Bomarc
Boeing	XB-47	Stratojet
Cessna	O-2A	Skymaster
Convair	F-102A	Delta Dagger
Convair	XRB-58A	Hustler
Douglas	A-4D	Skyhawk
Douglas	B-26C	Invader
Douglas	C-133A	Cargomaster
Douglas	RB-66A	Destroyer
Douglas	YC-47D	Skytrain
Fairchild	C-123K	Provider
General Dynamics	F-111	
Grumman	HU-16	Albatross
Lockheed	C-121K	Super Constellation
Lockheed	F-104A	Starfighter
Lockheed	P-80B	Shooting Star
Lockheed	T-33A	Shooting Star
Martin	B-57B	Canberra
McDonnell	F-101B	Voodoo
McDonnell	CRF-4C	Phantom II
North American	AT-6B	Texan
North American	B-25N	Mitchell
North American	CT-39A	Sabreliner
North American	F-86A	Sabre
North American	F-100C	Super Sabre
North American	F-100D	Super Sabre
North American	P-51H	Mustang
Northrop	T-38A	Talon
Republic	F-84A	Thunderjet
Republic	F-84F	Thunderstreak
Republic	F-105B	Thunderchief
Republic	F-105F	Thunderchief

Museum of Science and Industry

57th Street and Lake Shore Drive, Chicago, Illinois 60637
(312) 684-1414

The Museum of Science and Industry is segmented into 75 exhibition halls that contain exhibits illustrating scientific principles and industrial concepts. Areas addressed include nutrition, automobile, energy, marine, farm and railroad. Many of the exhibits elicit participation from the visitor.

Some of the more impressive exhibits include the coal mine, the circus, a 16-foot-tall model of the human heart, petroleum and the captured World War II German submarine U-505.

Space related exhibits are contained in the Henry Crown Space Center. Among the artifacts is the Apollo VIII Command Module that carried Frank Borman, James Lovell and William Anders to the first manned orbit around the moon. There is also the Aurora VII piloted by Scott Carpenter. Adjoining the Space Center is the Omnimax Theater which presents films on a screen that is three stories high (there is an admission fee for the theater).

All of the museum's aircraft are noteworthy, either by individual achievement or as a type of aircraft. The German Junkers Ju 87 Stuka in the museum is a very rare example of the infamous World War II dive bomber. The Lockheed F-104 Starfighter on display was the first airplane to exceed an altitude of 100,000 feet, and also set speed and time-to-climb records as well. The Supermarine Spitfire actually survived air combat during World War II. The plane was piloted to five victories over German opponents before being relegated to training duties when more advanced models flew combat missions. The Piccard balloon established a new altitude record in 1933 when it rose over 11-1/2 miles above earth.

DIRECTIONS TO MUSEUM: The museum is located just off Lake Shore Dr. on the south side of Chicago in Jackson Park.

ADMISSION COST: Museum is free. Omnimax: adults $4.75; senior citizens and children (3-12 yrs.) $3.25.

HOURS OF OPERATION: Open Monday-Friday 9:30am-4pm; Saturday, Sunday and holidays 9:30am-5:30pm. Henry Crown Space Center is open 6-9pm on Friday and Saturday if there are no conflicting events at museum. Closed Christmas.

MUSEUM NOTES: Display aircraft are indoors. Film is available in the gift shop. A cafe is in the building.

A brochure is available.

Display Aircraft

MANUFACTURER	MODEL	POPULAR NAME
Boeing	40-B4	
Curtiss	JN-4	"Jenny"
Curtiss Pusher		
Junkers	Ju 87B-2/Trop	Stuka
Lockheed	F-104	Starfighter
McDonnell	Mercury Capsule	*Aurora VII*
Morane-Saulnier		
North American Rockwell	Apollo VIII Command Module	
Piccard balloon		
Sikorsky	HH-52A	Sea Guard
Supermarine	Mk IA	Spitfire
Travel Air	*Texaco #13*	

Prairie Aviation Museum

P.O. Box 856, Bloomington, Illinois 61702
(309) 663-7632

The Prairie Aviation Museum was constructing a museum building at the time of this book's publication to house the organization's extensive collection of aviation related mementos and artifacts.

The museum's sole display airplane is a Douglas DC-3, although planes owned by museum members are sometimes on display. The plane was manufactured in 1942 as a C-53 and entered service with the Navy. After the war, the plane entered commercial service until purchased by the museum in 1984. Restoration was undertaken and in 1985 it was painted by Ozark Airlines in their colors to celebrate the airline's 35th Anniversary. Touring the plane provides a view of travel in the first important airplane in commercial air travel.

DIRECTIONS TO MUSEUM: The museum is located at Bloomington-Normal Airport.

ADMISSION COST: Free.

HOURS OF OPERATION: Open Saturday and Sunday 1-4pm from Memorial Day to Labor Day.

MUSEUM NOTES: The DC-3 is outdoors. Museum building under construction. A restaurant is located in the nearby terminal building.

A brochure is available.

Heritage Museum Foundation
Grissom Air Force Base, Indiana 46971-5000

The aircraft collection is located outside the front gate of Grissom Air Force Base. Originating as Bunker Hill Naval Air Station during World War II, the Air Force took over the base in 1954, then renamed it in 1968 in memory of Virgil "Gus" Grissom, astronaut. The base is currently home for an air refueling wing and tactical fighter squadron.

In the collection are a B-47 Stratojet and a B-58 Hustler. Stratojets were the first jet bombers in the Air Force inventory capable of carrying nuclear weapons. Over 2,000 B-47s were constructed and the last was retired from Strategic Air Command service in 1967. The B-58 was one the most sophisticated aircraft of its day. Built with honeycombed skin and containing complex avionics, the B-58 was capable of Mach 2 and was the first supersonic bomber. The decision to concentrate on missiles and a high accident rate resulted in a short service life for the B-58. There are only eight remaining on display.

The B-17 on display at Grissom is one of over 12,000 built collectively by Boeing, Douglas and Vega. Most of the inventory was destroyed after World War II, but several B-17s continued in service with Allied air forces and as search and rescue planes. Turning their load-carrying capabilities to peaceful use, some B-17s were converted to fire bombers and dropped loads of water on forest fires.

The Boeing B-47, the Air Force's first swept-wing bomber, was produced in greater numbers at the time than any other post-World War II bomber. Over two thousand were built by Boeing, Douglas and Lockheed.

DIRECTIONS TO MUSEUM: Grissom AFB is located approximately 13 miles north of Kokomo, Indiana, on US 31. The aircraft are displayed outside the base gate.

ADMISSION COST: Free

VIEWING HOURS: Daylight hours.

MUSEUM NOTES: All aircraft are outside. A museum building should be open in late summer 1991. There are no restaurants in the immediate vicinity.

A brochure is available.

Display Aircraft

MANUFACTURER	MODEL	POPULAR NAME
Boeing	B-17G	Flying Fortress
Boeing	B-47E	Stratojet
Boeing	KC-97L	Stratofreighter
Cessna	O-2A	Super Skymaster
Cessna	T-41	Mescalero
Cessna	U-3A	
Douglas	C-47D	Skytrain
Fairchild	C-119G	Flying Boxcar
General Dynamics	TB-58A	Hustler
Lockheed	F-104D	Starfighter
Lockheed	T-33A	Shooting Star
McDonnell	F-4C	Phantom II
North American	B-25J	Mitchell
North American	F-86H	Sabre
North American	F-100F	Super Sabre
Republic	F-84F	Thunderstreak
Republic	F-105	Thunderchief

Airpower Museum
Rt. 2, Box 172, Ottumwa, Iowa 52501
(515) 938-2773

The Airpower Museum is affiliated with the Antique Airplane Association (AAA). Formed in 1953, the AAA is the largest and oldest organization devoted to antique, classic and replica aircraft. Currently there are 42 chapters and eight type clubs associated with AAA (type clubs are interested in a specific airplane model).

While named the Airpower Museum, the aircraft collection actually provides a look at approximately 25 light-category airplanes constructed prior to 1950. Several of the planes are rare antiques. For the enthusiast who is interested in the early history of general aviation, the aircraft and memorabilia found in the Airpower Museum provide a

The musuem's Brewster B-1 Fleet is unique by virtue of its status as an antique airplane and its heritage. Fleet biplanes were originally manufactured by the Fleet company in the United States. A Fleet company in Canada also produced the plane, which was popular as a trainer. The ill-fated Brewster Corporation purchased manufacturing rights from the U.S. Fleet company, but never built the plane. When the plane shown was moved from Canada to the U.S., it was necessary to license it as a Brewster, since the type certificate was held by that company.

Bernie Pietenpol was a pioneer in the field of "homebuilt" aircraft. His goal was to design and build an airplane that used an automotive engine, unrealized until the introduction of the Ford Model A. He developed two planes, a two-seat Air Camper and a single-seat Sky Scout (pictured above). Rudimentary, but functional, the Pietenpol design reduced material costs as much as possible while remaining simple enough for a mechanically apt homebuilder to construct the plane. Pietenpol flew the first Air Camper in 1928 and hundreds of plans have been sold since then. The only major change to the design has been installation of a variety of powerplants. The scarcity of Model A engines and a desire for increased horsepower has resulted in the installation of an assortment of engines ranging from aircraft engines to the Corvair. There is also a club of Pietenpol Air Camper and Sky Scout builders and owners.

look back at some of the aircraft and people responsible for general aviation's development.

The museum is located at Antique Airfield, a rural airport with two grass runways. Prior to World War II, most airports consisted of grass or dirt strips. During World War II, the government constructed bases throughout the country with hard-surface runways so pilot training was less influenced by weather and intensive use. Most of these bases became municipal or regional airports after the war and the number of grass strips decreased. Today grass strips are usually operated by private owners. The grass found at Antique Airfield is the appropriate surface for antique airplanes.

The AAA and its chapters sponsor fly-ins throughout the year around the country. Fly-ins provide an opportunity to see rare airplanes in flight. Contact AAA at the phone number listed above to obtain information on their annual fly-in at Antique Airfield.

DIRECTIONS TO MUSEUM: Located east of Blakesburg. From Blakesburg follow county road H-41 east for four miles to airport. From Ottumwa follow county road H-47 west for ten miles to airport.

ADMISSION COST: Free (donation requested).

HOURS OF OPERATION: Open Monday-Friday 9am-5pm; Saturday 10-5pm; Sunday 1-5pm. Closed New Year's Day, Labor Day, Thanksgiving and Christmas.

MUSEUM NOTES: Display aircraft are indoors. There is a gift shop, but film is not available. Restaurants are located in Blakesburg and Ottumwa.

Display Aircraft

MANUFACTURER	MODEL	POPULAR NAME
Aeronca	7AC	Champion
Aeronca	11AC	Chief
Aeronca	65LA	
Aeronca	K	
Anderson	Z	
Backstrom/Van White	WB-1	Flying Plank II
Bede	BD-5	
Brewster	B-1	Fleet
Culver	LCA	Cadet
Culver	PQ-14	
Fairchild	71	
Fleet	7	
Lippisch	X-114	
Monoprep	218	
Pietenpol	Sky Scout	
Porterfield	CP-40	
Rearwin	8135	Cloudster
Rose	A-1	Parakeet
Ryan	PT-22	Recruit
Ryan	STA	
Smith	DSA-1	Miniplane
Stinson	S	Junior
Volmer Jensen	VJ-23	
Vultee	BT-13A	Valiant
Welch	OW-8	

Iowa Aviation Preservation Center

P.O. Box 31, Greenfield, Iowa 50849
(515) 343-7184

The Iowa Aviation Preservation Center highlights and commemorates the role and contribution Iowans have made in aviation history. A portion of the museum is devoted to the Iowa Aviators Hall of Fame.

All airplanes in the collection were manufactured before 1947. The Curtiss Robin is serial number 6 and the oldest Robin known to exist. The de Havilland Hornet Moth is one of only two in existence. Six Aetna-Timm Aerocraft trainers were built and the museum's is the last known to exist.

DIRECTIONS TO MUSEUM: The museum is located at Greenfield Municipal Airport, which is one mile north of Greenfield.

ADMISSION COST: Adults $2.00; children $1.50; 12 yrs. and under $1.00.

HOURS OF OPERATION: Open Monday-Friday 10am-5pm; Saturday-Sunday 1-5pm. Closed New Year's Day, Thanksgiving, Christmas Eve and Christmas.

MUSEUM NOTES: Display airplanes are indoors. There is a gift shop, but film is not available. A restaurant is nearby.

A brochure is available.

Display Aircraft

MANUFACTURER	MODEL	POPULAR NAME
Aetna-Timm	2SA	Aerocraft
Curtiss	Robin	
de Havilland	D.H.82	Tiger Moth
de Havilland	D.H.87	Hornet Moth
Mead glider		
Northrup glider		
Piper	J-2	Cub
Piper	J-3	Cub
Piper	J-5	Cub Cruiser
Schweizer glider		

National Balloon Museum
Box 149, Indianola, Iowa 50125
(515) 961-3714

Balloons provided man's first flight in lighter-than-air craft. The acknowledged pioneers in ballooning were the Montgolfier brothers and Jacques Alexandre Cesar Charles of France. The Montgolfier brothers explored hot-air balloons while the balloons of Charles were filled with the recently discovered gas hydrogen. In 1783 the Montgolfiers launched the first manned balloon, and "aeronauts" became national celebrities.

Until recent time, balloons were primarily used for research and military applications. Knowing the enemy's location and activity is a great military advantage, and although used sporadically during the Civil War, thousands of observation balloons were flown in World War I. During World War II balloons served as naval convoy guardians in the form of blimps, and in England, barrage balloons tethered by steel cables thwarted low-level airplane attacks.

It is the balloon's capability to reach altitudes formerly unattainable by other aircraft that have established the balloon's usefulness to scientific research. Manned balloons

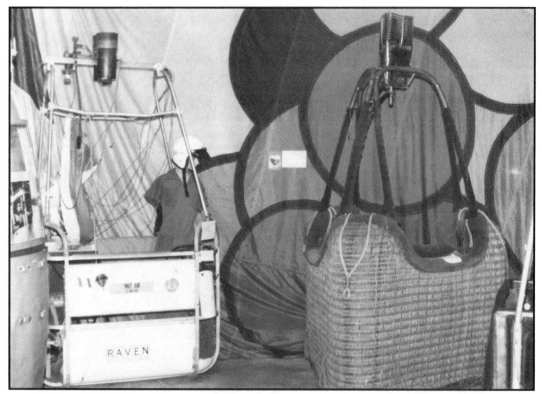

Among the artifacts in the National Balloon Museum are several ballon baskets.

provided information on the effects on their occupants in the cold, oxygen-lean altitudes of the upper atmosphere. Telescopes were carried aloft so stellar observations could be made without the distortion caused by the denser lower atmosphere.

Before the "Race into Space," there was the race to achieve the highest altitude by manned flight, possible only by balloon. Some of the flight gear used in early space flights was initially developed and tested in balloon ascents. During the record-setting ascension in 1960, Air Force Captain Joseph Kittinger Jr. reached an altitude of 102,800 feet. Nearing the peak of the ascension, Kittinger negatively responded to a command by quipping, "Come and get me." Kittinger left the gondola and fell until his parachute opened at 17,500 feet. Kittinger reached the ground after descending for nearly 14 minutes, setting both the altitude record and maximum height for a parachute jump.

With the development of lightweight, compact propane burners and rip-stop nylon, recreational ballooning took off in the 1960s to become the popular, colorful sport of today. Many companies have recognized the value of a silent, slow-moving billboard and have emblazoned the balloons with eye-catching logos. Ballooning has grown into a sport that draws hundreds of balloons to national events.

The National Balloon Museum is situated in Indianola, Iowa, which has hosted the U.S. National Hot Air Balloon Championships for several years. Housed in the museum are artifacts, mementos, displays and equipment related to ballooning. A collection of prints and photographs depicts ballooning scenes.

Each summer a major ballooning meet is held in Indianola. Contact the museum for the scheduled dates.

DIRECTIONS TO MUSEUM: The museum is located at 1601 N. Jefferson (US 65 & 69) in Indianola.

ADMISSION COST: Free (donation requested).

HOURS OF OPERATION: Open Monday-Friday 9am-4pm (closed noon-1pm); Saturday 10am-4pm; Sunday 1-4pm. Closed major holidays.

MUSEUM NOTES: All exhibits are indoors. There is a gift shop. Restaurants are nearby.

A brochure is available.

Combat Air Museum
P.O. Box 19142, Topeka, Kansas 66619
(913) 862-3303

On display at the Combat Air Museum are aircraft that flew during the Spanish Civil War, World War II, Korean War and the Vietnam War. A variety of military artifacts and memorabilia are also displayed.

Exhibited aircraft include a Lockheed EC-121 Super Constellation that is open for walk-through viewing. One of only two existing North American O-47B observation planes is on display. Also displayed is a Grumman F11F Tiger that was formerly flown by the Navy's Blue Angels demonstration team. Many of the aircraft are maintained in flying condition and may be absent while participating in flying shows.

The museum sponsors the Superbatics Air Show which usually highlights aerobatic performers and World War II era aircraft. Call the museum for show dates.

DIRECTIONS TO MUSEUM: The museum is located south of Topeka at Forbes Field. From US 75 enter airport at air terminal entrance. Proceed to air terminal. The museum is three blocks south of air terminal building on "J" St.

ADMISSION COST: Adults $2.50; senior citizens $2.00; children (6-16 yrs.) $1.00; free for military in uniform.

HOURS OF OPERATION: Open Monday-Saturday 9:30am-4pm; Sunday 12:30-4pm.

MUSEUM NOTES: Display aircraft are indoors and outdoors. Film is not available in the gift shop. There is a restaurant nearby.

A brochure is available.

Originally designed as a high-altitude, long-range escort fighter, the F-101 Voodoo was used as an interceptor and photo-reconnaisance plane. The Voodoo was the world's first supersonic photo-reconnaisance plane and was used extensively to provide photo intelligence during the Cuban Missile Crisis and the Vietnam War.

The Vultee-Stinson V77C Reliant was produced as the AT-19 and used by the Royal Navy as a trainer during World War II. The civilian version accommodated four or five passengers and was used as an executive airplane as well as a bush plane.

Display Aircraft

MANUFACTURER	MODEL	POPULAR NAME
Beech	C-45	Expeditor
Beech	RU-8D	Twin Beech
Curtiss	J-1	
de Havilland	Beaver	
Douglas	A-26	Invader
Douglas	C-47	Skytrain
Douglas	Honest John	
Grumman	F11F	Tiger
Grumman	F-9F	Panther
Grumman	S-2	Tracker
Heinkel	He 111	
Lockheed	EC-121	Constellation
Lockheed	T-33A	Shooting Star
McDonnell	F-101B	Voodoo

Messerschmitt	MC-G-10	
North American	AT-6	Texan, Harvard
North American	B-25J	Mitchell
North American	F-86H	Sabre
North American	O-47B	
North American	T-28B	Trojan
Republic	F-84F	Thunderstreak
Stinson	V77C	Reliant
Western Electric	Nike Ajax	

Kansas Cosmosphere and Space Center

1100 North Plum, Hutchinson, Kansas 67501
(316) 662-2305

Seemingly out-of-place is a world-class science and space center in a mid-sized prairie community. However, the Kansas Cosmophere and Space Center (KCSC) possesses the largest collection of space artifacts in the country outside the Smithsonian's Air and Space Museum. Thanks to efforts of local citizens, organizations and companies, and cooperation from NASA, this outstanding science and space center was constructed and is now outgrowing its present facility.

An outgrowth of the center is its capability to restore and replicate spacecraft and related equipment. It is the only permanent restoration facility of its type in the world and has restored many projects for other museums. This capability is apparent in the excellence of the articles on display at the center.

The center has on display the largest public collection of spacesuits, including spacesuits from the USSR. There are spacecraft from the Mercury, Gemini and Apollo missions, a Lunar Rover, a Lunar Module, a moon rock, and a variety of space artifacts.

Two other attractions in the center worth considering are the Omnimax theater and the planetarium. The Omnimax film is presented in such a way that the viewer feels more involved. Films are changed approximately every six months.

KCSC also sponsors educational programs for teachers and children. The children's camp is called the Future Astronaut Training Program and accepts students entering the 7th, 8th and 9th grades. The camp lasts five days and covers subjects related to astronaut training and space science. Contact KCSC for information.

DIRECTIONS TO MUSEUM: In Hutchinson at the intersection of IIth St. and Plum.

ADMISSION COST: Museum free. Omnimax: Adults $4.50; senior citizens & children $3.25. Planetarium: All ages $2.50.

HOURS OF OPERATION: Open Monday-Wednesday 9am-4pm (until 5pm during summer); Thursday-Friday 9am-9pm; Saturday 10am-9pm; Sunday noon-8pm. Closed Christmas.

MUSEUM NOTES: Spacecraft are indoors. Film is not available in the gift shop. There are vending machines on site and a restaurant is nearby.

A brochure is available.

Liberal Air Museum

P.O. Box 2585, 2000 West 2nd Street, Liberal, Kansas 67905
(316) 624-5263

During World War II, the central part of the country was dotted with airfields used to train thousands of aircrews. Liberal Army Air Field served as a training base for B-24 crews. During a reunion of B-24 aircrews, local citizens conceived the idea of a museum that chronicles Liberal's aviation history. Liberal was also the site of a Beech Aircraft factory, so the museum addresses both civilian and military aviation subjects.

The collection consists of over 60 aircraft on display with more undergoing restoration or promised to the museum. Noteworthy among the military airplanes is the last airworthy Douglas A-20 bomber and one of the few Japanese Mitsubishi "Zero" fighters in existence. Approximately 10,000 Zeros were built with 6,000 of those built by the Nakajima company. Fast and agile, the Zero was flown by experienced, combat-tested pilots at the outset of World War II resulting in superiority over Allied air forces. But the advent of better tactics, improved aircraft and experienced pilots, brought equality and eventually domination for the Allies. American fighters improved considerably during the war, but the Zero remained essentially the same throughout the war.

Several interesting civilian aircraft are present, including a Cessna Airmaster, Funk B75, Pietenpol Air Camper, Mooney Mite and Globe Swift. Several homebuilt airplanes are also displayed.

Each year the museum sponsors an air show. Contact museum for air show dates.

DIRECTIONS TO MUSEUM: The museum is located at Liberal Municipal Airport. From US 83 turn onto 2nd St. and follow to airport on west side of town. From US 54 turn north onto Western Ave. Follow Western Ave. to 2nd St. then turn left onto 2nd St. and travel west to airport.

ADMISSION COST: Adults $3.50; senior citizens $3.00; children (6-18 yrs.) $2.00.

HOURS OF OPERATION: Open Monday-Friday 8am-5pm; Saturday 10am-4pm; Sunday 1-4pm. Closed New Year's Day, Thanksgiving, Christmas Eve and Christmas.

MUSEUM NOTES: Display aircraft are indoors and outdoors. Film is not available in the gift shop. A restaurant is nearby.

A brochure is available.

Display Aircraft

MANUFACTURER	MODEL	POPULAR NAME
Aeronca	11AC	Chief
Aeronca	K	
Avid	Flyer	
Beech	35	Bonanza

Beech	C-45	Expeditor
Bell	H-13H	Sioux
Bell	UH-1E	Iroquois "Huey"
Bellanca	Cruisair	
Cavalier	SA102-5	
Cessna	120	
Cessna	140	
Cessna	175	
Cessna	195	
Cessna	Airmaster	
Cessna	UC-78	Bobcat
Culver	V	
Curtiss Pusher		
Douglas	A-4	Skyhawk
Douglas	A-20	Havoc
Dragonfly		
Fairchild	24-CAF	
Fairchild	PT-19A-FA	Cornell
Fairchild	PT-23	Cornell
Funk	B-75	
Globe	Swift	
Grumman (General Motors)	TBM	Avenger
Interstate	L-6	
Lockheed	QF-80	Shooting Star
Luscombe	Observor	
Luscombe	Sports Coupe	
McCulloch	J-2	Gyro-plane
McDonnell	F-4	Phantom II
Mitsubishi	A6M2	Zero "Zeke"
Mooney	M20B	
Mooney	Mite	
Mustang II		
North American	B-25	Mitchell
North American	D-16	Twin Navion
North American	L-17	Navion
Northrop	drone	
Northwest	Porterfield	
Phoenix hang glider		
Piasecki	HUP-3	
Pietenpol	Air Camper	
Piper	J-3	Cub
Piper	PA-22-135	
Piper	PA-23-150	Apache
Pober	Pixie	
Rally 3 ultralight		

Rand	KR-1	
Rearwin	Sportster 7000	
Republic	P-47	Thunderbolt
Rutan	VariEze	
Sky Bolt		
Stinson	L-5	Sentinel
Stinson	V-77	
Taylorcraft	L-2	Grasshopper
Thorp	T-18	
Vought	F-8	Crusader
Vultee	BT-13	Valiant
Willie II		

Don F. Pratt Museum

AFZB-DPT-MU, 26th and Tennessee Avenue, Fort Campbell, KY 42223
(502) 798-3215/4986

The museum is named in honor of Brigadier General Don F. Pratt who was assistant divisional commander of the 101st Airborne Division. Pratt was killed in World War II during the Normandy Invasion. The museum centers on the history of the 101st Airborne Division, the "Screaming Eagles."

The nearby air park contains a Douglas C-47 Skytrain and a Waco CG-4A glider. These two aircraft carried most of the paratroopers and airborne infantry during World War II. C-47s were the workhorses for transporting men and material throughout all theaters of the war. Skytrains were also used as tow planes for Waco gliders. The glider carried 13 infantryman, or a combination of men and equipment, at a towed speed of 150 mph. At the release point, the glider pilot disconnected the tow rope from the tow plane and glided to the landing zone.

In 1964 the Army realized a need for a fast, heavily-armed helicopter gunship to provide aerial fire support. In the museums's air park is one of the Lockheed AH-56 Cheyennes that was designed to fulfill the Army's requirements. But an inability to produce the helicopter quickly, as well as technical and expense problems, forced abortion of the program. The Army contracted with Bell Helicopter to produce the Huey Cobra and fill the gunship role, which it did for more than 15 years.

DIRECTIONS TO MUSEUM: Fort Campbell is south of Hopkinsville, Kentucky, on the Kentucky/Tennessee state line. From US 41 Alternate enter Fort Campbell at main gate (gate 4). Proceed on Chaffee Road/26th Street to first stop sign. Museum will be on right.

ADMISSION COST: Free.

HOURS OF OPERATION: Open Monday-Friday 7:30am-4:30pm; Saturday 9am-4:30pm; Sunday noon-4:30pm. Closed New Year's Day and Christmas.

MUSEUM NOTES: Display aircraft are outdoors. Film can be purchased in the gift shop. There is a restaurant nearby.

A brochure is available.

Display Aircraft

MANUFACTURER	MODEL	POPULAR NAME
Douglas	C-47	Skytrain
Lockheed	AH-56A	Cheyenne
Waco	CG-4A	

Museum of History and Science
727 West Main Street, Louisville, Kentucky 40202
(502) 561-6100

The museum presents a wide-ranging selection of exhibits devoted to local history and science. An IMAX big-screen theater runs movies that depict scientific and educational subjects through spectacular photography.

A variety of space equipment and models is on display. A Gemini capsule training unit is open so you can sit inside and visualize space travel.

DIRECTIONS TO MUSEUM: From I-64 westbound exit at 3rd St., Downtown, River Rd. exit and follow River Rd. to parking lot at 7th St. From I-64 eastbound exit onto 9th St. Turn left onto Market. Turn left onto 2nd St. Turn left onto River Rd. and follow to parking lot at 7th St.

ADMISSION COST: Adults $4.00; senior citizens and children (2-12 yrs.) $3.00. With IMAX Theater: adults $6.00; senior citizens and children (2-12 yrs.) $5.00.

HOURS OF OPERATION: Open Monday-Thursday 9am-5pm; Friday & Saturday 9am-9pm; Sunday noon-5pm. Closed Thanksgiving and Christmas.

MUSEUM NOTES: There is a gift shop, but film is not available. There are vending machines at the museum as well as nearby restaurants.

A brochure is available.

Display Aircraft

MANUFACTURER	MODEL
McDonnell	Gemini Capsule
Midget	Mustang
North American Rockwell	Apollo 13 Command Module
Sellers	Quadraplane

Eighth Air Force Museum
P.O. Box 10, Barksdale Air Force Base, Louisiana 71110
(318) 456-3067

Dedicated in 1933, Barksdale Air Force Base is home for one of the most famous Air Force units, the Eighth Air Force. The Eighth was responsible for the strategic bombing of Europe during World War II. The museum highlights and commemorates the efforts of the Eighth Air Force.

Two aircraft made up the bulk of the Eighth Air Force's bomber inventory in World War II, the Boeing B-17 Flying Fortress and the Consolidated B-24 Liberator. During the war it was necessary to allocate production to companies other than the original manufacturer to meet production goals. The museum's B-17G was constructed by Douglas Aircraft, which built close to 3,000 B-17s. The museum's B-24J was constructed by Ford, which built over 6,700 B-24s. The museum's B-47 is another airplane built by a secondary contractor. It was constructed by Douglas and not Boeing.

DIRECTIONS TO MUSEUM: Barksdale AFB is situated east of Shreveport on I-20. From I-20 exit onto Airline Dr. and follow signs to air base. Guard at gate will provide directions to museum.

ADMISSION COST: Free.

HOURS OF OPERATION: Open Monday-Friday 9am-4pm; Saturday 10am-4pm; Sunday noon-4pm. Closed Thanksgiving and Christmas.

MUSEUM NOTES: Display aircraft are outdoors. There is a gift shop, but film is not available. There are restaurants nearby.

A brochure is available.

Display Aircraft

MANUFACTURER	MODEL	POPULAR NAME
Beech	AT-11	Kansas
Beech	C-45	Expeditor
Boeing	B-29	Superfortress
Boeing (Douglas)	B-17G	Flying Fortress
Boeing (Douglas)	B-47	Stratojet
Consolidated (Ford)	B-24J	Liberator
Douglas	C-47	Skytrain
General Dynamics	FB-111	
Hawker Siddeley	MkII	Vulcan
Noorduyn	UC-64	Norseman
North American	P-51D	Mustang
Republic	F-84F	Thunderstreak

Wedell-Williams Memorial Aviation Museum

Box 394, Airport Circle, Patterson, Louisiana 70392
(504) 395-7067

The museum commemorates two men who are best known for their involvement in air racing, Jimmy Wedell, a barnstormer, and Harry Williams, a timber tycoon. They collaborated in producing a series of racing airplanes that dominated air races during 1932, 1933 and 1934. Their planes won the Bendix Trophy all three years and the Thompson Trophy in 1933 and 1934, as well as earning several second and third places. A hurricane wiped out the flying operation in 1934 and within two years both men died in air crashes.

The symbols of air racing achievement in the 1930s were the Bendix Trophy and Thompson Trophy. The Thompson Trophy was awarded to the winner of a closed-course race while the Bendix Trophy winner was the fastest participant in a cross-country race. The museum has on display a replica of the Wedell-Williams #44 air racer, one of the most famous racers of its day. The airplane won both the Bendix and Thompson races. Ironically, Jimmy Wedell won only one race in his own plane. All other victories in Wedell-Williams racers were piloted by other men.

DIRECTIONS TO MUSEUM: Located at Williams Memorial Airport. Museum is on Hwy. 182 west of Patterson.

ADMISSION COST: Adults $2.00; children 50¢.

HOURS OF OPERATION: Open Tuesday-Saturday 10am-4pm; closed Sunday, Monday and holidays.

MUSEUM NOTES: Display airplanes are indoors and outdoors. There is a gift shop, but film is not available. A restaurant is nearby.

A brochure is available.

Display Aircraft

MANUFACTURER	MODEL	POPULAR NAME
Aero Commander	680	
Beech	D17S	Staggerwing
Cessna	185E	
Farley Vincent	Starflight	
Focke-Wulf (replica)	190	
Stearman		
Volksplane		
Wedell-Williams (replica)	44	

Owls Head Transportation Muse[

P.O. Box 277, Rt. 73, Owls Head, Maine 04854
(207) 594-4418

Maine

The Owls Head Transportation Museum is a "working" museum. The m_____ _____ __self as having "one of the finest collections of antique aircraft, automobiles and engines on the Eastern Seaboard." Most of the artifacts date from the turn of the century. On weekends various planes, cars, tractors and engines are operated on the museum grounds. Throughout the summer the museum stages special events that bring together collectors who exhibit their antique planes, cars and other machinery. Contact the museum for a current calendar of events.

The airplane collection is comprised mainly of replicas and original airplanes predating World War II. The airplanes are in flying condition and during the summer they are often flying in an airshow. Call ahead for airshow dates and times. If interested in the biplane era of flight, then this museum is highly recommended.

DIRECTIONS TO MUSEUM: The museum is located two miles south of Rockland on Rt. 73 at the Knox County Airport. Follow signs.

ADMISSION COST: Adults $3.00; high school ages $2.00; children under 12 free.

HOURS OF OPERATION: Open 10am-5pm Monday-Friday November through April; open 10am-5pm all week May through October.

MUSEUM NOTES: Display aircraft are located indoors and outdoors. Film can be purchased in the gift shop. Refreshments are available during special events and several restaurants are nearby.

A brochure is available.

Display Aircraft

MANUFACTURER	MODEL	POPULAR NAME
Ace	Acesport	
Bellanca (replica)	Mono	
Bleriot (replica)	XI	
Breezy	Super	
Burgess-Wright (replica)	B	
Bushmaster	2000	Trimotor
Christen	Eagle	
Curtiss (replica)	D	
Curtiss	JN-4D	"Jenny"
de Havilland		Tiger Moth
Demenjos		Old Orchard Beach
Fokker (replica)	Dr.I	Triplane
Great Lakes		

...ken	Special	
...ooney	M-18	Mite
Nieuport (replica)	28	
North American	AT-6	Texan
Piper	J-3	Cub
Pitts	Special	
Royal Aircraft Factory (replica)	F.E.8	
Sopwith (replica)	Pup	
SPAD (replica)	XIII	
Standard	J-1	
Stearman	A75NI	
Waco	10	
Waco	UBF-2	
Wright (replica)		*Vin Fiz*

NASA Goddard Space Flight Center

Visitor Center, Goddard Space Flight Center, Code 130, Greenbelt, Maryland 20771
(301) 286-8981

Goddard Space Flight Center was established in 1959 and is the oldest NASA scientific laboratory devoted to space exploration.

The facility is named after Dr. Robert H. Goddard, whose achievements in rocket research are as important as the Wright Brothers in manned flight. Goddard scientists are investigating such areas as astronomy, solar physics, astrophysics, planetology, climatology and Earth sciences. Goddard is the only national laboratory capable of handling all tasks necessary to complete a space mission from conception to analyzing data.

The Visitor Center presents exhibits related to work conducted at Goddard. Visitors can retrieve satellites as well as direct spacecraft movement while sitting in a gyro-chair.

Tours of Goddard are conducted every Thursday, and intermittently on other days. Tour duration is approximately 1 hour. Model rocket launches are conducted on the first and second Sunday of each month. On the fourth Sunday of every month, officials at Goddard present a program outlining current Goddard projects.

DIRECTIONS TO MUSEUM: From Washington D.C. take the Baltimore-Washington Pkwy. north to Route 193 east. Stay on Route 193 for approximately two miles. Continue past the Goddard main entrance and turn left onto Soil Conservation Rd. The Visitor Center is on the left.

From Baltimore take the Baltimore-Washington Pkwy south to the Beltsville Agricultural Research Center exit and follow signs to Visitor Center.

ADMISSION COST: Free.

HOURS OF OPERATION: Open Wednesday-Sunday 10am-4pm. Closed New Year's Day, Thanksgiving and Christmas.

MUSEUM NOTES: Displays are indoors and outdoors. Film is available in the gift shop. There are a snack bar and a picnic area onsite.

A brochure is available.

Maryland

Naval Air Test and Evaluation Museum

Box 407, Naval Air Test Center, Patuxent River, Maryland 20670
(301) 863-7418

The museum is situated outside the main gate of the Patuxent River Naval Air Station. NAS Patuxent River is the site of the Naval Air Test Center which performs testing and evaluation of Navy aircraft and weapons systems.

The Test Center evaluates some of the most sophisticated aircraft in the world. The Navy must fly airplanes capable of operating from an aircraft carrier as well as equaling or exceeding the performance capabilities of land-based aircraft. The Center tests and evaluates new aircraft and equipment before they are accepted into the Navy's inventory, as well as analyzing aircraft modifications and troubleshooting problems with existing equipment.

The museum provides exhibits, artifacts and information related to the mission of the Naval Air Test Center and naval aviation. Among the airplanes displayed outside is a Douglas F-6A Skyray. Exemplifying the dual requirements of Naval combat aircraft, the Skyray served as an all-weather interceptor operating from aircraft carriers. In 1953 the prototype flew 753 mph and became the first airplane designed for use on aircraft carriers to set a world speed record.

DIRECTIONS TO MUSEUM: The museum is located in Lexington Park, Maryland, at intersection of Route 235 and Shangri-La Dr.

ADMISSION COST: Free.

HOURS OF OPERATION: July-September: open Tuesday-Saturday 10am-5pm; Sunday noon-5pm. October-June: open Tuesday-Saturday 11am-5pm; Sunday noon-5pm.

MUSEUM NOTES: Display aircraft are indoors and outdoors. There is a gift shop, but film is not available. A restaurant is nearby.

A brochure is available.

Display Aircraft

MANUFACTURER	MODEL	POPULAR NAME
Douglas	A-4M	Skyhawk
Douglas	F-6A	Skyray
Grumman	E-2B	Hawkeye
Grumman	S-2	Tracker
McDonnell	F-4	Phantom II
North American	RA-5C	Vigilante
Vought	A-7E	Corsair II

Paul E. Garber Facility

Silver Hill, Maryland
Mail address: National Air and Space Museum, Smithsonian In
Washington, D.C. 20560
(202) 357-1400

Someone visiting the National Air and Space Museum in Washington, D.C., might wonder what behind-the-scenes workforce produced the displays. After all, it's been decades since most of the like-new aircraft and spacecraft the public sees left the production line. The organization responsible is located just outside D.C. in Silver Hill, Maryland. Formerly named the Silver Hill Museum, the group of buildings was renamed the Paul E. Garber Preservation, Restoration and Storage Facility in 1980. Paul E. Garber, Historian Emeritus, was responsible for obtaining much of the museum's collection.

Actually, the aircraft on display at the National Air and Space Museum are a small percentage of the aircraft the Smithsonian possesses. The Smithsonian has first right to claim any available United States military aircraft, in addition to the acquisition of aircraft in private hands. Although a considerable number of aircraft are loaned to other museums, the exhibition area in the Air and Space Museum is too small to display all the aircraft in the Smithsonian inventory. The remaining restored aircraft, spacecraft and engines have been placed on display at the Garber Facility.

The Garber Facility comprises a staff of craftsmen and technicians experienced in the restoration and preservation of aircraft, a considerable task considering the wide realm of construction techniques and materials found in aviation manufacturing. A great deal of the restoration process is devoted to locating old factory drawings so the aircraft can be reconstructed to it's original condition.

Visiting the Garber Facility is by tour only. A portion of the tour includes a walk through the workshop area providing the visitor an opportunity to see some of the best craftsman in the nation at work. A limited number of visitors can be accommodated on a tour. The Smithsonian recommends calling ahead and making a reservation. During the summer months reservations may be needed two weeks in advance.

DIRECTIONS TO MUSEUM: From I-95 exit onto Pennsylvania Ave. eastbound or Suitland Pkwy. eastbound. Travel to Branch Ave. and turn right onto Branch. At Silver Hill Rd. turn left, go one block and turn left. Facility is at corner of intersection.

From I-495/95 northbound take exit 4B onto St. Barnabas Rd. northbound. Travel approximately three miles to Silver Hill Rd. Continue through intersection. Facility is on right.

From I-495/95 southbound exit at Branch Ave. and turn right onto Branch. Turn right onto St. Barnabas Rd. Travel to Silver Hill Rd. Continue through intersection. Facility is on right.

ADMISSION COST: Free.

HOURS OF OPERATION: Tours begin Monday-Friday at 10am; Saturday and Sunday at 10am and 1pm. Tours last 2-3 hours.

MUSEUM NOTES: Display aircraft are indoors. Buildings containing aircraft and exhibits are neither heated nor air conditioned.

A brochure is available.

Display Aircraft

MANUFACTURER	MODEL	POPULAR NAME
Abraes	Explorer	
Aeronca	C-2	
Aikerman	Tailless	
Antonov	AN-2	Colt
Applebay	Zuni II	
Arado	234-B	Blitz
Arlington	1A	Sisu
Arrow	A2-60	Sport
Bachem	BA 349(BP 20)	Natter
Baldwin	Red Devil	
Bede	BD-5	
Beech	35	Bonanza
Beech (cutaway)	V35B	Bonanza
Bell	30	
Bell	ATV	VTOL
Bell	P-39Q	Airacobra
Bell	P-63A	Kingcobra
Bell	UH-1M	Iroquois "Huey"
Bell	VH-13J	Sioux
Bellanca	C.F.	
Benoist-Korn		
Berliner helicopter		
Bertelson	Aerobile	
Boeing	B-29	Superfortress *Enola Gay*
Boeing-Vertol	VZ-2A	VTOL
Bowlus	Baby Albatross	
Bowlus-duPont	Albatross I	*Falcon*
Bücker	Bu 181	Bestmann
Caudron	G-4	
Cessna	150L	Commuter
Cessna	180	*Spirit of Columbus*
Cessna	O-1A	Bird Dog
Convair	240	*Caroline*
Culver	TD2C-1	
Curtis	XP-55	Ascender

Curtiss	F6C-1	*Gulfhawk IA*
Curtiss	JN-4D	"Jenny"
Curtiss-Wright	CW-1	Junior
Curtiss-Wright	X-100	
Custer	CCW-1	Channel Wing
Dassault	Falcon 20	
de Havilland	D.H.98	Mosquito
de Havilland	DHC-1A	Chipmunk
Douglas	B-26B	Invader
Eipper-Formance	Cumulus 10	
Erco	415	Ercoupe
Farman	Sport	
Felixstowe (N.A.F.)	F-5L	Flying Boat
Fieseler	Fi 156	Storch
Focke-Wulf	Fw 190F-8	
Fowler-Gage	Tractor	
Frankfort	TG-1A	
Franklin	PS-2	*Texaco Eaglet*
Grumman	F6F-3	Hellcat
Grumman	F8F-2	Bearcat *Conquest I*
Grumman	TBF-1	Avenger
Grunau	Baby IIb	
Hawker	Mk.IIC	Hurricane
Heinkel	He 162A	Volksjager
Helio	No. 1	
Herrick	HV2A	Convertoplane
Hiller	Flying Platform	
Hiller	HOE-1	
Hispano	HA-200B	Cairo
Hughes	H-1	Racer
Kaman	K-225	
Kreider-Reisner	KR-34C	
Kugisho	11 (22)	Ohka
Laird	LCDW 500	*Super Solution*
Langley	Aerodrome	
Lockheed	P-38J	Lightning
Lockheed	T-33	Shooting Star
Lockheed	XC-35(10E)	Electra
Mahoney		*Sorceress*
Martin, J.V.	K-III Kitten	
McDonnell	XV-1	Convertiplane
Messerschmitt	Me 163B	Komet
Mikoyan-Gurevich	MiG-15	"Fagot"
Mooney	M-18C	Mite
Nakajima	J1N1-S	Gekko "Irving"

NASA	Parasev	
Nelson	BB-1	Dragonfly
Nelson	PG-185B	Hummingbird
Nieuport	28C-1	
North American	F-86A	Sabre
North American	SNJ-4	Texan
Northrop	N-1M	Flying Wing
Piper	J-3	Cub
Piper	PA-12	*City of Washington*
Piper	PA-18	Super Cub
Pitcairn	AC-35	
Pitts Special	S-1C	*Little Stinker*
Pitts Special	S-1S	
Princeton	Air Scooter	
Radioplane	DQ-14	
Republic	P-47D	Thunderbolt
Republic	RC3	Seabee
Rotorway	Scorpion Too	
Rutan	Quickie	
Rutan	VariEze	
Saab	J-29	
Schulgleiter	SG.38	
Schweizer	2-22	
Sikorsky	JRS-1	(S-43)
Sikorsky	XR-5(VS-317)	Dragonfly
Sopwith	Snipe	
Standard	J-1	
Stearman	N2S-5	Kaydet
Stearman-Hammond	Y	
Stinson	L-5	Sentinel
Stinson	SR-10F	Reliant
Stout	Skycar	
Turner	RT-14	Meteor
Valkyrie		
Verville		
Vought	F4U-1D	Corsair
Vought	OS2U	Kingfisher
Waco	9	
Waco	UIC	Cabin
Waterman	Aeromobile	
Weedhopper	C	
Windecker	Eagle I	
Wiseman-Cooke		
Yakovlev	Yak-18	"Max"
Zimmerman	Flying Platform	

Henry Ford Museum & Greenfield Village

20900 Oakwood Boulevard, P.O. Box 1970, Dearborn, Michigan 48121
(313) 271-1620

Displayed at the Henry Ford Museum & Greenfield Village are Americana dating from the 1600s to the present. Special emphasis is placed on the relationship between industrial technology and American history as reflected in the collections of automobiles, locomotives and aircraft. Changes in transportation, agriculture, industry, leisure, entertainment and domestic living are traceable in the collections and exhibits. Glass blowing, printing, weaving and pottery are among the crafts demonstrated. Visitors

Among the Ford Museum's aircraft is this 1931 Pitcairn Autogiro. Designed by Spaniard Juan de la Cierva, the autogiro utilizes the rotating blades to produce lift. Later versions were capable of vertical takeoffs and landings, if the needed headwind was available. The autogiro was developed into a safe aircraft and demand exceeded production in the late 1920s (approximately 240 were built in Japan where the autogiro was most popular). The Detroit News *used their autogiro to fly reporters to sites of major stories. The Depression and failure to obtain a military contract produced insufficient demand for the Pitcairn Autogiro and it passed into history. The development work performed on the autogiro rotor and blade system enhanced the similar system found on helicopters.*

The Ryan NYP in the Ford Museum is a sister ship of Charles Lindbergh's Spirit of St. Louis, *which hangs in the Air and Space Museum in Washington, D.C. Lindbergh attempted in 1926 to find an aircraft company that would build for him an airplane capable of crossing the Atlantic, and finally found the small manufacturer Ryan Airlines in San Diego, California. Ryan had constructed the M-2 mailplane and the NYP was an outgrowth designed for later commercial sales. Price for the airplane with one of the newly developed Wright Whirlwind J-5C engines was $10,580. Lindbergh made partial payment for the* Spirit of St. Louis *and a St. Louis sponsor contributed the remainder. Two months after work began the plane was ready for flight testing.*

may enter such notable structures as Edison's laboratory, the Wright Brothers' Cycle Shop and the Henry Ford farmhouse.

The bulk of the airplane collection predates 1930 and contains several airplanes of historical significance. The Fokker Trimotor was the first airplane to overfly the North Pole while the Ford Trimotor *Floyd Bennett* was the first airplane to overfly the South Pole. The Junkers *Bremen* made the first east-to-west Atlantic crossing. The Lockheed Vega was the second constructed and was flown by noteworthy aviators Jimmy Doolittle, Amelia Earhart, Billy Mitchell and Charles Lindbergh.

At one time, Henry Ford envisioned airplanes providing transportation on a personal basis. In 1927, three airplanes called "Flivvers" were constructed as prototypes for the "everymans" airplane. Powered by a four-cylinder engine, the plane was a single-place monoplane. Unfortunately, a test pilot was killed in one of the prototypes and the project was dropped. One of the remaining prototypes is hanging in the museum.

DIRECTIONS TO MUSEUM: From eastbound I-94 exit onto northbound Southfield (M-39); go three miles to northbound Oakwood then go two miles.

From westbound I-94 exit onto northbound Oakwood then go three miles.

From northbound I-75 exit onto northbound Southfield (M-39); go eight miles to northbound Oakwood then go two miles.

From eastbound I-96 exit onto southbound Southfield (M-39); go west on Michigan Avenue then turn left onto Oakwood and go 1/2 mile.

ADMISSION COST: Adults $10.50; senior citizens $9.50; children (5-12 yrs.) $5.25. Tickets are separate but priced the same for either Henry Ford Museum or Greenfield Village. Combination tickets for admission available at reduced cost.

HOURS OF OPERATION: Open daily 9am-5pm. Some structures closed January 2-March 16. Closed Thanksgiving and Christmas Day.

MUSEUM NOTES: Display aircraft are indoors. Film is available in the gift shop. Restaurants are located on the grounds. Contact museum for special events and exhibits.

A brochure is available.

Display Aircraft

MANUFACTURER	MODEL	POPULAR NAME
Baumann	RB-1	
Bleriot	XI	
Boeing	40-B2	
Curtiss	Canuck(JN-4)	
Curtiss Flying Boat		
Douglas	DC-3	
Fokker	Trimotor	
Ford	Trimotor	*Floyd Bennett*
Ford	"Flivver"	
Junkers	*Bremen*	
Laird		
Lockheed	Vega	
Piper	J-3	Cub
Pitcairn	PCA-2	Autogiro
Ryan		
Sikorsky		
Standard	J-1	
Stinson	Detroiter	*Pride of Detroit*
Stinson	Detroiter diesel	

Kalamazoo Aviation History Museum

3101 East Milham Road, Kalamazoo, Michigan 49002
(616) 382-6555

The Kalamazoo Aviation History Museum is dedicated to the restoration, preservation and display of flying and static aircraft from World War II. The museum opened in 1979, and besides displaying award-winning aircraft, also exhibits engines, uniforms, cockpits, equipment and other artifacts.

Also known as the Kalamazoo "Air Zoo" for its collection of Grumman 'Cats, the museum possesses examples of all four Grumman piston-engine airplanes; namely, the Wildcat, Hellcat, Tigercat and Bearcat. All of the 'Cats are in flying condition. One of only two flying P-39 Airacobras also resides at the museum.

On occasion, guided tours of the restoration facility are conducted.

The quality of the restorations has gained the museum six Grand Champion Warbird Awards at the annual EAA (Experimental Aircraft Association) Air Show in Oshkosh, Wisconsin.

One of the unique fighter designs of World War II was the Bell P-39 Airacobra. The engine was located near the midpoint of the fuselage and drove the propeller through a drive shaft. The design permitted better aerodynamics and the use of tricycle landing gear. Slow climb speed and lack of speed at high altitudes relegated the plane to low altitude missions. Most of the Airacobras were shipped to Allied air forces, particularly the Soviet Union.

The Grumman F4F Wildcat was the Navy's front-line fighter at the outbreak of World War II. The Wildcat's flying capabilities were inferior to the Japanese Mitsubishi Zero, but superior flying tactics utilizing the Wildcat's superior firepower and rugged construction resulted in a respectable combat record.

A "Flight of the Day" usually occurs at 2:00 pm, when weather permits and a pilot and airplane are available. Most of the airplanes are in flying condition and often participate in flying shows. Call ahead if a particular airplane interests you to be sure it is present.

DIRECTIONS TO MUSEUM: From I-94 exit onto Portage Rd. Travel south past the entrance of the Kalamazoo County Airport to Milham Rd. Turn left (east) and follow Milham Rd. to museum.

ADMISSION COST: Adults $5.00; senior citizens $4.00; children (13-18 yrs.) $2.00, (6-12 yrs.) $1.00.

HOURS OF OPERATION: Open Monday-Saturday 10am-5pm; Sunday 1-5pm. Closed major holidays.

MUSEUM NOTES: Display aircraft are indoors and outdoors. Film is available in the gift shop. There is a snack area onsite and restaurants are located nearby.

A brochure is available.

Display Aircraft

MANUFACTURER	MODEL	POPULAR NAME
Aeronca	O-58B	Grasshopper
Bell	RP-39Q	Airacobra
Cessna	OE-1	Bird Dog

The last of the piston-engine Grumman 'Cat series was the F7F Tigercat. Designed as a multirole fighter, Tigercats entered service too late to see action in World War II, and were too slow to duel with jet fighters in the Korean War. Production ceased in 1946.

Curtiss	P-40N	Warhawk
Douglas	AD-4NA	Skyraider
Douglas	C-53	Skytrooper
Fairchild	PT-23	Cornell
Grumman	F6F-5N	Hellcat
Grumman	F7F-3P	Tigercat
Grumman	XF8F-1D	Bearcat
Grumman (General Motors)	FM-2	Wildcat
Hispano	HA-1112-M1L	Buchón
Messerschmitt	Bf 108	
North American	B-25H	Mitchell
North American	SNJ-5	Texan
North American	T-28A	Trojan
Republic	F-84F	Thunderstreak
Republic	P-47D	Thunderbolt
Stearman	PT-13	Kaydet
Timm	N2T-1	Tutor
Vought	F8U-2NE	Crusader
Vought (Goodyear)	FG-1D	Corsair
Vultee	BT-13	Valiant

Michigan Space Center
2111 Emmons Road, Jackson, Michigan 49201
(517) 787-4425

Claiming to be the "Biggest Little Space Center on Earth," the Michigan Space Center is situated on the campus of Jackson Community College. In 1977 the Center opened its doors with the intent of educating visitors to the past, present and future technological aspects of space exploration. The Center is housed in a 40-foot-high geodesic dome that reflects the futuristic contents on display.

Many exhibits invite "hands-on" inspection, including viewing a moon rock through a microscope, sitting in a space capsule and trying on an astronaut helmet. Outside stands an imposing Redstone rocket similar to the rockets that carried Mercury capsules into space. Inside are Mercury, Gemini and Apollo modules, a Lunar Rover, satellites, and a variety of space related artifacts and equipment. A special exhibit constructed with funds contributed by public donations memorializes the crew of the Space Shuttle *Challenger*.

DIRECTIONS TO MUSEUM: Traveling east or west on I-94 take exit 142 southbound onto US 127. Exit onto M50 (McDewitt) westbound. Follow M50 and turn south onto Hague Ave. Turn right at Emmons Rd. and follow signs.

Traveling north on US 127 turn left onto Wetherby. Turn left onto Crouch Rd. and then right onto Hague Ave. Turn left at Emmons Rd. and follow signs.

ADMISSION COST: Adult $3.00; senior citizen $2.00; student $2.00; children under 6 yrs. free.

HOURS OF OPERATION: Open Monday 10am-5pm (10am-6pm from Memorial Day to Labor Day; closed Mondays from December thru March); Tuesday-Friday 10am-5pm (10am-6pm from Memorial Day to Labor Day); Saturday 10am-5pm; Sunday 11am-5pm. Closed New Year's Day, Easter, Thanksgiving and Christmas.

MUSEUM NOTES: Displays, except Redstone rocket, are indoors. The gift shop does not stock film. There are vending machines onsite and a restaurant is nearby.

A brochure is available.

Display Aircraft

MANUFACTURER	MODEL
Chrysler	Mercury Redstone
McDonnell	Mercury Capsule
McDonnell	Gemini Capsule
North American Rockwell	Apollo 9 Command Module

Selfridge Military Museum

127 TRW/MU, Box 43, Selfridge ANG Base, Michigan 48045
(313) 466-5035

The museum sits on the grounds of one of the earliest military airfields, Selfridge Army Air Field. The field is named for Lieutenant Thomas Selfridge, the first military officer to pilot an engine-driven aircraft, and also the first to die in a crash. The museum chronicles the base's history beginning with activation in 1917.

Most of the aircraft in the aircraft collection were flown by the Michigan Air National Guard (ANG), which demonstrates the diverse aircraft and missions the ANG has performed since World War II. Historically, Air Guard and Reserve units were equipped with equipment no longer desirable to the regular Air Force. However, recent policy changes have resulted in first-line equipment also appearing in Guard and Reserve units.

DIRECTIONS TO MUSEUM: Selfridge ANG Base is northeast of Detroit. From I-94 northbound take Exit 240 onto Rosso Hwy. Follow Rosso east to main gate. Obtain a visitor's pass and directions from guard at gate. From I-94 southbound take Exit 241 onto 21 Mile Rd. and travel east, then veer south to Selfridge.

ADMISSION COST: Free (donation requested).

HOURS OF OPERATION: Open only on Sunday 1-5pm from April 1 to November 1. Closed remainder of year and on Easter.

MUSEUM NOTES: Display aircraft are outdoors. There is a gift shop, but no film is available. A restaurant is nearby.

A brochure is available.

Display Aircraft

MANUFACTURER	MODEL	POPULAR NAME
Cessna	O-2A	
Cessna	U-3A	
Convair	C-131D	Samaritan
Convair	F-106A	Delta Dart
Convair	TF-102A	Delta Dagger
Douglas	A-4D	Skyhawk
Douglas	B-26C	Invader
Grumman	S-2A	Tracker
Lockheed	C-130A	Hercules
Lockheed	T-33A	Shooting Star
Martin	RB-57A	Canberra
McDonnell	RF-101C	Voodoo
McDonnell	F-4C	Phantom II
North American	F-86A	Sabre

North American	F-100D	Super Sabre
North American	F-100F	Super Sabre
Republic	F-84F	Thunderstreak
Republic	RF-84F	Thunderflash
Sikorsky	HH-52A	Sea Guard
Vought	A-7D	Corsair II
Vought (Goodyear)	FG-1D	Corsair

Yankee Air Force Museum

P.O. Box 1100, Ypsilanti, Michigan 48197
(313) 483-4030

The Yankee Air Force Museum is located at Willow Run Airport, which is just east of Ypsilanti. The museum is situated in a hanger that was a part of the complex that produced over 8,700 B-24 Liberator bombers during World War II. The Yankee Air Force was started in 1981 to promote the restoration and preservation of historic aircraft. Membership in YAF exceeds 1,600.

The B-24 Liberator was produced in greater numbers than any other American aircraft during World War II. Originally designed by Consolidated Aircraft Company, Ford Motor Company was enlisted to manufacture the airplane and a factory at Willow Run Airport

A trip to the Yankee Air Force Museum may offer a look at a restoration project underway. Visible here is the inside starboard engine of a Boeing B-17G Flying Fortress. The engine is a Wright nine-cylinder radial that produces 1,200 horsepower. The four engines of the B-17G powered it to a top speed of 287 mph at an altitude of 25,000 feet. More of the G models were built (8,680 manufactured at three locations) than any other B-17 variation.

was constructed. A portion of the museum is devoted to the manufacture of the B-24 and the people who participated.

Among the museum's aircraft is a rare example of a Consolidated PB4Y-2 Privateer. The PB4Y-2 is a modified version of the B-24 Liberator and was used as a patrol bomber. The Privateer had a single vertical tail in place of the characteristic twin tails of the Liberator. Another notable aircraft on display is the Grumman F7F-3N Tigercat, the only twin, piston-engine fighter to serve with the Marine Corps.

At any given time, the museum's hanger will have several airplanes undergoing maintenance, overhaul or restoration. Visitors are allowed to walk around the hanger and observe work in progress.

Some of the display aircraft are flyable and may be away performing at airshows, particularly on weekends.

DIRECTIONS TO MUSEUM: The museum is located at the Willow Run Airport at the corner of Ecorse and Beck Rds. From I-94 exit onto Belleville Rd., then travel north on Belleville to Tyler Rd. Turn left onto Tyler and follow signs.

ADMISSION COST: Adults $3.50; senior citizens $2.50; children (3-12 yrs.) $1.50.

HOURS OF OPERATION: Open Tuesday-Saturday 10am-4pm; Sunday noon-4pm.

Closed Monday. Closed New Year's Day, Easter, Thanksgiving, Christmas Eve, Christmas.

MUSEUM NOTES: Display aircraft are indoors and outdoors. Film is available in the gift shop. Restaurants are found at I-94 and Belleville Road.

A brochure is available.

Display Aircraft

MANUFACTURER	MODEL	POPULAR NAME
Bell	HTL-3	
Boeing	B-17G	Flying Fortress
Boeing	B-52D	Stratofortress
Consolidated	PB4Y-2	Privateer
Convair	TF-102	Delta Dagger
Douglas	C-47D	Skytrain
Douglas	DC-6A	Liftmaster
Fairchild	PT-19	Cornell
Fairchild	PT-23	Cornell
Grumman	F7F-3N	Tigercat
Grumman	F-11A	Tiger
Howard	GH-2	Nightingale
Lockheed	T-33A	Shooting Star

McDonnell	F-101B	Voodoo
Naval Aircraft Factory	N3N-3	
North American	B-25D	Mitchell
North American	F-86F	Sabre
North American	T-6	Texan
North American	T-28	Trojan
Pou de Ciel (Flying Flea)		
Republic	F-84F	Thunderstreak
Republic	RF-84F	Thunderflash
Vultee	BT-13A	Valiant

Minnesota Air Guard Museum

P.O. Box 11598, St. Paul, Minnesota 55111
(612) 725-5609

The Minnesota Air Guard was the first air unit to be federally recognized as a segment of the National Guard. On January 17, 1921, the Minnesota Air Guard was established and began military service to the state and nation that continues today.

The museum reflects the aircraft flown by the Minnesota Air Guard. During the early fifties the primary threat to the United States was from long-range Russian bombers. The Guard was responsible for interception and three examples of 1950s interceptors are exhibited. The F-94C, F-89H and F-102 on display are examples of the first all-weather, jet interceptors flown by squadrons in Canada and the northern U.S. to meet Russian bombers flying a polar route.

DIRECTIONS TO MUSEUM: Museum is located on the northeast corner of Minneapolis/St. Paul International Airport. At intersection of Crosstown and Hiawatha Aves. travel south on Hiawatha to Air Guard Base and follow directions.

ADMISSION COST: Free (donations requested).

HOURS OF OPERATION: Open mid-April through mid-September. Open only on Saturday and Sunday 11am-5pm. Call ahead for holiday schedule.

MUSEUM NOTES: Display aircraft are primarily outside. There is a gift shop, but film is not available. A restaurant is nearby.

A brochure is available.

Display Aircraft

MANUFACTURER	MODEL	POPULAR NAME
Beech	C-45	Expeditor
Convair	F-102	Delta Dagger
Douglas	C-47	Skytrain
Lockheed	C-130	Hercules
Lockheed	F-94A	Starfire
Lockheed	T-33	Shooting Star
McDonnell	F-4C	Phantom II
McDonnell	F-101	Voodoo
North American	BC-1A (AT-6)	
North American	P-51	Mustang

Planes of Fame Air Museum

14771 Pioneer Trail (County Rd. #1), Eden Prairie, Minnesota 55344
(612) 941-2633 weekends, 941-7820 weekdays

The Planes of Fame Air Museum focuses on World War II era aircraft. Most of the aircraft have been restored to flying condition.

Unique among the museum's airplanes are a Supermarine Spitfire and a Russian Yak-11 trainer. The Spitfire is the famous British World War II fighter. Over 20,000 Spitfires were built in a number of variations, but very few are found in U.S. museums. The Yak is also very rare. It was produced after World War II as an advanced trainer for the Russian and Warsaw Pact air forces.

Some aircraft may be away participating in airshows at other airfields. Call ahead if you are interested in a particular airplane.

The museum offers rides in their Stearman biplane. Call for times and prices.

DIRECTIONS TO MUSEUM: The museum is located on the northwest corner of Flying Cloud Field. From I-494 exit onto Hwy. 169 south and travel south to County Road #1 (Pioneer Trail). Follow Co. Rd. #1 west and watch for signs to museum.

ADMISSION COST: Adults $5.00; children (7-17 yrs.) $2.00.

HOURS OF OPERATION: Open during summer Saturday and Sunday 11am-5pm; open weekdays by appointment only, call ahead.

MUSEUM NOTES: Display aircraft are indoors and outdoors. Film is available in the gift shop. Restaurants are nearby.

A brochure is available.

Display Aircraft

MANUFACTURER	MODEL	POPULAR NAME
Beech	T-34B	Mentor
Curtiss	P-40N	Warhawk
Douglas	C-47	Skytrain
EKW	C3605	
Grumman	F6F-5	Hellcat
Grumman	F8F	Bearcat
Grumman (General Motors)	FM-2	Wildcat
Grumman (General Motors)	TBM-3	Avenger
Lockheed	P-38	Lightning
North American	AT-6	Texan
North American	B-25J	Mitchell
North American	P-51D	Mustang

North American	T-28B	Trojan
Piper	J-3	Cub
Republic	P-47D	Thunderbolt
Stearman	N2S	
Supermarine	Mk.XIV	Spitfire
Vought (Goodyear)	FG-1D	Corsair
Yakovlev	Yak-11	"Moose"

NASA Stennis Space Center

Visitors Center, Bldg. 1200, Stennis Space Center, Mississippi 39529
(601) 688-2370

Formerly named the National Space Technology Laboratories, the site was renamed the Stennis Space Center in honor of John C. Stennis, senator of Mississippi from 1947 to 1989. Stennis was a member of the Armed Services and Appropriations Committees and a strong supporter of the nation's efforts in space.

The prime mission of the Stennis Space Center is developmental testing of Space Shuttle main engines and other large propulsion systems. All main engines for the Space Shuttle are proven acceptable for flight at Stennis. The facility was originally created as a site for test firing the first and second stage rocket engines of the Saturn V rockets used on the Apollo missions.

The Visitors Center provides exhibits related to space flight and the ongoing research performed at Stennis. Several spacecraft are displayed, including the Apollo IV Command Module, as well as rocket engines and a moon rock. Also contained in the Visitors Center are informative displays describing the work performed by other agencies at Stennis. The Naval Oceanographic Office, National Weather Service, National Mapping Division and U.S. Geological Survey are present at Stennis and they and other organizations make use of the facilities and personnel.

Tours of the facility are offered, and for those with good timing, the tour includes viewing a test firing of a Space Shuttle rocket engine, provided the test is conducted during the Center's operating hours.

DIRECTIONS TO MUSEUM: Stennis Space Center is approximately 45 miles east of New Orleans. From I-59 exit onto Hwy. 607 southbound. From I-10 exit onto Hwy. 607 northbound. Follow signs to Visitors Center.

ADMISSION COST: Free.

HOURS OF OPERATION: Open daily 9am-5pm. Closed Christmas.

MUSEUM NOTES: Spacecraft are indoors. Film can be purchased in the gift shop. A snack bar is located in the building.

A brochure is available.

National Agricultural Aviation Museum
1150 Lakeland Drive, Jackson, Mississippi 39216
(601) 354-6113

Agricultural aviation has had significant impact on United States agriculture. Aerial application provides the means to combat infestation over a wider area than ground application, as well as reaching areas that are inaccessible to ground vehicles.

Prior to World War II, aerial application was crude due to a lack of suitable airplanes, rudimentary equipment and insufficient chemical research. Huff-DaLand was the only company manufacturing airplanes specifically intended for aerial application. After World War II, thousands of surplus airplanes were available, and chemicals developed during the war became available for agricultural use. During the 1950s and 1960s airplanes specifically designed for aerial application were manufactured by Ayres, Callair, Cessna, Piper, Schweizer and Snow. Agricultural aviation grew into an important segment of the aviation industry.

For any aviation enthusiast, the name "Stearman" identifies the typical biplane of the late 1920s and 1930s. After World War II, thousands of the Stearman trainers were available at surplus prices. Converted to agricultural spraying, Stearmans provided hundreds of operators the opportunity to enter the business of aerial application. The conical apparatus attached to the Stearman's wings shown above are venturi that disbursed the spray.

One of the aircraft on display is a Schweizer (Grumman) Ag-Cat. First built in 1957, the Ag-Cat was designed by Grumman and manufactured by Schweizer. It was specifically designed as an "agplane" and the sturdier landing gear and greater payload made it more desirable than the older Stearman (also on display). Hundreds of Ag-Cats have been produced while establishing the record of longest produced aircraft in U.S. history.

DIRECTIONS TO MUSEUM: From I-55 take exit 98-B onto Lakeland Dr. At traffic light just east of freeway turn left into parking lot adjacent to baseball stadium.

ADMISSION COST: Adults $3.00; senior citizens $2.75; children (6-18 yrs.) $1.00.

HOURS OF OPERATION: Open Monday-Saturday 9am-5pm; Sunday 1-5pm.

MUSEUM NOTES: Display aircraft are indoors. Film can be purchased in the gift shop. Restaurants are nearby.

A brochure is available.

Display Aircraft

MANUFACTURER	MODEL	POPULAR NAME
Bell	47	
Piper	PA25-235	Pawnee
Schweizer (Grumman)	Ag-Cat	
Stearman		

St. Louis Aviation Museum
P.O. Box 5867, St. Louis, Missouri 63134
(314) 524-1559

The purpose of the museum is to display artifacts and memorabilia representative of aviation history in the St. Louis area.

The greatest influence on recent St. Louis area aviation history is McDonnell Douglas at Lambert International Airport. James McDonnell started the McDonnell Aircraft Company in 1939 at Lambert Field. The company served as a subcontractor during World War II while developing plans for airplanes of their design. In 1947 McDonnell delivered to the Navy the FD-1 (FH-1) Phantom, the first purpose-built, all-jet, carrier-based airplane. Production of an improved version of the Phantom, the F2H Banshee, established McDonnell as a significant military aircraft manufacturer. In the late 1950s, McDonnell conceived the highly successful F-4 Phantom II. Then after the merger with Douglas Aircraft in 1967, the F-15 Eagle was developed and currently flies as the Air Force's front-line fighter.

The museum has on display four airplanes produced by McDonnell. The Phantom and Banshee reflect early naval aviation during the subsonic era. The F-101 Voodoo entered service with the Air Force in 1957 and served as a supersonic interceptor and reconnaissance airplane.

Also displayed is a Hawker Siddeley AV-8A Harrier. Originally designed and manufactured in Great Britain, the Harrier is capable of vertical take-off and landing and saw combat in the Falklands War. The AV-8A version was purchased for the U.S. Marine Corps. McDonnell Douglas upgraded the design and built a later version for the Marines, the AV-8B Harrier.

DIRECTIONS TO MUSEUM: From I-70 take Earth City Expressway south to Creve Coeur Mill Rd. Go two miles to Creve Coeur Airport. Museum is at 3127 Creve Coeur Mill Rd.

ADMISSION COST: Free.

HOURS OF OPERATION: Open weekends 10am-4pm June-November.

MUSEUM NOTES: Display aircraft are indoors and outdoors. There is a gift shop, but film is not available. No restaurants are nearby.

A brochure is available.

Display Aircraft

MANUFACTURER	MODEL	POPULAR NAME
Cavalier		
Curtiss	JN-4	"Jenny"
Demoiselle		

Glasair		
Hawker Siddeley	AV-8A	Harrier
McDonnell	F2H-2	Banshee
McDonnell	F-101B	Voodoo
McDonnell	FH-1	Phantom
Meyers		
Rawdon		
Rutan	VariEze	
Stinson	L-5	Sentinel
Taylor	Titch	

Save A Connie

480 Richards Road, Kansas City, Missouri
Mail address: P.O. Box 9144, Riverside, Missouri 64168
(816) 421-3401

Save A Connie is a non-profit organization dedicated to restoring and preserving the last flying Lockheed Super Constellation (all versions of Constellations were known as "Connie"). A significant segment of the organization is comprised of retired Trans World Airlines employees who worked on Constellations during their airline careers.

The plane was named *Star of America* by Save A Connie. Configured as a cargo hauler during its commercial life, the Connie is being restored as the passenger version. Save A Connie plans to fly the plane to air shows as long as practicable, then donate it to a museum, hopefully, to an air transport museum under consideration in Kansas City.

Star of America is parked on a ramp at Kansas City's Downtown Airport. The airport was formerly the main commercial airport for the city as well as headquarters for TWA.

The organization also possesses a Martin 404. The 404 could accomodate 48 passengers and was an upgraded version of the earlier Martin 202. Both the 202 and 404 saw service as short to medium route airliners.

DIRECTIONS TO MUSEUM: Save A Connie is located at Kansas City Downtown Airport which is just across the Missouri River from downtown. From I-70 take Exit 2C and turn onto Broadway heading across the river. At north end of bridge fol-

Prominent in this view of Save A Connie's Lockheed Constellation are the three vertical stabilizers, the most identifiable feature of Constellations. Constellations and Douglas DC-7s were the last and most highly refined of the multi piston-engined airliners.

low sign for Richards Road/Downtown Airport. After stop sign veer around circle onto Richards Road. Follow road past terminal building to 480 Richards Road. Go around to ramp side of building and enter through door with "Save A Connie" above it.

ADMISSION COST: Free (donation requested).

HOURS OF OPERATION: Open 9:30am-4pm Monday-Friday. Closed Saturday, Sunday and major holidays.

MUSEUM NOTES: Display aircraft are outdoors.

Malmstrom AFB Museum and Air Park

840 CSG/CDR, Malmstrom Air Force Base, Montana 59402
(406) 731-2705

Originally named Great Falls Army Air Base, the base has hosted units assigned missions in training, transport, air defense, refueling and missile deployment. Renamed Malmstrom Air Force Base in 1955, the installation has been under the authority of the Strategic Air Command for several years and was the first base to be equipped with the Minuteman intercontinental ballistic missile.

In the air park are several aircraft representative of those that served at Malmstrom AFB. Rarely on display in museums is the Minuteman III missile. A Minuteman III is capable of a range of over 7,000 miles and will reach a speed of approximately 15,000 miles-per-hour and an altitude of 700 miles during flight. The nose separates to allow three separate pods to seek individual targets.

DIRECTIONS TO MUSEUM: Malmstrom AFB is on the east side of Great Falls. From US 87 Bypass turn east onto Second Avenue North and follow to main gate of air base. Museum is inside air base and a pass must be obtained at main gate where directions will be provided.

ADMISSION COST: Free.

HOURS OF OPERATION: Open Monday-Saturday noon-3pm. Closed Sunday.

MUSEUM NOTES: Display aircraft are outdoors. There is a gift shop, but film is not available. A restaurant is nearby.

A brochure is available.

Display Aircraft

MANUFACTURER	MODEL	POPULAR NAME
Bell	UH-1F	Iroquois "Huey"
Boeing	KC-97G	Stratofreighter
Lockheed	T-33	Shooting Star
Martin	EB-57B/E	Canberra
McDonnell	F-101B/F	Voodoo
North American	B-25J	Mitchell
Republic	F-84F	Thunderstreak

Harold Warp Pioneer Village

Highways 6 & 34, Minden, Nebraska 68959
(308) 832-1181

A collector's paradise is the best description of the Harold Warp Pioneer Village. Here on display is Americana at its best. There are comprehensive collections of autos, tractors, toys, sewing machines, guns, snowmobiles, musical instruments and aircraft. Many of the artifacts are exhibited in restored buildings and rooms.

Among the aircraft is a version of the first jet airplane produced in the United States, the Bell P-59 Airacomet. Underpowered and ungainly, Airacomets were never flown in combat. Another unique aircraft is the Pitcairn Autogiro. Although marginally successful commercially in the 1920s, the autogiros stimulated public awareness in the possibilities of rotorcraft. Also on display is a Sikorsky HNS-1, circa 1944, an example of successful early helicopters.

DIRECTIONS TO MUSEUM: Located near intersection of US 6 & 34 and Hwy. 10.

ADMISSION COST: Adults $5.00; children (6-16 yrs.) $2.50.

HOURS OF OPERATION: Open daily 8am-sundown.

MUSEUM NOTES: Display aircraft are indoors. Film can be purchased in the gift shop. A motel, campground and restaurant are present on the grounds.

A brochure is available.

Display Aircraft

MANUFACTURER	MODEL	POPULAR NAME
Alon	Aircoupe	
Bell	P-59	Airacomet
Benson	B-6	Gyrocopter
Benson	B-7	Gyrocopter
Cessna	MDLA	
Curtiss		
Curtiss	JN-4D	"Jenny"
Curtiss	N-9	
Hartman		
Piper	PA-23-150	Apache
Pitcairn	Autogiro	
Sikorsky	HNS-1	Hoverfly
Stinson	Detroiter	
Swallow		
Taylorcraft	J-2	
Wright	B	

Strategic Air Command Museum

2510 Clay Street, Bellevue, Nebraska 68005
(402) 292-2001

Located adjacent to Offutt Air Force Base, headquarters of the Strategic Air Command (SAC), the museum displays the airplanes and missiles flown by SAC on past and present missions.

Noteworthy airplanes in the museum's collection are the first operational B-52, a record-setting B-58, one of only three British Vulcan bombers on display in the USA, an XF-85 experimental parasite fighter, and one of only four remaining B-36 bombers.

Among the indoor displays are found a B-52 cockpit you can sit in, a replica of the SAC underground command post, an ICBM launch room and SAC memorabilia, including artifacts of General Curtis LeMay.

DIRECTIONS TO MUSEUM: I-80 westbound: exit south on Kennedy Fwy. (US 75) in Omaha. I-80 eastbound: exit east on Hwy. 370 to Bellevue. I-29 northbound and southbound: take exit 42 onto Hwy. 370 westbound to Bellevue; follow signs in Bellevue to museum.

ADMISSION COST: Adults $3.00; children (6-12 yrs.) $1.75; senior citizen and group discounts.

HOURS OF OPERATION: Open daily 8am-8pm from Memorial Day to Labor Day and 8am-5pm remainder of year. Closed New Year's Day, Thanksgiving and Christmas.

MUSEUM NOTES: Display aircraft are located inside and outside. Vending machines are onsite with restaurants nearby. Film can be purchased at gift shop.

A brochure is available.

This B-58 Hustler on the SAC Air Museum's display ramp was the previous coast-to-coast record holder before a SR-71 Blackbird bettered the record in 1990.

Display Aircraft

MANUFACTURER	MODEL	POPULAR NAME
Boeing	AGM-86B	Cruise Missile
Boeing	B-17G	Flying Fortress
Boeing	B-29	Superfortress
Boeing	B-47E	Stratojet
Boeing	B-52B	Stratofortress
Boeing	CIM-10A	Bomarc
Boeing	KC-97G	Stratofreighter
Consolidated	T-29A	
Convair	B-36J	Peacemaker
Convair	B-58A	Hustler
Convair	F-102A	Delta Dagger
Douglas	B-26B	Invader
Douglas	C-47	Skytrain
Douglas	C-54D	Skymaster
Douglas	C-124C	Globemaster II
Douglas	C-133	Cargomaster
Douglas	SM-75	Thor
Fairchild	C-119G	Flying Boxcar
General Dynamics	SM-65	Atlas I
Grumman	SA-16B	Albatross
Hawker Siddeley	MkII	Vulcan
Lockheed	SR-71	Blackbird
Lockheed	T-33	Shooting Star
Lockheed	U-2C	
Martin	B-57E	Intruder
Martin Marietta	SM-68	Titan I (storm damaged)
McDonnell	ADM-20	Quail
McDonnell	F-101B	Voodoo
McDonnell	XF-85F	Goblin
North American	B-25 (cutaway)	Mitchell
North American	B-25J	Mitchell
North American	CT-39	Sabreliner
North American	F-86H	Sabre
North American	RB-45C	Tornado
Northrop	SM-62A	Snark
Piasecki	CH-21	Workhorse
Republic	F-84F	Thunderstreak
Rockwell	AGM-28	Hound Dog
Sikorsky	H-19B	Chicasaw
Vought	SLV-1	Blue Scout

Aviation Hall of Fame & Museum of New Jersey

Teterboro Airport, Teterboro, New Jersey 07608
(201) 288-6344

New Jersey is rich with aviation history. The museum presents artifacts and memorabilia reflecting aviation in New Jersey.

Included in the artifacts exhibited are engines from the Bell X-1 and the X-15. The aviation collection of entertainer/pilot Arthur Godfrey is on display as well as the largest collection of Curtiss-Wright engines. There is also a complete collection of ARC radios. The museum's artifacts are contained in two buildings on east and west sides of the airport.

The main museum collection is located in the old control tower for Teterboro airport (on west side of airport), one of the busier general aviation airports in the country. Visitors can sit in the old tower and watch the airplanes and helicopters come and go while listening to a radio tuned to the airport tower frequency. Listen to the radio on a particularly busy day at Teterboro and you'll appreciate the job controller's perform. The museum building on east side of airport is only open on weekends, or for special tours.

DIRECTIONS TO MUSEUM: From I-80 exit onto Green St. and follow signs (Note: Stay in I-80 "Local" lanes; don't use "Express" or you won't be able to exit onto Green St.). The museum is located in the old control tower portion of a hanger occupied by Atlantic Aviation. Ask for directions to building on east side of airport.

ADMISSION COST: Adults $3.00; senior citizens and children $2.00.

HOURS OF OPERATION: Open 10am-4pm daily. Closed New Year's Day, Easter, July 4th and Christmas.

MUSEUM NOTES: Display aircraft are outdoors. There is a gift shop, but film is not available. A restaurant is nearby.

A brochure is available.

Display Aircraft

MANUFACTURER	MODEL
Lockheed	Bushmaster
Martin	202

Confederate Air Force
(New Mexico Wing)
P.O. Box 1260, Hobbs, New Mexico 88240
(505) 397-7180

The Confederate Air Force (CAF) was organized to preserve World War II military aircraft. Headquarters for the CAF is Odessa/Midland, Texas, but to promote interest nationwide, wings have been formed. Members can actively participate in aircraft restoration and display through their local wings.

The New Mexico Wing of the CAF has several aircraft and memorabilia on display at their facility at Lea County Airport. Of interest is the replica of a Japanese "Val" dive bomber. Originally manufactured by the Aichi aircraft company as the model D3A, the designation "Val" is the US military identifying code word. Code words were assigned to all enemy aircraft to avert miscommunication, particularly when Americans attempted to pronounce Japanese names. The Aichi D3A was a highly effective dive bomber during the early stages of the war, especially at Pearl Harbor.

DIRECTIONS TO MUSEUM: Follow US 62/180 west from Hobbs to Lea County Airport.

ADMISSION COST: Free.

HOURS OF OPERATION: Open daily during daylight hours. Call ahead for holiday schedule.

MUSEUM NOTES: Display aircraft are indoors and outdoors. Film is not available onsite. A restaurant is located on airport grounds.

A brochure is available.

Display Aircraft

MANUFACTURER	MODEL	POPULAR NAME
Aichi (replica)	D3A	"Val"
Beech	C-45	Expeditor
Martin	AM-1	Mauler
North American	SNJ	
Ryan	PT-22	
Stinson	L-5	Sentinel

National Atomic Museum

P.O. Box 5400, Kirtland Air Force Base, Abuquerque, New Mexico 87115
(505) 845-6670

The museum was created in 1969 to chronicle the history of nuclear weapons. The exhibits trace the evolution of nuclear weapons from the early 1940s to the present, using only unclassified information. Particularly emphasized is the Manhattan Project—the World War II undertaking that produced the first atomic bomb.

Delivering the atomic bomb to a target is primarily accomplished by aircraft or missiles, although cannons and torpedoes have also been utilized. Two airplanes that were originally designed to carry nuclear weapons are on display, the Boeing B-52 Superfortress and the Republic F-105 Thunderchief. Both airplanes entered service during the 1950s, and while the F-105 is no longer in the Air Force inventory, B-52s remain a nuclear deterrent with over 250 still flying in Air Force units. A number of missiles are exhibited that were or are used as delivery devices for nuclear weapons.

DIRECTIONS TO MUSEUM: From I-25 exit onto Gibson Blvd. and travel east on Gibson to gate of Kirtland AFB. From I-40 exit onto Wyoming Blvd. and travel south on Wyoming to gate of Kirtland AFB. Stop at gate for pass and directions to museum.

The Boeing B-52B Stratofortress was the first U.S. plane to drop a thermonuclear weapon (H-bomb). The event occurred on May 20, 1956, at Bikini Island. The B-52 was designed to deliver an H-bomb to any target in the world, using aerial refueling to extend its range. However, the only bombing missions B-52s have flown in combat consist of dropping conventional bombs into Vietnam, Iraq and Kuwait. The B-52 cannot survive in Soviet air space, so to extend its usefullness as a nuclear delivery system, cruise missiles are carried. The cruise missiles penetrate the air defenses rather than exposing the B-52.

ADMISSION COST: Free.

HOURS OF OPERATION: Open 9am-5pm daily. Closed New Year's Day, Easter, Thanksgiving and Christmas.

MUSEUM NOTES: Display aircraft are indoors and outdoors. A restaurant is nearby.

A brochure is available.

Display Aircraft

MANUFACTURER	MODEL	POPULAR NAME
Boeing	CIM-10	Bomarc
Boeing	LGM-30A	Minuteman I
Boeing	B-52B	Stratofortress
Chrysler	Redstone	
Douglas	MGR-1	Honest John
Lockheed	Polaris	
Martin	MGM-13	Mace
Northrop	SM-62	Snark
Republic	F-105D	Thunderchief
Rockwell	AGM-28	Hound Dog

Cradle of Aviation Museum

Museum Lane, Mitchel Field, Garden City, New York 11530
(516) 222-1190

Aircraft from virtually all eras of aviation history are on display at the Cradle of Aviation Museum. Currently undergoing renovation, but remaining open, the museum will encompass an air and space exhibition hall plus an Omnimax theater. Completion is expected in 1993.

The collection is housed in early era hangers that are situated on the site of what was originally Hazelhurst Field, a World War I training field. Hazelhurst Field was renamed Mitchel Field and later Mitchel Air Force Base. Formerly centered in a hotbed of aviation activity, the field has been closed since 1982. New buildings and roads now cover the old base.

Among the airplanes on display are airplanes constructed by three of the pioneers of flight: Wright, Bleriot and Curtiss. An interesting comparison of airplane construction can be noted when examining the wood, wire and fabric of the first airplanes, the met-

At the end of World War II, the Allies discovered German research planes and data that indicated the advantages of swept wings. Several American airplane designs, as well as Soviet, were influenced by the German work. Shortly after World War II, Grumman produced for the Navy the straight-wing F9F Panther, a jet fighter-bomber. Grumman then produced a swept-wing version designated the F9F-6/8 Couger. The original fuselage and tail assembly remained the same, but the wing incorporated a sweepback of 35 degrees. Maximum speed increased approximately 50 mph over the earlier Phantom. Cougars entered service in 1951 and flew as front-line fighters for several years. A trainer version of the Cougar was in service until 1974.

The Lunar Module (LM) in the museum was destined for use on Apollo 18, but the mission was cancelled. Note that the LM lacks aerodynamic streamlining. With no atmosphere on the moon there was no need to accommodate air movement in the design. The LM was separated into two major sections. When the astronauts left the lunar surface, rockets attached to the top half (Ascent Module), lifted it up away from the lower half, which remained behind. The Ascent Module then docked with the Command Module orbiting the moon.

al fabrication of the World War II fighters, and the composite construction of the contempory Rutan VariEze.

A substantial number of spacecraft are on display, notably a Mercury capsule and a Lunar Module. Significant progress in manned spaceflight is apparent when comparing these two spacecraft. The Lunar Module in the museum was destined for use on Apollo 18, but the mission was cancelled.

DIRECTIONS TO MUSEUM: From Meadowbrook Pkwy. take exit M4 and follow signs for Nassau Coliseum onto Charles Lindbergh Blvd. After first traffic light turn right to hangers 3 and 4 on the Nassau Community College campus (formerly Mitchell AFB).

ADMISSION COST: Free (donation requested).

The Thomas-Morse S-4C Scout was a training plane that served as an intermediate training step between the less demanding "Jenny" and faster fighter planes. Maximum speed of the Scout was 95 mph and it could reach an altitude of 15,000 feet.

HOURS OF OPERATION: Open May-September on Friday, Saturday and Sunday, noon-5pm.

MUSEUM NOTES: Display aircraft are indoors. There is a gift shop, but film is not available. A restaurant is nearby.

A brochure is available.

Display Aircraft

MANUFACTURER	MODEL	POPULAR NAME
Aeronca	7AC	Champion
Bede	BD-5	
Boeing	Lunar Roving Vehicle	
Breese	Penguin	
Brock	Gyroglider	
Commonwealth	Skyranger	
Convertawings	Quadrotor	
Curtiss	JN-4D	"Jenny"
Fairchild-Republic	T-46	

Fleet	2	
Goddard rocket	A Series	
Grumman	Echo Cannister	
Grumman	F4F-3	Wildcat
Grumman	F6F-5	Hellcat
Grumman	F9F-7	Cougar
Grumman	F-11A	Tiger
Grumman	FTV-17	Rigel
Grumman	G-63	Kitten
Grumman	JRF	Goose
Grumman	Habitat Space Station	
Grumman	LM-13	Ascent Stage
Grumman	LM-17	Lunar Module
Grumman	LTA-1,-11	Lunar Module
Grumman	Molab	
Grumman (General Motors)	TBM-3E	Avenger
Gyrodyne	QH-50C	Dash
Herring-Curtiss	Golden Flyer	
Kohm	Lady Godiva	
Martin-Boeing	Dyna-Soar	
Maxson	A6M-12C	Bullpup
Maxson	AQM-37A	Drone
McDonnell	Mercury Capsule	
North American Rockwell	Command Module	
Peel	Z-1	Glider Boat
Philips	Hellkat	
Queen-Bleriot	XI	Dragonfly
Republic	F-84F	Thunderstreak
Republic	F-105B	Thunderchief
Republic	JB-2	Loon
Republic	P-47N	Thunderbolt
Republic	RC3	Seabee
Rogallo		
Rotec	Ralley	
Rotorway	Scorpion	
Rutan	VariEze	
Ryan	B-1	Brougham *Spirit of St. Louis*
Sperry	Aerial Torpedo	
Sperry	Messenger	
Thomas-Morse	S-4C	Scout
Veligdans (Monerai)		
Waco	CG-4	Glider
Wright (replica)	B	*Vin Fiz*
Wright	Flyer	

Dart Airport Aviation Museum
P.O. Box 211, Mayville, New York 14757
(716) 753-2111

Dart Airport is a turf-strip facility that serves as home base for a wide variety of flying machinery. Flying around Dart is everything from helicopters to ultralights, antiques to gliders. There's also the museum, as well as a glider club that offers rides and flight instruction.

The museum focuses on antique airplanes and includes two examples of the Erco Ercoupe 415. Designed by noted designer Fred Weick, the salient feature of the Ercoupe is its FAA certified inability to spin. The absence of a spin capability, plus ease of flying, characterized the plane as suitable for the first-time plane buyer with limited piloting experience.

The Ercoupe was built prior to World War II by the Engineering Research Corporation (Erco), then manufactured again after the war in anticipation of the post-war flying boom. Aircraft manufacturers hoped to cash in on aviation-minded servicemen after World War II, but GIs decided to invest in homes instead, and the great rush to purchase planes never materialized. The plane was subsequently manufactured by Forney Aircraft, Alon and finally by Mooney. Although produced sporadically, there were over 6,000 built.

DIRECTIONS TO MUSEUM: The museum is located at Dart Airport which is 1.6 miles east of Mayville on Route 430.

ADMISSION COST: Free.

HOURS OF OPERATION: No set operating hours, but usually open. Call ahead.

MUSEUM NOTES: Display aircraft are indoors and outdoors. There is a gift shop, but film is not available. There are vending machines onsite and a restaurant is nearby.

A brochure is available.

Display Aircraft

MANUFACTURER	MODEL	POPULAR NAME
Curtiss	CW-1	
Erco	415	Ercoupe
Erco	415-C	Ercoupe
Fleet	16B	
Heath	Super Parasol	
Mead		
Piper	J-2	Cub

Empire State Aerosciences Museum

130 Saratoga Road, Scotia, New York 12302
(518) 377-2191

The Empire State Aeroscience Museum strives to preserve the heritage of aviation in New York as well as provide an educational forum for aerospace technology. The museum membership is dedicated to the promotion of aviation and its future through retrospection and education.

The museum is located at Schenectady Airport, the site of what was formerly the General Electric Flight Test Facility. General Electric has been at the forefront of aircraft engine development as well as a leader in avionics for aircraft and spacecraft. Much of GE's development work was performed at Schenectady Airport. From 1946 to 1964 the installation was one of the country's premier aviation research facilities.

The museum possesses a 1910 biplane constructed by John Von Pomer. The plane is probably one of the first built-from-plans homebuilts. Eighteen-year-old Von Pomer built the plane as a replica of a Curtiss Pusher, flew his creation for two years, then stored it at the urging of his parents who feared for his safety. The plane suffered severe deterioration after decades in a barn, but the museum plans to rebuild Von Pomer's plane for display.

DIRECTIONS TO MUSEUM: The museum is located at Schenectady Airport which is on Hwy. 50 northeast of Scotia. At Socha Plaza traffic light, turn right to museum.

ADMISSION COST: Free.

HOURS OF OPERATION: Open Tuesday-Saturday 10am-4pm. Closed major holidays.

MUSEUM NOTES: Display aircraft are indoors and outdoors. There is a gift shop, but film is not available. A restaurant is located nearby.

A brochure is available.

Display Aircraft

MANUFACTURER	MODEL	POPULAR NAME
de Pischof (replica)	Avionette	*Flying Motorcycle*
Fisher	303	
Mooney	M18	Mite
Peterson	J-4	Javelin
Rensselaer Polytechnic Institute	RP-1	
Sonerai II		
Star-Lite		
Von Pomer		

Glenn H. Curtiss Museum

41 Lake Street, Hammondsport, New York 14840
(607) 569-2160

Glenn Curtiss was a famous pioneer aviator. A contemporary and competitor of the Wright brothers, Curtiss was a bicycle and motorcycle builder who joined Alexander Graham Bell in conducting aeronautical experiments. Curtiss subsequently went on to build his own aircraft while setting records and gaining awards along the way. The museum contains a collection of airplanes and memorabilia reflecting Curtiss' life and accomplishments.

Perhaps the most famous Curtiss airplane was the JN-4 "Jenny". The Jenny trained thousands of pilots and was the predominate barnstorming airplane following World War I. A cutaway version of a 1918 JN-4 fuselage in the museum provides an inner view of the wood, wire and fabric structure that comprised an early airplane.

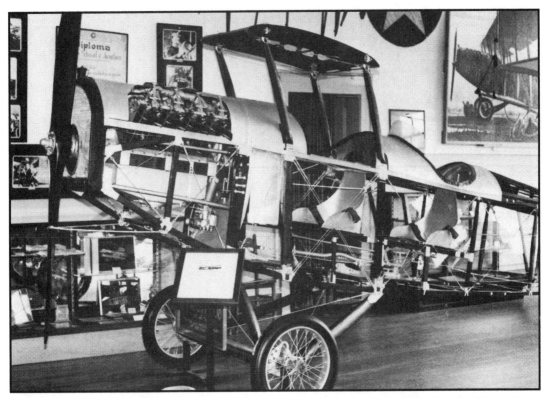

Carpentry was a needed skill in the manufacture and repair of early aircraft. Note the extensive use of wood in the fuselage of the Curtiss Museum's DH-4. Also note the wires that strengthen the box structure by distributing forces imposed on the fuselage.

Many of Glenn Curtiss' accomplishments occurred in and around Hammondsport, New York. Curtiss developed seaplanes on nearby Keuka Lake, as well as flying from its frozen surface during the winter. The sign documenting Curtiss' achievements stands outside the museum.

In addition to the Curtiss airplane museum, there are also exhibits in the museum devoted to Curtiss motorcycles and local history.

DIRECTIONS TO MUSEUM: Museum is located at the corner of Lake and Main Sts..

ADMISSION COST: Adults $3.00; senior citizens $2.50; students $2.00; children (7-12 yrs.) $1.00.

HOURS OF OPERATION: Open mid-April through October 9am-5pm; not open on Sunday in April, May and June. Call ahead for holiday schedule.

MUSEUM NOTES: Display aircraft are indoors. There is a gift shop, but film is not available. Vending machines are onsite and restaurants are nearby.

A brochure is available.

Display Aircraft

MANUFACTURER	MODEL	POPULAR NAME
Curtiss	*June Bug II*	
Curtiss	Oriole	
Curtiss	Robin	
Curtiss	D	
Curtiss	JN-4	"Jenny"
Dopple	Raab	
Mercury	Chic	
Ohm/Krapf Special		

Intrepid Sea-Air-Space Museum

West 46th Street and 12th Avenue, New York, New York 10
(212) 245-2533

The mainstay of the current Navy is the aircraft carrier. Moored at pier 86
son River is the aircraft carrier *Intrepid*, now decommissioned from Navy service and
open for public viewing. There is only one other aircraft carrier on public display in the
country, the *Yorktown* in Charleston, South Carolina, so touring the *Intrepid* is a unique
opportunity.

The *Intrepid* was commissioned during World War II as an Essex-class aircraft carrier.
The Essex-class carriers were the heart of Naval aviation during the war due to their
size and speed. The *Intrepid* participated in Navy operations in the Pacific during the
war and also saw service during the Vietnam War. Originally constructed with the typical inline flight deck design of the World War II era, the *Intrepid* was modified during
the 1950s to add an angled, strengthened flight deck. The modification permitted safer
flight operations for heavier, faster jet aircraft. The *Intrepid* participated in the space
program as a recovery ship during the Gemini flights.

The aircraft collection is one of the largest collections of Navy aircraft in the country,
particularly in the area of jet-powered airplanes. Noteworthy airplanes include a Curtiss
1911 Pusher, the first airplane to land on a ship. Significant among the museum's

A view of the jets lining the port side of the Intrepid's *flight deck. Off the bow and
in the background is a portion of the Manhattan skyline.*

McDonnell Demons, like the one sitting on the Intrepid's *catapult, were underpowered at the outset of production and suffered from engine problems. Crashes occured and the program was in jeopardy of cancellation. A more powerful engine was installed, several hundred Demons were built and McDonnell went on to develop its most famous fighter, the Phantom II.*

World War II era airplanes is a Grumman SB2C Helldiver. Not often seen in museums, the Helldiver was found in all Navy bombing squadrons at the end of the war.

Distinctive among the jet-powered airplanes is a North American RA-5C Vigilante. The Vigilante was one of the most advanced aircraft of its day. Vigilantes are the only supersonic bombers to have operated from a carrier deck. Originally designed to provide strategic bombing capabilities for the Navy, all Vigilantes were later reconfigured for reconnaissance when the Navy decided to embrace the Polaris missile for nuclear bomb delivery. Vigilantes were flown by the Navy during the 1960s and 1970s, including participation in the Vietnam War. At over 79,000 pounds gross weight, they were the second heaviest airplane to fly from carriers.

The hanger deck of the *Intrepid* has been converted into a large exhibition hall. Airplanes, artifacts and a theater are found on the hanger deck. Several decks of the Intrepid are open for self-guided tours, including a portion of the island where bridge and flight operations were located. All visitors with even basic knowledge of aircraft carrier

Nicknamed "Scooter" by Navy pilots, the Douglas A-4 Skyhawk was originally conceived as a low-cost, expendable deliverer of nuclear bombs. However, its role changed and the A-4 served during Vietnam as a ground support attack bomber. The Navy's Blue Angels air demonstration team flew Skyhawks for 12 years from 1974 to 1986, longer than any other airplane flown by the team.

flight operations will be impressed by the limited space available on the *Intrepid* for launching and recovering jet airplanes.

Alongside the *Intrepid* as part of the museum are the destroyer U.S.S. *Edson* and the submarine U.S.S. *Growler*. Both vessels offer interesting tours for visitors interested in naval ships.

Please note that stairways must be climbed to reach the various decks. Appropriate footwear is recommended, particularly during damp weather.

DIRECTIONS TO MUSEUM: The museum is located off of 12th Ave. on the west side of Manhattan at pier 86, which is near 46th St. There are signs along 12th Ave. noting the museum. Parking in the lot at the pier is expensive (over $10). If you are driving into the city, Sunday morning is probably the best day to visit the museum.

ADMISSION COST: Adults $7.00; children $4.00. Military personnel in uniform enter free.

HOURS OF OPERATION: Open Wednesday-Sunday 10am-5pm. Closed Monday and Tuesday. Closed major holidays.

The McDonnell F-4 Phantom II is one of the most versatile fighters ever built. Phantoms have flown missions as fighters, bombers and interceptors, as well as performing photo-reconnaisance and electronic countermeasures missions. The F-4 was originally designed for naval carrier operations and was equipped with an arresting hook under the tail. Air Force versions of the F-4 retain the hook as an emergency option during landing at airfields equipped with an arresting wire system.

MUSEUM NOTES: Display aircraft are in-doors and outdoors. Film is available in the gift shop. There are vending machines on the *Intrepid* and street vendors outside the museum grounds.

A brochure is available.

Display Aircraft

MANUFACTURER	MODEL	POPULAR NAME
Bell	OH-13	Sioux
Bell	UH-1A	Iroquois "Huey"
Curtiss	SB2C-3	Helldiver
Curtiss Pusher (replica)		
Demoiselle (replica)		
Douglas	A-3	Skywarrior
Douglas	A-4	Skyhawk
Douglas	F3D(F-10)	Skynight
Grumman	A-6	Intruder
Grumman	E-1B	Tracer
Grumman	F6F-5	Hellcat
Grumman	F11F-1	Tiger
Grumman	HU-16	Albatross
Grumman	S-2E	Tracker
Grumman	TS-2A	Tracker

Lockheed	SP-2E	Neptune
Lockheed	T-33	Shooting Star
McDonnell	F-3B	Demon
McDonnell	F-4N	Phantom II
McDonnell Douglas	AV-8C	Harrier
North American	FJ-3	Fury
North American	RA-5C	Vigilante
Northrop	YF-17	Cobra
Republic	F-84F	Thunderstreak
Royal Aircraft Factory (replica)	S.E.5a	
Sikorsky	HH-52A	Sea Guard
Sikorsky	HUS-1	
Piasecki	CH-21C	Shawnee
Vickers-Supermarine	Scimitar F.1	
Voisin Pusher		

National Soaring Museum
Harris Hill Road #3, Elmira, New York 14903
(607) 734-3128

The National Soaring Museum has the largest collection of classic and contemporary sailplanes in the world. Soaring is the sport of flying in a non-powered airplane with only the pilot's skill at reading and anticipating air movement determining the duration and outcome of the flight.

The museum is located adjacent to Harris Hill soaring field, the site of many soaring championships. The field is very active during the summer soaring season and visitors can observe sailplane takeoffs and landings, weather permitting. Sailplane rides are available all week during the summer and on weekends the rest of the year. Call for prices.

The museum presents exhibits that explain the principles of flight and the aspects of atmospheric conditions that affect the performance of a sailplane in flight. There are also exhibits tracing the history of soaring and the evolution of sailplane construction. A full scale simulator allows a visitor to experience sitting in a sailplane cockpit.

Among the sailplane collection is a replica of the Wright 1911 glider #5. There is also the Bowlus-duPont Albatross. The Albatross was built in 1933 and won the National

The Albatross was one of the significant soaring planes of its day. Built in 1933, the Albatross was piloted by Richard duPont in 1933 to a world distance record of 121.6 miles. This was the first soaring record achieved by an American. It later won the U.S. National Soaring Championship in 1934 and 1935.

Soaring Championship in 1934 and 1935. In 1933 Richard duPont piloted Albatross to a world soaring distance record of 121.6 miles, the first soaring record achieved by an American.

The museum and field are a portion of Harris Hill Park. The park comprises a recreational park with miniature golf, batting cages, driving range and picnic facilities.

DIRECTIONS TO MUSEUM: From Hwy. 17 take exit 51 and go south on Chambers Rd. (away from the shopping mall). Turn right onto County Rd. 14 and go about 1 1/2 miles. Turn left at museum sign onto Harris Hill Rd. Turn right at top of steep hill and follow signs to Harris Hill Park and museum. Proceed through park and follow signs to museum.

ADMISSION COST: Adults $3.00; senior citizens $2.50; children (10 yrs. and up) $2.00.

HOURS OF OPERATION: Open daily 10am-5pm.

MUSEUM NOTES: Display aircraft are indoors. There is a gift shop, but film is not available. No restaurants are nearby.

A brochure is available.

Display Aircraft

MANUFACTURER	MODEL	POPULAR NAME
Baker-McMillen	Cadet	
Bowlus-duPont	Albatross	
Briegleb	BG-12/16	
Briegleb	BG-12/BD	
Franklin	PS-2	
Herring-Arnot (replica)		
Huetter	H-17	
Laister	Nugget	
Nelson	Hummingbird	
Ridgid Midget		
Schempp-Hirth	Goppingen III	*Minimoa*
Schweizer	SGP 1-1	
Schweizer	SGS 1-19	
Waco (fuselage)	CG-4A	
Wright glider (replica)		

National Warplane Museum
P.O. Box 159, Geneseo, New York 14454
(716) 243-0690

The National Warplane Museum is dedicated to the preservation and restoration of World War II airplanes in flying condition. As such, the museum recommends that you call ahead if there is a particular airplane you wish to see. It's possible that the airplane may be participating in an airshow elsewhere. However, if your timing is right, you may see planes leaving on Friday and returning on Monday.

Noteworthy among the museum's airplanes is the Consolidated PBY-6A Catalina. Over 3,200 Catalinas were produced, more than any other seaplane. The first Catalina was delivered to the Navy in 1936 and the last was retired from Navy service in 1957. Catalinas participated in every Navy campaign while performing search, rescue and patrol missions. Flying or static examples of the Catalina are scarce and unique. The Catalina of the National Warplane Museum is in flying condition.

Free tours are available that include a walk through the maintenance and restoration shops. The museum sponsors an airshow each year during the summer; call for show dates. An interesting sidenote is the grass surface of the runway and ramp area. Many older airplanes were designed for grass field operation and watching the museum's B-17 traverse the grass is a scene you'll not find at other airfields.

DIRECTIONS TO MUSEUM: Located off Route 63 at Geneseo Airport, which is just west of town.

ADMISSION COST: Adults $3.00; children under 12 yrs. $1.00.

The National Warplane Museum has one of the few flying Catalinas. During World War II, the Consolidated PBY Catalinas filled the need for a patrol plane to search the thousands of miles of ocean and coastline. After the war, they were flown as island-hopping transport planes and fire-bombers.

HOURS OF OPERATION: Open Monday-Friday 9am-5pm; Saturday & Sunday 10am-5pm. Call ahead for holiday schedule.

MUSEUM NOTES: Display airplanes side and outside. There is a gift sho film is not available. A restaurant is nearby.

A brochure is available.

Display Aircraft

MANUFACTURER	MODEL	POPULAR NAME
Aeronca	L-3	
Beech	C-45	Expeditor
Boeing	B-17G	Flying Fortress
Consolidated	PBY-6A	Catalina
Curtiss	C-46	Commando
Curtiss	P-40E	Warhawk
Douglas	A-1D	Skyraider
Douglas	A-26	Invader
Fairchild	PT-19	Cornell
Fairchild	PT-26	
Grumman	G44	Widgeon
Stearman	PT-17	Kaydet
Taylorcraft	L-2	Grasshopper
Vultee	BT-13	Valiant

Old Rhinebeck Aerodrome

Stone Church Road, Rhinebeck, New York 12572
(914) 758-8610

The Old Rhinebeck Aerodrome provides both theatrical and historical entertainment. During the week the collection of World War I and other antique aircraft is on display, and on weekends an airshow is presented.

The Sunday air show is the centerpoint for a melodramatic play complete with heroes, heroines and villains. Set in World War I, the costumes, buildings and machinery reflect the last era of chivalry in the air. The play is entertaining for all ages while airplane enthusiasts will enjoy watching the early aircraft performing above the grass airfield. Saturday's airshow presents airplanes from the Pioneer and Lindbergh eras.

The aircraft collection includes many original World War I airplanes such as a SPAD XIII, Sopwith Snipe, Thomas Morse Scout, Nieuport 83E and Morane-Saulnier. Accurate replicas of a Fokker Triplane, Fokker D.VII, Sopwith Dolphin and Avro 504K are also displayed. Old engines, cars, equipment, and artifacts of the era are also on display.

For those wishing to experience the thrill of flight in an open-cockpit airplane, rides are offered in a 1929 biplane before and after the airshow. Contact Aerodrome for price.

DIRECTIONS TO MUSEUM: The Aerodrome is located north of Rhinebeck on US 9 then follow Stone Church Rd. The Aerodrome is also accessible off of Route 199 between US 9 and the Taconic Pkwy.

ADMISSION COST: Weekend airshows: Adults $8.00; children (6-10 yrs.) $4.00. Weekdays: Adults $3.00; children (6-10 yrs.) $1.00.

HOURS OF OPERATION: Open daily May 15 through October 10am-5pm. Weekend airshows 2:30pm (approximately 1 1/2 hrs. duration).

MUSEUM NOTES: Display aircraft are inside and outside. A restaurant is at the Aerodrome and other restaurants are in nearby towns. Film is available in the gift shop.

A brochure is available.

Display Aircraft

MANUFACTURER	MODEL	POPULAR NAME
Avro	504K	
Bleriot	XI	
Curtiss	JN-4	"Jenny"
Fokker	D.VII	
Fokker	Dr.I	Triplane
Morane-Saulnier		

New Standard	D-25
Nieuport	10
Nieuport	83E
Sopwith	Dolphin
Sopwith	Snipe
SPAD	XIII
Thomas-Morse	Scout

82nd Airborne Division War Memorial Museum
Bldg. C-6841 Ardennes Street, P.O. Box 70119, Fort Bragg, North Carolina 28307
(919) 868-4785

Fort Bragg is "Home of the Airborne." All the major airborne divisions of World War II trained at Bragg, and one of the most famous, the 82nd Airborne Division, is permanently stationed there. The first military parachute jump took place at Bragg in 1923 from a balloon, and the evolution of parachutes from escape device to the means for airborne assault began.

World War II was the greatest showcase for airborne operations utilizing paratroopers (while airborne troops were used in Vietnam, large paratroop operations were conducted only early in the war). On most missions, paratroopers were transported to their drop zones in either a Douglas C-47 Skytrain or a Curtiss C-46 Commando. Examples of both airplanes are present in the museum. C-46s and C-47s served throughout the world during the war. After the war, surplus planes were quickly purchased by commercial transport companies. Many are still flying today.

DIRECTIONS TO MUSEUM: Follow Hwy. 24 to Fort Bragg and turn left onto Gruber Rd. Follow Gruber Rd. then turn right onto Reilly St. Follow Reilly St. then turn left onto Ardennes St. Travel approximately 1 1/2 miles to museum.

ADMISSION COST: Free.

HOURS OF OPERATION: Open Tuesday-Saturday 10am-4:30pm; Sunday 11:30am-4pm. Closed Monday. Closed New Year's Day and Christmas.

MUSEUM NOTES: Display aircraft are indoors and outdoors. Film can be purchased in the gift shop. A restaurant is nearby.

A brochure is available.

Display Aircraft

MANUFACTURER	MODEL	POPULAR NAME
Bell	UH-1	Iroquois "Huey"
Curtiss	C-46	Commando
de Havilland	C-7A	Caribou
Douglas	C-47	Skytrain
Fairchild	C-119	Flying Boxcar
Fairchild	C-123	Provider
Waco	CG-15A	

North Carolina Museum of Life and Science

433 Murray Avenue, P.O. Box 15190, Durham, North Carolina 27704
(919) 477-0431

The Museum of Life and Science presents exhibits in the areas of natural history and the sciences. Live animals representative of wildlife in North Carolina may be viewed in their natural habitat. "Hands-on" displays adressing a variety of life sciences educate and entertain the visitor. The Ellerbee Creek Railway offers a trip through an adjacent nature park (included in admission price to museum).

The aviation exhibits are dedicated primarily to space travel. On display are spacecraft, as well as engines used to power missiles and spacecraft. Also displayed are space suits and a moon rock.

The museum has two airplanes on display, a Douglas DC-3 and a Grumman F11A Tiger. The DC-3 is painted in the colors of Piedmont Airlines, a post-World War II regional air carrier. The Douglas DC-3 was the first highly successful airliner because it appealed to air travelers seeking reliability (a DC-3 has never crashed due to structural failure) and comfort. Airline operators could realize a profit by carrying passengers, and not need an airmail contract to bring in extra revenue.

DIRECTIONS TO MUSEUM: From I-85 exit onto Duke St. Travel north on Duke St. then turn right at Murray Ave. Follow Murray to flashing yellow lights.

ADMISSION COST: Adults $3.75; children (3-12 yrs.) $2.50.

HOURS OF OPERATION: Open 10am-5pm Monday-Saturday; 1-5pm Sunday (open until 6pm from Memorial Day to La-bor Day). Closed New Year's Day, Thanksgiving and Christmas.

MUSEUM NOTES: Display aircraft are indoors and outdoors. There is a gift shop, but film is not available. There are vending machines onsite and restaurants nearby.

A brochure is available.

Wright Brothers National Memorial
Rt. 1, Box 675, Manteo, North Carolina 27954
(919) 441-7430

Knowing they needed a steady wind to conduct their flying experiments, the Wright brothers studied national Weather Bureau records and selected the sand dunes on the Outer Banks of North Carolina. Although Kitty Hawk is most noted for the birth of powered flight, the flying was actually performed farther south on the Kill Devil Hill sand dunes.

On display are replicas of the 1902 Wright Glider and 1903 Wright Flyer plus artifacts related to the Wright brothers presence at the site. The hanger, workshop and living quarters of the 1903 camp have been reconstructed. The flight path of the first sustained, controlled powered flight is marked. A sixty-foot gray granite monument shaft identifies Kill Devil Hill, the site of numerous glider experiments.

In the foreground is a replica of the Wright Flyer and in the background a replica of the 1902 Wright Glider. Perhaps the Wrights greatest achievement was the development of control systems. Manned gliders had flown short distances before the Wrights flew, but their instability detered their builders, at times fatally. Through experimentation and research with their gliders, the Wrights solved the problems that stymied their efforts to sustain controlled flight, then successfully undertook powered flight.

DIRECTIONS TO MEMORIAL: Located on US 158 near Kill Devil Hills.

ADMISSION COST: Adults (17-61 yrs.) $1.00; children and senior citizens free; car load $3.00.

HOURS OF OPERATION: Open daily 9am-5pm September-June 15; 9am-7pm June 15-Labor Day. Open all holidays except Christmas.

MEMORIAL NOTES: Display aircraft are inside. Film is available in the gift shop. A restaurant is nearby.

A brochure is available.

Bonanzaville, U.S.A.

Box 719, West Fargo, North Dakota 58078
(701) 282-2822

Bonanzaville, U.S.A., is a collection of original, restored and reconstructed buildings that present a historical perspective of life in the Northern Plains. The sod house, log cabins and wood-frame houses show the various types of home construction found in the area. The barber shop, harness shop, creamery, hotel, country store, newspaper, blacksmith and drug store acquaint the visitor with life in an early town. A number of other buildings contain artifacts and memorabilia such as automobiles, tractors, telephones, engines, dolls and farm implements. The museum contains one of the largest Midwest collections of American Indian artifacts. The wide range of exhibits should provide something of interest to everyone in the family.

The aircraft collection is as diverse as Bonanzaville. There are World War II airplanes as well as homebuilt airplanes. The Curtiss Pusher is representative of aviation in 1911, while the Standard J-1 is a typical 1917 biplane. The Piper J-3 Cub entered production in 1938 and has been flown by thousands of pilots. World War II era aircraft include a Douglas A-26 Invader, Douglas C-47 Skytrain, Vultee BT-13 Valiant, Beech C-45 Expeditor, Aeronca PT-19A Cornell and Pratt-Reed PR-G-1 training glider. The Pitts S-1 Special airplane is an example of one of the best aerobatic airplanes in the world.

DIRECTIONS TO BONANZAVILLE: From I-94 take exit 85 onto US 10 eastbound and follow road to Bonanzaville.

ADMISSION COST: Adults $3.25; children $1.25.

HOURS OF OPERATION: May-October: Monday-Friday 9am-8pm, Saturday-Sunday 9am-5pm. November-April: Tuesday-Friday 9:30am-4pm (during winter village is closed and aircraft are not on display, but museum is open).

BONANZAVILLE NOTES: Display aircraft are indoors. Film can be purchased in the gift shop. A restaurant is nearby.

A brochure is available.

Display Aircraft

MANUFACTURER	MODEL	POPULAR NAME
Aeronca	PT-19A	Cornell
Beech	C-45	Expeditor
Bowers	Fly Baby	
Briegleb	BG-12	
Curtiss	D-III	
Douglas	A-26	
Douglas	C-47	Skytrain
Freed	Snowplane	

McKinnie	165	
Piper	J-3	Cub
Pitts	S-1	Special
Pratt-Reed	PR-G-1	
Standard	J-1	
Stits	SA-3B	
Swallow		
Vultee	BT-13A	Valiant
Weedhopper		

Frederick C. Crawford Auto-Aviation Museum

10825 East Boulevard, Cleveland, Ohio 44106
(216) 721-5722

The Crawford Museum has evolved over the last fifty years into a major transportation museum. The museum focuses on automotive artifacts and memorabilia with over 120 automobiles on display, as well as motorcycles, bicycles and airplanes.

Frederick Crawford was employed by Thompson Products, whose owner, Charles Thompson, instituted the Thompson Trophy Race in 1930 at the National Air Races in Cleveland. The Thompson was a closed course race from 1930 to 1949, except for the war years, that featured the nation's fastest airplanes. Air racing caught the nation's attention and crowds upwards of 100,000 crammed airfields to watch the planes dash around the pylons. Cleveland served as the site for numerous Thompson races and as the terminus for the Bendix Trophy Race, the cross country equivalent of the Thompson.

The museum has on display one of the series of Wedell-Williams air racers. The Wedell-Williams racers were highly successful, winning the Bendix in 1932 and both the Bendix and Thompson in 1933 and 1934. Harry Williams provided the funds and Jimmy Wedell built and piloted the planes. Planes were built for other competitors, and although Wedell won the 1933 Thompson, he was often beaten by pilots flying planes he built. The Wedell-Williams planes were the dominant racers of their time, stopped only by the death of Wedell in a training accident in 1934.

DIRECTIONS TO MUSEUM: From I-90 exit onto Martin Luther King Dr. and travel south. At circle turn right onto East Blvd. Turn left at East 108th St. then right onto Magnolia Dr.

ADMISSION COST: Adults $4.00; children $2.00.

HOURS OF OPERATION: Open Tuesday-Saturday 10am-5pm; Sunday noon-5pm. Closed major holidays.

MUSEUM NOTES: Display airplanes are indoors. There is a gift shop and a restaurant is nearby.

A brochure is available.

Display Aircraft

MANUFACTURER	MODEL	POPULAR NAME
Curtiss	E Hydro	
Howard	DGA-3	*Mike*
North American	P-51K	Mustang
Wedell-Williams		

NASA Lewis Research Center

Visitor Center, 21000 Brookpark Rd., Cleveland, Ohio 44135
(216) 433-2001

The Lewis Research Center is a National Aeronautics and Space Administration (NASA) facility that conducts research in aeronautics and space technology. Research is centered around aircraft structures and power and propulsion in space. Research for the future space station is also conducted at Lewis.

The Visitor Center includes exhibits on Earth-orbiting satellites, space exploration, technology utilization, power systems (such as solar cells), materials research, propulsion and the Space Shuttle. The exhibits appeal to a variety of ages. Information on tours is available by calling the telephone number listed above.

DIRECTIONS TO MUSEUM: The Center is near Cleveland Hopkins International Airport on Brookpark Rd. (Route 17). From I-480 South exit onto Grayton Rd. and go south to Brookpark Rd.

ADMISSION COST: Free

HOURS OF OPERATION: Open Monday-Friday 9am-4pm; Saturday 10am-3pm; Sunday 1pm-5pm. Closed New Year's Eve, New Year's Day, Easter, Thanksgiving, Christmas Eve and Christmas.

MUSEUM NOTES: Spacecraft are located inside and outside. There is a gift shop, but film is not available. Restaurants are nearby.

A brochure is available.

Display Spacecraft

MANUFACTURER	MODEL
General Dynamics	Centaur
Lockheed	Agena
North American Rockwell	Apollo

Neil Armstrong Air & Space Museum
P.O. Box 1978, I-75 & Bellefontaine St., Wapakoneta, Ohio 45895
(419) 738-8811

Situated in the hometown of Neil Armstrong, Wapakoneta, Ohio, the museum commemorates the aviation and space achievements of Neil Armstrong and other Ohioans. The museum is housed in an architecturally unique building that combines earth-covered structures with a 60-foot dome.

The emphasis of the museum is astronaut Neil Armstrong, the first human to touch the moon. Among the artifacts is the Gemini VIII capsule flown by Armstrong and Major David Scott, the Aeronca 7AC Champion in which Armstrong learned to fly, and several items from Armstrong's aviation past.

Suspended from the ceiling is the airframe of the *Toledo II*. The *Toledo* was one of the 1920s dirigibles that were touted to be the last word in aviation travel. They eventually lost favor as several dirigibles, most notably the *Hindenburg*, met with tragic accidents.

The Astro Theater provides the visitor with an imaginary trip to the moon through the use of a multi-media presentation.

DIRECTIONS TO MUSEUM: The museum is located at exit 111 off of I-75.

ADMISSION COST: Adults $3.00; children (6-12 yrs.) $1.00.

HOURS OF OPERATION: Open Monday-Saturday 9:30am-5pm; Sunday and holidays noon-5pm. Closed December through February.

MUSEUM NOTES: Display aircraft are indoors and outdoors. Film is available in the gift shop. There are vending machines onsite and a restaurant is nearby.

A brochure is available.

Display Aircraft

MANUFACTURER	MODEL	POPULAR NAME
Aeronca	7AC	Champ
Douglas	F5D	Skylancer
McDonnell	Gemini Capsule VIII	
Toledo	II	
Wright	G	Aero-boat

Ohio History of Flight Museum

4275 Sawyer Rd., Port Columbus International Airport
Columbus, Ohio 43219
(614) 231-1300

The museum features aircraft and artifacts that reflect aviation history in Ohio.

On display is the world's first inflatable airplane, the Goodyear "Inflato-plane". The airplane pioneered the use of the rubberized fabric that was used later in blimps.

A French Caravelle twin-engine jetliner is open for public viewing on weekdays from 9 to 11 am. Built by Sud-Est, Caravelles went into service in 1959 and were the first successful short-range jet airliners.

The oldest airplane on display in the United States is the museum's Curtiss Model D built in 1911.

DIRECTIONS TO MUSEUM: From I-270 take Exit 37 and travel south on Hamilton Rd. Turn right onto Sawyer Rd. and follow to museum.

ADMISSION COST: Adults $2.00; children 50¢.

HOURS OF OPERATION: Open weekdays 9am-4pm.

MUSEUM NOTES: Display aircraft are indoors and outdoors. There is a gift shop, but film is not available. A restaurant is nearby.

A brochure is available.

Display Aircraft

MANUFACTURER	MODEL
Aeronca	C-2
Alliance	Argo
American	Eaglette
Benson	B-8
Culver	Cadet
Culver	Dart
Curtiss Pusher	D
Goodyear	Inflato-plane
Smith	Termite
Sud-Est	Caravelle
Waco	9
Waco	10

United States Air Force Museum
Wright-Patterson Air Force Base, Ohio 45433
(513) 255-3286

For the avid aviation enthusiast, a trip to the Air Force Museum can easily occupy two days viewing the exhibits in the 10 1/2 acres of indoor space. On display are most of the aircraft that served in this country's Air Force (and Air Corps) from the early 1900s. The museum is the largest and oldest (established 1923) military aviation museum in the world. Nearly one and a half million visitors annually toured the museum in 1988 and 1989.

The Air Force Museum is situated on a portion of historic Wright Field. Wright was the primary testing facility for military aircraft until flight testing began in the Southern California desert. The installation was renamed Wright-Patterson Air Force Base in 1948

Standing outside the Air Force Museum are these five missles. From nearest to farthest is a Minuteman III, Minuteman I, Jupiter, Titan and Thor. The solid-fuel Minuteman III is the heart of the land-based missile deterent force.

Early in its life, the Mustang was better suited to lower altitudes due to its unsupercharged Allison engine. During early production the A-36 variant ("A" signifying attack) was built in greater numbers than the P-51. Flown on dive bombing missions, the A-36s were equipped with slotted dive brakes that extend from the upper and lower surfaces of the wing as shown in the photograph above.

and currently serves as the spearhead for research and development of Air Force projects. With approximately 27,000 military and civilian personnel employed, Wright-Patterson is the largest air force base in the world in terms of manpower.

There are over 200 aircraft on display, some of which are unique and found in no other museum. Particularly noteworthy displays are the North American XB-70 supersonic bomber prototype, the Presidential airplanes, the last surviving Martin B-10, the Boeing B-29 *Bockscar* that dropped the atomic bomb on Nagasaki, a Messerschmitt Me 262 jet fighter and Billy Mitchell's SPAD XVI.

Across the airfield is the Annex which houses another large group of aircraft. A short bus trip provides the only method of transportation permitted to reach the Annex. The Presidential airplanes plus other unique aircraft are located in the Annex so the extra time taken is worthwhile.

In addition to the displayed aircraft, the museum has a theater which shows military and aviation related films daily. Guest lecturers and special events are also presented. Artifacts in the museum include such items as military equipment, uniforms, aircraft insignia and personal mementos.

The Kawanishi N1K2-J was one of the finest fighters flying in the Pacific Theater of World War II. Only 428 were built by the Japanese and were not sufficient to affect the War's course. The airplane was highly maneuverable due to a unique device containing a manometer. Sensing air pressure, the device actuated the wing's flaps to increase lift when needed.

Alongside the main building is a memorial park. Started originally by planting a tree to remember Vietnam POWs and MIAs, members of Air Force units and family members have commissioned or constructed symbols of remembrance for units serving throughout the Air Force's history.

DIRECTIONS TO MUSEUM: From I-75 exit onto Needmore Rd. (exit 58) and follow Needmore Rd. six miles to Springfield St. Follow signs to entrance. From other locations in Dayton, the museum is located on Springfield St., one mile from the Harshman Rd. exit off of Ohio Rte. 4.

ADMISSION COST: Free.

HOURS OF OPERATION: Open daily 9am-5pm. Closed New Year's Day, Thanksgiving and Christmas.

MUSEUM NOTES: Display aircraft are located indoors and outdoors. Film is available in the gift shop. A cafe is located onsite and restaurants are nearby.

A brochure is available.

Display Aircraft

MANUFACTURER	MODEL	POPULAR NAME
Aeronca	L-3B	Grasshopper
Beech	AT-11	Kansas

The MiG-21, code-named "Fishbed," was developed by the Soviet manufacturer Mikoyan-Gurevich to intercept strategic bombers. Characterized by its simplicity and low cost, the plane has been produced over thirty years and served in the air forces of 34 countries. Although lacking sophisticated electronics, the high speed and maneuverability of the MiG-21 make it a potent opponent for all but the very latest Allied fighters.

Beech	C-45H	Expeditor
Beech	T-34A	Mentor
Beech	UC-43	Traveler
Beech	VC-6A	
Bell	P-39Q	Airacobra
Bell	P-59B	Airacomet
Bell	P-63A	Kingcobra
Bell	UH-1P	Iroquois "Huey"
Bell	UH-13J	Sioux
Bell	X-1B	
Benson	X-25A	
Bleriot		
Boeing	B-17G	Flying Fortress
Boeing	B-29	Superfortress
Boeing	B-47E	Stratojet
Boeing	B-52D	Stratofortress

Boeing	KB-50J	Superfortress
Boeing	KC-97L	Stratofreighter
Boeing	NKC-135A	Stratotanker
Boeing	P-12E	
Boeing	WB-50D	Superfortress
CASA	YA-37A	Dragonfly
Cessna	O-1G	Bird Dog
Cessna	O-2A	
Cessna	T-37B	
Cessna	U-3A	
Cessna	UC-78B	Bobcat
Consolidated	B-24D	Liberator
Consolidated	PBY-5A	Catalina
Consolidated	PT-1	Trusty
Convair	B-36J	
Convair	B-58A	Hustler
Convair	C-131D	Samaritan
Convair	F-102A	Delta Dagger
Convair	F-106A	Delta Dart
Culver	PQ-14B	
Curtiss	C-46D	Commando
Curtiss	JN-4D	"Jenny"
Curtiss	O-52	Owl
Curtiss	P-6E	Hawk
Curtiss	P-36A	Hawk
Curtiss	P-40E	Kittyhawk
Curtiss (replica)	D	
Curtiss-Wright	AT-9	Fledgling
de Havilland	C-7A	Caribou
de Havilland	D.H.98	Mosquito
de Havilland	DH-4	
de Havilland	U-6A	Beaver
Douglas	A-1E	Skyraider
Douglas	A-20G	Havoc
Douglas	A-26A	Counter-Invader
Douglas	A-26C	Invader
Douglas	B-18A	Bolo
Douglas	B-23	Dragon
Douglas	C-39A	
Douglas	C-47D	Skytrain
Douglas	C-124C	Globemaster II
Douglas	C-133A	Cargomaster
Douglas	O-38F	
Douglas	O-46A	
Douglas	RB-66B	Destroyer

Douglas	VC-118	Liftmaster
Douglas	X-3	Stilleto
Fairchild	C-82A	Packet
Fairchild	C-119J	Flying Boxcar
Fairchild	C-123K	Provider
Fairchild	PT-19	Cornell
Fairchild	PT-26	Cornell
Fairchild-Republic	A-10A	Thunderbolt II
Fieseler	Fi 156	Storch
Fisher	P75A	Eagle
Focke-Achgelis	Fa 330A-1	Bachstelze
Focke-Wulf	Fw 190D-9	
General Dynamics	F-111A	
Grumman	HU-16B	Albatross
Grumman	J2F-6(OA-12)	Duck
Halberstadt	CL IV	
Hawker	XV-6A	Kestrel
Helio	U-10D	Courier
Hispano	HA-1112K(Bf 109G)	
Junkers	Ju 88D-1	
Kaman	HH-43F	Huskie
Kawanishi	N1K2-J	Shinden Kai
Kugisho	MXY7-K1	Ohka II
Lockheed	C-60A	Lodestar
Lockheed	EC-121D	Constellation
Lockheed	F-80C	Shooting Star
Lockheed	F-94A	Starfire
Lockheed	F-94C	Starfire
Lockheed	F-104C	Starfighter
Lockheed	JC-130A	Hercules
Lockheed	P-38L	Lightning
Lockheed	P-80R	Shooting Star
Lockheed	T-33A	Shooting Star
Lockheed	U-2A	
Lockheed	VC-121E	Constellation
Lockheed	VC-140B	Jetstar
Lockheed	YF-12A	
Loening	OA-1A	
Martin	B-10	
Martin	B-26G	Marauder
Martin	EB-57B	Canberra
Martin	SV-5J	
Martin	X-24B	
McDonnell	F-4C	Phantom II
McDonnell	F-101B	Voodoo

McDonnell	RF-101C	Voodoo
McDonnell	XF-85	Goblin
McDonnell	XH-20	
McDonnell	YF-4E	Phantom II
McDonnell Douglas	F-15A	Eagle
Messerschmitt	Me 262A	Schwalbe
Mikoyan-Gurevich	MiG-15	"Fagot"
Mikoyan-Gurevich	MiG-17	"Fresco"
Mikoyan-Gurevich	MiG-21F-13	"Fishbed"
Nieuport	28	
Noorduyn	UC-64A	Norseman
North American	A-36A	Apache
North American	B-25D	Mitchell
North American	B-45C	Tornado
North American	BT-14	
North American	F-82B	Twin Mustang
North American	F-86A	Sabre
North American	F-86D	Sabre
North American	F-86H	Sabre
North American	F-100C	Super Sabre
North American	F-100D	Super Sabre
North American	F-107A	
North American	O-47B	
North American	P-51D	Mustang
North American	T-6G	Texan
North American	T-28A	Trojan
North American	T-28B	Trojan
North American	T-39A	Sabreliner
North American	X-15A	
North American	XB-70	Valkyrie
Northrop	F-89J	Scorpion
Northrop	P-61C	Black Widow
Northrop	X-4	
Northrop	YF-5A	
Piasecki	CH-21A	Workhorse
Piper	L-4	Grasshopper
Republic	F-84E	Thunderjet
Republic	F-84F	Thunderstreak
Republic	F-105B	Thunderchief
Republic	F-105G	Thunderchief
Republic	P-47D	Thunderbolt
Republic	XF-91	Thunderceptor
Republic	YRF-84F	Thunderflash
Rockwell International	B-1A	
Royal Aircraft Factory (Eberhardt)	SE-5E	

Ryan	L-17A	Navion
Ryan	PT-22	Recruit
Ryan	ST-A	
Schweizer	TG-3A	
Seversky	P-35A	
Sikorsky	R-4B	Hoverfly
Sikorsky	R-6A	Hoverfly II
Sikorsky	UH-19B	Chickasaw
Sikorsky	YH-5A	Dragon Fly
Sopwith (replica)	F.1	Camel
SPAD	VII	
SPAD	XVI	
Sperry-Verville	M-1	Messenger
Standard	E-1	
Standard	J-1	
Stearman	PT-13D	Kaydet
Stearman	PT-17	Kaydet
Stinson	L-5	Sentinel
Supermarine	Mk LF.XVIE	Spitfire
Taylorcraft	L-2M	Grasshopper
Thomas-Morse	S-4C	Scout
Vought	A-7D	Corsair II
Vought	XC-142A	
Vultee	BT-13B	Valiant
Vultee	L-1A	Vigilant
Waco	CG-4A	Hadrian
Westland	MkIII	Lysander
Wright Flyer	B	
Wright Flyer (replica)		

Fort Sill Museum
437 Quanah Road, Fort Sill, Oklahoma 73503
(405) 351-5123

Fort Sill is home for the Army's artillery branch. Established in 1869 and situated in a historic region of the Southwest, Fort Sill was an important Army installation during the settling of the area and the resulting conflicts with the local Indians. Geronimo was imprisoned here and is buried in the nearby Apache cemetary. Many of the original buildings still stand and have been preserved as National Historic Landmarks.

The museum presents historical items related to the Army field artillery and missiles. Also on display are cavalry and Indian artifacts reflecting the early years of the fort.

DIRECTIONS TO MUSEUM: The museum is two miles north of Lawton on US Hwy. 281 and situated in the Old Post historic area. The missile exhibit is located south of the Old Post on Randolph Rd.

ADMISSION COST: Free (donation requested).

HOURS OF OPERATION: Open daily 9am-4pm. Closed New Year's Eve, New Year's Day, Christmas Eve and Christmas.

MUSEUM NOTES: Aircraft are inaccessible until sometime in fall 1991 when remodeled building should be open. Missiles are exhibited outside. There is a gift shop, but film is not available. There is a restaurant nearby.

A brochure is available.

Display Aircraft & Missiles

MANUFACTURER	MODEL	POPULAR NAME
Bell	UH-1B	Iroquois "Huey"
Cessna	L-19	Bird Dog
Cessna	T-41B	Mescalero
Douglas	M3A1	Honest John
Firestone	M2	WAC Corporal
Hiller	OH-23F	Raven
LTV Aerospace	Lance	
Martin Marrieta	PI	Pershing
Martin Marrieta	PIA	Pershing
Martin Marrieta	PII	Pershing
Martin Orlando	XM-4	Lacrosse
Piper	L-4	Grasshopper
Redstone Arsenal	M47	Little John
Republic	JB-2	Loon
JPL/Sperry	Sergeant	

45th Infantry Division Museum

2145 N.E. 36th Street, Oklahoma City, Oklahoma 73111
(405) 424-5313

Proudly quoting the famous Army General George Patton, "The 45th is one of the best, if not actually the best division in the history of American arms," the museum's focus is the military history of the 45th Infantry Division during World War II and the Korean War.

Known as the Thunderbirds for the emblem on their shoulder patch, the men of the 45th comprised one of the more highly decorated units during both wars.

The museum possesses artifacts related to the 45th as well as military items that date back to the Revolutionary War. Of special interest is the area set aside to display over 200 original cartoons drawn by Bill Mauldin. Mauldin served with the 45th during World War II and won his first of two Pulitzer Prizes for editorial cartoons in 1945.

The outdoor exhibit area consists of aircraft, trucks, tanks, cannon and other paraphernalia typically found in the Army's inventory during and after World War II. The aircraft also represent the types of airplanes and helicopters flown in greatest numbers by the Army in the same period. The most recognized helicopter on display, at least to the general public, is the Bell UH-1, better known as the "Huey." Thousands were manufactured and their steady appearance on nightly news during the Vietnam War and in subsequent movies formed the public's perception of the modern airborne Army.

The de Havilland Beaver was manufactured from 1948 to 1969. The Beaver is outfitted with floats and used in great numbers by bush pilots in Canada and Alaska. The Army purchased the plane for utility use and designated it U-6.

DIRECTIONS TO MUSEUM: From I-35 exit onto N.E. 36th St. and travel west to museum.

ADMISSION COST: Free.

HOURS OF OPERATION: Open Tuesday-Friday 9am-5pm; Saturday 10am-5pm; Sunday 1-5pm; closed Monday. Closed from Christmas through New Year's Day.

MUSEUM NOTES: Display aircraft are out-doors. There is a gift shop, but film is not available. A restaurant is nearby.

A brochure is available.

Display Aircraft

MANUFACTURER	MODEL	POPULAR NAME
Bell	OH-13E	Sioux
Bell	UH-1	Iroquois "Huey"
Cessna	L-19	Bird Dog
de Havilland	U-6	Beaver
Hiller	OH-23C	Raven
Piper	L-4B	Grasshopper
Ryan	L-17	Navion
Sperry	MGM-29	Sergeant

Oklahoma Air Space Museum

2100 N.E. 52nd Street, Oklahoma City, Oklahoma 73111
(405) 427-5461

The Oklahoma Air Space Museum is one of four major museums comprising the Kirkpatrick Center Museum Complex. The Kirkpatrick Center comprises areas of art, science, photography and history, as well as a planetarium and botanical gardens.

A wide variety of air and spacecraft are on display. The spacecraft displayed range from a replica of a German World War II V-2 rocket to a cockpit exhibit of the Challenger Space Shuttle. A Lunar Module sits on the museum floor with mockups of Gemini and Mercury capsules suspended overhead.

Of interest among the aircraft exhibited are several early airplanes, notably a replica of a Nieuport 11 World War I fighter, a Wiley Post biplane and an American Eagle A-101 biplane. Several homebuilt aircraft are possessed by the museum and one of the more interesting is the Cricket. Looking like an overgrown radio-controlled model, the Cricket is probably one of the smallest twin-engine airplanes ever built. Powered by two two-stroke engines, the plane is capable of 100 miles-per-hour.

German-built Bucker Jungmeisters were the most maneuverable, aerobatic airplanes prior to World War II. Luftwaffe pilots were trained in Jungmeisters, and after the war, the planes were the dominant entrants in aerobatic competitions.

Several other museums, such as the Cowboy Hall of Fame, Firefighters Museum, Softball Museum and 45th Infantry Division Museum (included in this book) are in the area and marked on the Kirkpatrick Center brochure.

DIRECTIONS TO MUSEUM: The Complex is located just south of the Remington Park racetrack and west of the Oklahoma City Zoo. From I-44 exit onto Martin Luther King Blvd. and travel south to N.E. 52nd St. From I-35 exit onto N.E. 50th St. and follow signs.

ADMISSION COST: Adults $5.00; senior citizens $3.00; children (5-12 yrs.) $3.00.

HOURS OF OPERATION: Open daily except Thanksgiving and Christmas. From Memorial Day to Labor Day open 9am-6pm Monday-Saturday, noon-6pm Sunday. Remainder of year open 9:30am-5pm Monday-Friday, 9am-6pm Saturday, noon-6pm Sunday.

MUSEUM NOTES: Aircraft and spacecraft are located inside the museum. There are vending machines and a restaurant located in the Complex, as well as restaurants situated nearby. Film can be purchased in the gift shop.

A brochure is available. A discount coupon is a part of the brochure.

Display Aircraft

MANUFACTURER	MODEL	POPULAR NAME
American Eagle	A-101	
Bede	BD5B	
Bücker (4/5 replica)	DH1	Jungmeister
Bücker	Bu 133c	Jungmeister
Cirrus	3	
Cloud Cutter		
Coffman Monoplane		
Cri Cri Cricket	MC12	
Curtiss (replica)	D	
Fokker (replica)	DR.1	
Lockheed	F-104G	Starfighter
Lockheed	T-33	Shooting Star
Mitchell Wing	B-10	
Mong	MS3	Sport
Nieuport (replica)	11	
Parker Pusher		
Pierce-Sawyer	JP-51	
Radioplane Surveillance Drone		
Schweizer	I-19	
Star	Cavalier	
Stinson	108-2	
Wiley Post	A	

Oklahoma State Fair Park

Oklahoma City, Oklahoma

Oklahoma City and the surrounding area have significant roots in aviation. Wiley Post, born in Texas but calling Oklahoma home, was a famous aviator during the thirties. Tinker Field was established during World War II and has served as a manufacturing, modification and overhaul base for the Army and Air Force. At Wiley Post Airport in the nearby suburb of Bethany, the Aero Commander company began manufacturing the highly successful line of Commander airplanes in 1948. The air park serves to mark Oklahoma City's aviation history.

The air park has a B-52, B-47, C-47 and Commander on display. The three military airplanes reflect the importance of Tinker Air Force Base to Oklahoma City and the nation. Thousands of people in the Oklahoma City area are or have been employed at the facility.

The "Blue Goose" Commander on display was the first Aero Commander airplane certified by the FAA as airworthy. The Commander was the first twin-engine airplane targeted towards business flying. The line of airplanes evolved into turboprop and jets before economic pressures in the aircraft market resulted in production cessation, although some models were continued by other manufacturers.

DIRECTIONS TO AIR PARK: The air park is located on the state fairgrounds. From I-40 exit onto Meridian and travel north to Reno (first intersection). Turn right onto Reno and follow Reno to fairgrounds. Turn left at Delmar Gardens and follow to air park.

The airplanes are located inside the fair complex and supported by pedestals. The Aero Commander was built in nearby Bethany, C-47s were built at the Douglas plant in Oklahoma City, while B-47s were built by Douglas in Tulsa.

ADMISSION COST: Free.

VIEWING HOURS : Daylight hours.

AIR PARK NOTES: Display aircraft are outdoors. There are restaurants nearby.

Display Aircraft

MANUFACTURER	MODEL	POPULAR NAME
Aero Commander	Commander	
Boeing	B-47	Stratojet
Boeing	B-52	Stratofortress
Douglas	C-47	Skytrain

Allied Air Force

Queen City Airport, 1730 Vultee St., Allentown, Pennsylvania 18103
(215) 791-5122

Anticipating construction of a museum building in 1991, the Allied Air Force currently displays their aircraft outdoors at the Queen City Airport in Allentown. The organization plans to increase their collection with the intent to preserve historic military and civilian aircraft.

Of significance in the collection is the Sikorsky CH-3B Sea King helicopter. This is the only Sea King known to be displayed. With over one thousand manufactured, the Sea King has been one of the more popular large helicopters. Over twenty-five countries have utilized the Sea King in their military forces. Originally designed as an amphibious anti-submarine helicopter, variants have been assigned roles of search-and-rescue, VIP transport, transport, utility and anti-ship.

Some of the aircraft are in flyable condition and may be absent while performing at an airshow.

DIRECTIONS TO MUSEUM: From I-78 exit onto Hwy. 309 southbound. Follow Hwy. 309 to Lehigh St. and turn left onto Lehigh. Follow Lehigh to Vultee (fire station) and turn left onto Vultee. Follow to end of Vultee.

ADMISSION COST: Adults & children over 11 yrs. $3.00.

HOURS OF OPERATION: Open Tuesday-Sunday 10am-4pm, May 1 through October 31.

MUSEUM NOTES: Display aircraft are outdoors.

A brochure is available.

Display Aircraft

MANUFACTURER	MODEL	POPULAR NAME
de Havilland	U-6A	Beaver
Douglas	DC-3	
Grumman	S2-D	Tracker
Sikorsky	CH-3B	Sea King
Sikorsky	UH-34J	Seabat

Franklin Institute Science Museum

20th & Benjamin Franklin Parkway, Philadelphia, Pennsylvania 19103
(215) 448-1200

The Franklin Science Museum was the first "hands-on" science center in America. From the walk-through beating heart to the 350-ton locomotive, the museum provides educational and entertaining exhibits for all ages. For the aviation enthusiast, you can sit in the cockpit of the Lockheed T-33 on display.

In addition to the exhibits is the Omniverse Theater that presents "big" screen, wide angle film shows that include space flight as well as exciting land and sea segments.

DIRECTIONS TO MUSEUM: The museum is located at 20th & Benjamin Franklin Pkwy. The museum has taped directions available by calling (215) 448-1200.

ADMISSION COST: Ticket prices vary according to attraction and time of day. Typical prices are adults $8.50 and children $7.00. Omniverse Theater is extra.

HOURS OF OPERATION: Call (215) 448-1200 for times.

MUSEUM NOTES: Display aircraft are indoors. There are gift shops and restaurants onsite. Film is available in the gift shops.

A brochure is available.

Display Aircraft

MANUFACTURER	MODEL	POPULAR NAME
Boeing Vertol	BO 105	Executaire
Lockheed	T-33	Shooting Star
Wright	B	

Mid-Atlantic Air Museum

Reading Regional Airport, Rd. #9, Box 9381, Reading, Pennsylvania 196
(215) 372-7333

Founded in 1980, the members of the Mid-Atlantic Air Museum have undertaken an ambitious plan devoted to acquiring and preserving noteworthy aircraft. In one instance, they traveled to the jungle of New Guinea to resurrect the museum's P-61 Black Widow.

Several aircraft are noteworthy in the collection. Among them are the P-61 Black Widow, the B-25J Mitchell, the P2V-7 Neptune and the UC-78 Bobcat. Cessna manufactured thousands of the UC-78s for use by the Air Force during World War II as a trainer and utility plane. The wings and fuselage formers were made of wood thereby generating the nickname "Bamboo Bomber." A UC-78 was the original "Song Bird" of the Sky King television series.

Shown above is the Custer CCW-5 Channel Wing. Note the "channel" in the wing around the engine nacelle. The normal engine position is reversed so the propeller is located behind the wing. Theoretically, air pulled through the channels increases the lifting power of the wing. This increased lifting power can be used to decrease the runway length required for take off. Advocates claim that if the concept had been fully explored since its inception in 1925, airplanes rather than helicopters would be chosen for short-take-off situations. The other surviving Channel Wing is found at the Air and Space Museum in Washington, D.C.

A noticeably different airplane on display is the CCW-5 Channel Wing. Manufactured by the Custer company in 1964, the channel wing was an effort to prove the concept of enhanced lift using rear-mounted engines to pull air over the wing. Theoretically, increased lift would improve take-off and landing capability. The concept did not result in production and only two airplanes are currently in museums.

The museum also possesses a collection of Piper aircraft. Among them is the Tri-Pacer once owned by William Piper, Sr.

DIRECTIONS TO MUSEUM: The museum is situated at the Reading Airport which is one-half mile northwest of Reading on Hwy. 183. Follow signs to museum.

ADMISSION COST: Adults $3.00; children (6-12 yrs.) $2.00.

HOURS OF OPERATION: Open daily 9:30am-4pm. Closed major holidays.

MUSEUM NOTES: Display aircraft are indoors and outdoors. There is a gift shop, but film is not available. A restaurant is nearby.

A brochure is available.

Display Aircraft

MANUFACTURER	MODEL	POPULAR NAME
Cessna	UC-78	Bobcat
Custer	CCW-5	Channel Wing
de Havilland	L-20	Beaver
Douglas	R4D	Dakota
Fairchild	PT-19	Cornell
Lockheed	P2V-7	Neptune
Messerschmitt	Bf 108	Taifun
Nord	1101	Noralpha
North American	B-25J	Mitchell
North American	F-86F	Sabre
North American	SNJ-4	Texan
North American	T-28D	Nomad
Northrop	P-61B	Black Widow
Piasecki	H-21A	Workhorse
Piper	L-21B	Super Cub
Piper	PA-22	Tri-Pacer
Piper	PA-23-250	Aztec
Piper	PA-34	Seneca
Piper	PA-38-112	Tomahawk
Sikorsky	UH-34J	Seabat
Stearman	PT-13	Kaydet
Vultee	SNV-1	Valiant

Willow Grove Air Park

Office of Public Affairs, Willow Grove Naval Air Station, Pennsylvania 19090
(215) 443-1776

The base was commissioned in 1943 as the Willow Grove Naval Air Station, and now serves as a base for several reserve units as well as a training facility.

The aircraft collection is located in an air park situated adjacent to the perimeter fence near the main gate. Unfortunately, you cannot enter the base without someone on the base vouching for you. However, you can park in the turnout next to the fence and view the aircraft from there.

Several noteworthy airplanes are in the collection. The Convair YF2Y-1 Sea Dart existed only as prototypes for a jet-powered seaplane. Designed to take off and land on skis, the Sea Dart prototypes were the only water-based jet fighters ever built. Also on display is a Messerschmitt Me 262 jet fighter. The Me 262 was capable of reversing the course of World War II, but operational mismanagement, dwindling fuel reserves, and lack of experienced pilots lessened its impact.

DIRECTIONS TO AIR PARK: From I-276 leave turnpike at Willow Grove exit. Follow Hwy. 611 north to Willow Grove NAS. The air park is on the east side of Hwy. 611 before main gate entrance to base.

ADMISSION COST: Free.

VIEWING HOURS: Sunrise to sunset.

AIR PARK NOTES: Display aircraft are outdoors. There are restaurants nearby.

Display Aircraft

MANUFACTURER	MODEL	POPULAR NAME
Arado	Ar 196	
Convair	YF2Y-1	Sea Dart
Grumman	F9F-2	Panther
Grumman	S-2	Tracker
Kawanishi	N1K1	Kyofu "Rex"
Lockheed	TV-1(P-80)	Sea Star
Messerschmitt	Me 262	
North American	FJ-4B	Fury
Vought	F7U-3	Cutlass
Vought	F8U	Crusader

Charleston AFB Air Park

Charleston Air Force Base, South Carolina 29404
(803) 566-5571

The mission of units stationed at Charleston Air Force Base since the early 1950s has been military airlift. The base is an element of the Military Airlift Command. The wing at Charleston AFB utilizes the massive C-141 Starlifter to perform its global mission.

Three notable airplanes that served in a transport capacity are exhibited in an air park on the base. Of interest is the C-124 Globemaster. Prior to the arrival of the C-141, the C-124 was the primary airlifter of massive, bulky cargo due to its large fuselage and the clam shell doors in its nose.

DIRECTIONS TO AIR PARK: Charleston AFB is located north of Charleston. From I-26 exit at Charleston AFB sign. At base gate the Security Police will provide directions to park.

ADMISSION COST: Free.

VIEWING HOURS : Open daily 7:30am-4:30pm.

AIR PARK NOTES: Display aircraft are outdoors. There are vending machines and a restaurant nearby.

A brochure is available.

Display Aircraft

MANUFACTURER	MODEL	POPULAR NAME
Douglas	C-47	Skytrain
Douglas	C-124	Globemaster II
Lockheed	C-121	Constellation

Florence Air and Missile Museum

P.O. Box 1326, Florence, South Carolina 29503
(803) 665-5118

Begun in 1963, the Florence Air and Missile Museum has grown into a museum that not only possesses an extensive collection of aircraft, but also displays a considerable number of missiles.

The missile collection encompasses a wide range of types, from mighty intercontinental ballistic missiles, such as the Titan, to anti-tank missiles. An assortment of space related artifacts are also displayed including a Gemini capsule, Saturn V rocket engines, space parachutes and launch computers.

Among the twenty airplanes on display is a rare Douglas BTD-1 Destroyer. During World War II, the Navy desired an airplane that could deliver both bombs and torpedoes, missions that were then performed by two planes, the Douglas SBD Dauntless and Grumman TBM Avenger. The Douglas BTD-1 was first flown in March 1943. Twenty-eight were produced before the Navy canceled the contract at the end of the war.

DIRECTIONS TO MUSEUM: The museum is located on the east side of Florence at Florence Regional Airport off of East Palmetto St. From I-95 take exit 170 and follow signs to museum.

ADMISSION COST: Adults $5.00; children $3.00.

HOURS OF OPERATION: Open daily 9am-5pm.

MUSEUM NOTES: Display aircraft are indoors and outdoors. Film can be purchased in the gift shop. A restaurant is nearby.

A brochure is available.

Display Aircraft

MANUFACTURER	MODEL	POPULAR NAME
Boeing	B-29	Superfortress
Boeing	B-47	Stratojet
Boeing	C-97	Stratofreighter
Convair	F-102	Delta Dagger
Douglas	B-26	Invader
Douglas	B-66	Destroyer
Douglas	BTD-1	Destroyer
Grumman	C-1	
Grumman	F11F	Tiger
Grumman	HU-16	Albatross
Lockheed	EC-121	Super Constellation
Lockheed	F-104	Starfighter

Lockheed	T-33	Shooting Star
Martin	B-57	Canberra
McDonnell	F-101	Voodoo
North American	F-86	Sabre
North American	F-100	Super Sabre
Northrop	F-89	Scorpion
Republic	F-84F	Thunderstreak

Patriots Point Naval and Maritime Museum

P.O. Box 986, 40 Patriots Point Road, Mt. Pleasant, South Carolina 29464
(803) 884-2727

Called the "World's Largest Naval and Maritime Museum," the Patriots Point Museum is a collection of five naval vessels, including the aircraft carrier *Yorktown*. The *Yorktown* served during World War II and the Vietnam War. The other ships in the museum are the *Savannah*, the first nuclear powered merchant ship, the destroyer *Laffey*, the submarine *Clamagore* and the Coast Guard cutter *Comanche*. All ships are open for tours.

Touring the *Yorktown* presents an exceptional opportunity to view the heart of naval aviation, the aircraft carrier. Here is the chance to see first hand the limited area available for flight operations and understand the need for precise, coordinated action by deck and air crews. An aircraft carrier is a small floating city (the *Yorktown's* ship complement was approximately 3,400 men). The self-guided tours allow you to view several decks and learn more about the crew and construction of an aircraft carrier.

Be aware that touring any of the ships requires climbing stairs that may be slippery in damp conditions. Appropriate footwear is advised.

DIRECTIONS TO MUSEUM: From Business US 17 follow Patriots Point Rd.

ADMISSION COST: Adults $8.00; children (6-11 yrs.) $4.00.

HOURS OF OPERATION: Open daily 9am-6pm. Closed Christmas.

MUSEUM NOTES: Display aircraft are indoors and outdoors. Film can be purchased in the gift shop. There is a cafe onsite and a restaurant is nearby.

A brochure is available.

Display Aircraft

MANUFACTURER	MODEL	POPULAR NAME
Douglas	A-4	Skyhawk
Grumman	E-1B	Tracer
Grumman	F6F	Hellcat
Grumman	F9F	Cougar
Grumman	F-11	Tiger
Grumman	S-2E	Tracker
Grumman (General Motors)	TBM	Avenger
North American	B-25	Mitchell
North American	FJ	Fury
Sikorsky	UH-34D	Seahorse
Vought	F-8	Crusader
Vought (Goodyear)	FG-1D	Corsair

South Dakota Air and Space Museum

P.O. Box 872, Box Elder, South Dakota 57719
(605) 385-5188

The museum is adjacent to Ellsworth Air Force Base, which began air operations during World War II. Ellsworth is the largest operational base in the Strategic Air Command. Units on the base fly the B-1B bomber and control Minuteman missiles.

Among the aircraft on display is the first B-52 assigned to Ellsworth AFB. General Eisenhower's personal B-25 is also in the collection. An intriguing oddity is a 3/5 scale mockup of the B-2 stealth bomber built by Honda Motor Co. for a television advertisement, before the highly secret B-2 bomber was actually rolled out for public viewing.

An interesting sidetrip is a bus tour of Ellsworth AFB. The tour begins at the museum and includes the base flightline and the museum's restoration hanger. The tour is only offered from mid-May to mid-September.

DIRECTIONS TO MUSEUM: Ellsworth AFB is east of Rapid City. From I-90 take exit 66 and drive towards Ellsworth AFB. Museum is near entrance to main gate.

ADMISSION COST: Free.

HOURS OF OPERATION: Open daily mid-May to mid-September 8:30am-6pm; mid-September to mid-May 8:30am-4pm.

Closed New Year's Day, Easter, Thanksgiving and Christmas.

MUSEUM NOTES: Display aircraft are indoors and outdoors. Film can be purchased in the gift shop. From mid-May to mid-September a snack bar is open.

A brochure is available.

Display Aircraft

MANUFACTURER	MODEL	POPULAR NAME
Beech	C-45	Expeditor
Beech	U-8	Seminole
Bell	UH-1	Iroquois "Huey"
Boeing	B-29	Superfortress
Boeing	B-52D	Stratofortress
Cessna	O-2	Skymaster
Cessna	U-3	
Convair	C-131	Samaritan
Douglas	B-26	Invader
Douglas	C-47	Skytrain
Lockheed	T-33	Shooting Star
Martin	EB-57B	Canberra
McDonnell	F-101	Voodoo

North American	B-25	Mitchell
North American	F-86	Sabre
Republic	F-84F	Thunderstreak
Republic	F-105	Thunderchief
Rockwell	Quail	
Stinson	L-5	Sentinel
Vultee	BT-13	Valiant
Western Electric	Nike	

Graceland

3764 Elvis Presley Boulevard, Memphis, Tennessee 38116
(901) 332-3322; outside TN (800) 238-2000

Graceland was the home of Elvis Presley for 20 years. Opened to the public in 1982, it now houses memorabilia of "The King of Rock 'n' Roll." Graceland is an entertaining 90-minute tour for anyone interested in popular music.

Elvis possessed two airplanes at the time of his death, a Convair 880 and a Lockheed Jet Star. The Convair 880 is a four-engine jetliner that was formerly operated by Delta Airlines. Here is an opportunity to look at a former airliner that has been converted to celebrity status. Purchased by Elvis for $250,000 in 1975, the plane was named *Lisa Marie* after Elvis' daughter and customized at a cost of $850,000. Installed equipment includes a satellite receiver, closed-circuit television, quadraphonic sound system, galley, telephones, bedroom, two bathrooms, shower and a dining room. A crew of four was required and annual operating cost for 1976 was over $400,000.

DIRECTIONS TO MUSEUM: Graceland is approximately ten miles south of downtown Memphis. From I-55 take exit 5B onto US 51 (Elvis Presley Blvd.) and go south one mile to Graceland.

ADMISSION COST: Airplanes: adults $4.25; children (4-12 yrs.) $2.75. All attractions package: adults $15.95; children (4-12 yrs.) $10.95.

HOURS OF OPERATION: Open seven days a week except closed Tuesday from November 1 through February. Closed New Year's Day, Thanksgiving and Christmas.

Opening time: May-August 8am; September-April 9am. Closing time: September-May 6pm; June-August 7pm (until 8pm June 15-August 11).

Note: last tour of Graceland begins one hour prior to closing time.

MUSEUM NOTES: Display aircraft are outdoors. Film can be purchased in gift shop. There is a restaurant at Graceland.

A brochure is available.

Memphis Belle

Memphis, Tennessee
(901) 579-3114

Few, if any, airplanes that flew during World War II are more famous than the *Memphis Belle*. During World War II, Air Force bomber crews completing 25 combat missions were removed from combat status. The crew of the *Memphis Belle*, a Boeing B-17F Flying Fortress, was one of the first crews to reach the goal. Attrition was high during the early years of the War for bomber crews (one out of three didn't reach the 25-mission mark), so surviving 25 missions was a highly recognized accomplishment. The *Belle* and aircrew returned to the United States from England and were sent around the country to fund raising and public relations events. Its mission served, the plane was declared scrap at the end of the War and scheduled for destruction. Recognized amongst the other cast-off planes, however, the *Belle* was secured by private parties so it could be restored as a historic artifact.

Two movies have told the story of the *Memphis Belle*, the original documentary was shown in 1943 while a retelling of the last mission was recently released. In the exhibit area the 1943 movie is shown.

PLEASE NOTE: The *Memphis Belle* is situated at what was formerly called Mud Island, an attraction park on the bank of the Mississippi River. The park is scheduled for remodeling and opening in the summer of 1991, but with a new name. Call the telephone number above for information concerning park.

Staggerwing Museum

P.O. Box 550, Tullahoma, Tennessee 37388
(615) 455-1974,-0691,-3594

The Staggerwing Museum Foundation operates the museum and serves as a resource for the restoration, preservation and maintenance of Beech Staggerwing and Travel Air airplanes. Contact museum for information on annual convention/fly-in.

The Beech Staggerwings were the high-water mark of the biplane era. Produced as executive class transportation, the Staggerwing provided fast, comfortable transportation and retractable landing gear. The identifying feature of the Staggerwing is the location of the upper wing which is noticeably farther back on the fuselage than the lower wing.

The museum has several Staggerwing and Travel Air airplanes on display as well as artifacts reflecting the history of those airplanes. Noteworthy airplanes include the first Staggerwing produced, serial number 1. First flown in 1932, the airplane crashed in 1935 and was buried. An extensive search located the plane and several years of restoration effort began. The plane should be on display during 1992.

The museum is presently restoring the Travel Air *Mystery Ship*, winner of the 1929 Thompson race. The plane was constructed behind closed doors at Walter Beech's Travel Air factory in Wichita. The *Mystery* defeated two favored military entries and heralded an era of dominance by civilian constructed planes in air racing. Components of the plane are sometimes on display. The fully renovated *Mystery* should be displayed in 1992.

DIRECTIONS TO MUSEUM: The museum is adjacent to Tullahoma Municipal Airport which is northwest of Tullahoma. From US 41 Alternate, turn onto Hwy. 55. Follow Hwy. 55 then turn onto Hwy. 130 and follow for 3/4 mile to museum at Parish Aerodrome.

ADMISSION COST: Adults $4.00; children under 13 free.

HOURS OF OPERATION: Open Saturday and Sunday 1-4pm. Closed December, January and February. May open by appointment; call 455-3594.

MUSEUM NOTES: Display aircraft are indoors. There is a gift shop. Restaurants are nearby.

A brochure is available.

Display Aircraft

MANUFACTURER	MODEL	POPULAR NAME
Beech	17 (all models)	Staggerwing
Travel Air	4000	
Travel Air	6000	

Admiral Nimitz State Historic Park

P.O. Box 777, Fredericksburg, Texas 78624
(512) 997-4379

The park is dedicated to Admiral Chester Nimitz and to those who served during World War II in the Pacific under his command. Nimitz was born in Fredericksburg and the museum is located in the Steamboat Hotel that was built by his grandfather in the 1850s. Artifacts and exhibits document the history of the Pacific Theater of war and Nimitz' role.

Although the aircraft collection consists of but four airplanes, two are extremely rare Japanese planes. The Aichi D3A2 Model 22 "Val" is original and one of two known to exist in the world (the Smithsonian's has been extensively rebuilt). The Aichi D3A2 was used by the Japanese as a dive bomber during World War II. An earlier variation, the D3A1, exacted extensive damage on the U.S. Navy fleet at Pearl Harbor. The other Japanese plane also flew during World War II. The Kawanishi N1K1 Kyofu "Rex" was a fighter built as a floatplane, a concept that apparently was unsatisfactory as very few were manufactured.

Also on display are examples of two important Navy airplanes of World War II, a Douglas SBD/A-24 Dauntless dive bomber and a General Motors TBM Avenger torpedo bomber. Dauntless dive bombers participated in carrier operations until mid-1944 and saw action in all the critical early naval engagements in the Pacific. Avengers were designed and built by Grumman and designated "TBF." To increase production, General Motors was enlisted to manufacture Avengers and those planes were designated "TBM." By war's end over 9,800 had been built.

DIRECTIONS TO MUSEUM: Located at Main St. and Washington.

HOURS OF OPERATION: Open daily 8am-5pm.

ADMISSION COST: Adults $2.00; children $1.00. Free for senior citizens and children under 7 yrs.

MUSEUM NOTES: Display aircraft are indoors and outdoors. Film is not available in the gift shop. A restaurant is nearby.

A brochure is available.

Display Aircraft

MANUFACTURER	MODEL	POPULAR NAME
Aichi	D3A2	Model 22 "Val"
Douglas	SBD/A-24	Dauntless
Grumman (General Motors)	TBM	Avenger
Kawanishi	N1K1	Kyofu "Rex"

Combat Jets Flying Museum

8802 Travelair, Houston, Texas 77061
(713) 645-0549

The Combat Jets Flying Museum collects significant fighter jet airplanes, plus flies them. A unique undertaking considering the expense and maintenance required.

Among the museum's airplanes are two MiG fighters, a MiG-15 and a MiG-21. The MiG designation is derived from the names of the Russian designers Artem Mikoyan and Mikhail Gurevich. The MiG-15 sweptwing design evolved from research and development conducted by the Germans during World War II. The public debut of the MiG-15 in 1948 startled the Allies and hastened efforts to construct the North American F-86 Sabre, the MiG's formidable adversary during the Korean War.

The museum possesses two examples of the F-86 Sabre. Originally designed with a straight wing, the wing was reconfigured into a 35-degree sweptback wing using research material captured from the Germans at the cessation of World War II. The Sabre was the first American fighter plane to break the sound barrier. During the Korean War, U.S. pilots flying Sabres established a 10-1 kill ratio against North Korean and Chinese pilots. Over 8,000 Sabres were manufactured and the plane remained in service with foreign countries into the late 1970s.

NOTE: The museum is a "working" facility to maintain the planes in flying condition. Due to safety and space considerations, the facility may be temporarily closed. The museum suggests calling ahead, particularly for large groups, for operating hours.

DIRECTIONS TO MUSEUM: The museum is located at Hobby Airport off Telephone Road.

ADMISSION COST: Free (donation requested).

HOURS OF OPERATION: Normally open 8am-5pm Monday-Friday.

MUSEUM NOTES: Display aircraft are indoors. There is a restaurant nearby.

Display Aircraft

MANUFACTURER	MODEL	POPULAR NAME
de Havilland	Mk.35	Vampire
Douglas	A-4C	Skyhawk
Hawker	Mk.51	Hunter
Lockheed	CF-104D	Starfighter
Lockheed (Canadair)	T-33	Silver Star
Mikoyan-Gurevich	MiG-15	"Fagot"
Mikoyan-Gurevich	MiG-21	"Fishbed"
North American	F-86	Sabre

Confederate Air Force Museum

One Heritage Way, P.O. Box CAF, Harlingen, Texas 78551
(512) 425-1057

Formed in 1957 to preserve historic World War II combat aircraft in flyable condition, the Confederate Air Force (CAF) currently lists approximately 143 aircraft in its inventory and over 8,000 members. Originally intending to collect only combat aircraft of the United States, the CAF now collects non-combat aircraft of both the Allied and Axis nations.

The CAF is supported nationally by Wings (chapters) that are scattered around the country. Each Wing supports the national organization through its own local preservation of aircraft and participation in airshows.

A unique facet of the CAF is the sponsorship program. Contributions may be directed to specific aircraft resulting in several people sharing in the cost of purchase, restoration and maintenance of one airplane. The CAF credits the sponsorship program with the extensive number of aircraft now flying in its "Ghost Squadron." Sponsors need not be members of the CAF to participate.

There are usually 25 to 40 aircraft onsite for display. The remaining aircraft are assigned to the various Wings or are participating in air shows. Some of the CAF aircraft are the only flying examples of certain World War II airplanes and are in high demand

Among the aircraft in the CAF inventory is this F4U Corsair, named Ace Maker. *Designed by Vought Aircraft, the Corsair's distinctive gull-wing shape was developed to accommodate the large propeller required for the high horsepower engine. Were it not for the bent wing, the plane would require tall landing gear so the propeller wouldn't strike the ground.*

during the air show season. One of the highlights of the season is the airshow presented by the CAF in Harlingen in the fall. Call the CAF for specific dates.

In addition to the aircraft is a vast collection of World War II artifacts and memorabilia.

DIRECTIONS TO MUSEUM: The CAF Museum is located at Valley International Airport two blocks north of the passenger terminal. The airport is situated adjacent to Texas Highway Loop 499 near the intersection of Farm-to-Market Road 502 on the northeast side of Harlingen.

HOURS OF OPERATION: Open Monday-Saturday 9am-5pm; Sunday and holidays noon-5pm.

MUSEUM NOTES: Display aircraft are indoors and outdoors. Film is available in the gift shop. There is a cafe onsite.

ADMISSION COST: Adults $4.00; senior citizens $3.00; teenagers $3.00; children (6-12 yrs.) $2.00.

A brochure is available.

Display Aircraft

MANUFACTURER	MODEL	POPULAR NAME
Aerocoupe	YO-55	
Aichi	D3A	"Val"
Beech	AT-7	Navigator
Bell	P-39	Airacobra
Bell	P-63	Kingcobra
Boeing	B-17	Flying Fortress
Boeing	B-29	Superfortress
Consolidated	LB-30	Liberator
Consolidated	PBY	Catalina
Curtiss	C-46	Commando
Curtiss	P-40	Warhawk
Curtiss	SB2C	Helldiver
de Havilland	D.H.94	Moth Minor
Douglas	A-26	Invader
Douglas	B-23	Dragon
Douglas	C-47	Skytrain
Douglas	C-54	Skymaster
Douglas	SBD	Dauntless
Fairchild	PT-19	Cornell
Fieseler	Fi 156D	Storch
Fleet	16B	Finch
Focke-Wulf	Fw 44	Stieglitz
Focke-Wulf	Fw 190	
Grumman	F6F	Hellcat
Grumman	F8F	Bearcat

Grumman (General Motors)	FM-2	Wildcat
Grumman (General Motors)	TBM	Avenger
Heinkel	He 111	
Junkers	Ju 52	
Lockheed	C-45	Lodestar
Lockheed	P-38	Lightning
Lockheed	PV-2	Harpoon
Martin	B-26	Marauder
Messerschmitt	Bf 108	Taifun
Messerschmitt	Bf 109	
Mitsubishi	A6M2	Zero "Zeke"
Nakajima	B6N	Tenzan "Jill"
Naval Aircraft Factory	N3N	
North American	AT-6	Texan
North American	B-25	Mitchell
North American	P-51	Mustang
North American	P-82	Twin Mustang
Piper	L-4	Grasshopper
Republic	P-47	Thunderbolt
Ryan	PT-22	Recruit
Sikorsky	R-4B	Hoverfly
Stearman	PT-17	Kaydet
Stinson	AT-19	Reliant
Stinson	L-5	Sentinel
Stinson	S-108	Voyager
Supermarine	Mk IX	Spitfire
Taylorcraft	L-2	Grasshopper
Vought (Goodyear)	FG-1	Corsair
Vultee	BT-13	Valiant
Waco	TG-3	

Corpus Christi Museum of Science & Industry
1900 N. Chaparral, Corpus Christi, Texas 78401
(512) 883-2862

The Corpus Christi Museum of Science & Industry contains exhibits that outline the scientific and historical aspects of South Texas. Recent additions include maritime displays of artifacts from Spanish shipwrecks circa 1554, and an area devoted to Navy aviation training.

The aviation exhibit area is titled "Navy Wings Over South Texas." Two major training bases for Navy aviators are located in the area, Corpus Christi Naval Air Station and Kingsville Naval Air Station. Both installations were opened during the early years of World War II. Corpus Christi NAS trained more Navy pilots than any other training base, and counted George Bush among those undergoing pilot training. The exhibit focuses on the Navy's aviation presence through a variety of artifacts, including a cockpit simulator for a McDonnell F-4 Phantom.

Two airplanes are on display, a North American SNJ Texan and a Naval Aircraft Factory N3N. Nicknamed the "Yellow Peril" by thousands of Navy aviation cadets, N3Ns served as the Navy's primary trainer during the late 1930s and most of the 1940s. The nickname was prompted by the plane's color and the need to master the plane before proceeding to further training. The Texan was flown as an advanced pilot trainer. North American built over 16,000 Texans which were designated by the Navy as SNJ and by the Air Force as AT-6.

DIRECTIONS TO MUSEUM: From I-37 exit onto Shoreline and follow to Chaparral. From Hwy. 181 southbound, exit onto Shoreline after crossing Harbor Bridge and follow to Chaparral.

ADMISSION COST: Adults $2.00; children (6-12 yrs.) 50¢. Admission is free on Saturday from 10am to noon.

HOURS OF OPERATION: Open Tuesday-Saturday 10am-5pm; Sunday 1-5pm. Closed Sunday and major holidays.

MUSEUM NOTES: Display aircraft are indoors. There is a gift shop, but film is not available. There are restaurants nearby.

A brochure is available.

Dyess Linear Air Park

96 BMW/CVM, Dyess Air Force Base, Texas 79607
(915) 696-2196

Dyess Air Force Base is a part of the Strategic Air Command and was the first base to serve as home for an operational wing of B-1B bombers.

Three bombers that were mainstays for the Air Force in fulfilling its strategic bombing capability are on display. The B-17, B-47 and B-52 are prominently displayed in areas adjacent to the base's main gate. B-17s and B-47s were retired long ago, but B-52s remain on active flying status over thirty years after entering service. B-52s are no longer stationed at Dyess, but you can occasionally see and hear in the distance the B-1 strategic bombers that operate from the base.

DIRECTIONS TO AIR PARK: The air park is situated on Dyess AFB. Travel west of Abilene on I-20 and exit at ramp to base.Follow Arnold Blvd. to main gate and stop at the visitors center for a pass. A map of the air park is available at the visitors center. If there is an operational exercise at the base, the base may be temporarily closed.

ADMISSION COST: Free.

HOURS OF OPERATION: Daylight hours.

MUSEUM NOTES: Display aircraft are outdoors. There are restaurants nearby in Abilene.

The crew of a B-47 consisted of a pilot, a co-pilot and a navigator/bombardier. The copilot also controlled the guns in the tail turret by remote control. The navigator/bombardier was also the radar operator. The pilot and copilot sat underneath the canopy while the navigator was located in the nose. If difficulty in flight required ejection, the pilot and co-pilot would exit upward after the canopy blew off. The navigator was ejected downward through an opening in the fuselage.

Display Aircraft

MANUFACTURER	MODEL	POPULAR NAME
Beech	T-34B	Mentor
Boeing	B-17G	Flying Fortress
Boeing	B-47E	Stratojet
Boeing	B-52D	Stratofortress
Boeing	KC-97L	Stratofreighter
Cessna	O-2	Skymaster
Convair	T-29C	Flying Classroom
Douglas	A-26C	Invader
Douglas	C-47A	Skytrain
Fairchild	C-123K	Provider
Grumman	HU-16	Albatross
Lockheed	C-130A	Hercules
Lockheed	F-104A	Starfighter
Lockheed	T-33A	Shooting Star
Martin	EB-57B	Canberra
McDonnell	F-4D	Phantom II
McDonnell	F-101B	Voodoo
North American	F-86L	Sabre
North American	F-100C	Super Sabre
North American	T-6F	Texan
North American	T-39A	Sabreliner
Northrop	F-89	Scorpion
Republic	F-84F	Thunderstreak
Republic	F-105D	Thunderchief
Republic	RF-84F	Thunderflash

Edward H. White II Memorial Museum

Brooks Air Force Base, Texas 78235
(512) 536-2203

Brooks Air Force Base is the aerospace medical research center for the Air Force. Opened over sixty-five years ago, the base originally served as a flight training center (Charles Lindbergh was a student). The School of Aviation Medicine moved to Brooks in 1926, and was later renamed the School of Aerospace Medicine.

The museum is housed in historic Hanger 9. The hanger was constructed during World War I and is the oldest existing hanger. Restored in 1969, the hanger now contains exhibits related to aerospace medicine. The artifacts, memorabilia and displays address the special medical problems and solutions resulting from manned flight.

DIRECTIONS TO MUSEUM: Brooks AFB is in southeast San Antonio. From I-37 exit onto S.W. Military Dr. Turn left at second traffic light onto North Road. Turn left at Fifth St. Turn right at next street and follow to Hanger 9.

ADMISSION COST: Free.

HOURS OF OPERATION: Open Monday-Friday 8am-4pm. Closed weekends and holidays.

MUSEUM NOTES: Display aircraft are indoors and outdoors. There is a restaurant nearby.

A brochure is available.

Display Aircraft

MANUFACTURER	MODEL	POPULAR NAME
Curtiss	JN-4	"Jenny"
North American	F-100	Super Sabre

Frontiers of Flight Museum

Love Field Terminal Building, LB-38, Dallas, Texas 75235
(214) 350-3600

The Frontiers of Flight Museum is an outgrowth of the massive aviation history collection of the University of Texas at Dallas. Only the Smithsonian collection ranks ahead in significance.

In the museum is a variety of photographs, artifacts and memorabilia that chronicle aviation history. Aviation pioneers as well as space exploration are addressed by the museum's exhibits. Among the displays you'll find a propeller from the dirigible U.S.S. *Shenandoah* and dinnerware from the *Hindenburg*. The museum covers all aspects of aviation history.

The museum is located on the upper mezzanine of the main terminal building at Love Field. Love Field was the major area airport before the Dallas-Fort Worth Intercontinental airport was constructed. Love Field remains very active. An excellent vantage point to view airliners and other airplanes using the airport is the upper parking level of the parking lot adjacent to the terminal.

DIRECTIONS TO MUSEUM: Love Field is northwest of downtown Dallas. From I-35 exit onto Mockingbird. Travel east to Cedar Springs Rd. Turn left onto Cedar Springs Rd. and follow signs to main terminal building.

ADMISSION COST: Adults $2.00; children (under 12 yrs.) $1.00.

HOURS OF OPERATION: Open Tuesday-Saturday 10am-5pm; Sunday 1-5pm. Closed Monday and major holidays.

MUSEUM NOTES: All displays are indoors. Film can be purchased in the gift shop. A restaurant is located in the terminal building.

A brochure is available.

History and Traditions Museum

AFMTC/LGMH, Lackland Air Force Base, San Antonio, Texas 78236
(512) 671-3444

Lackland Air Force Base is the basic training center for the Air Force as well as a training center for technical specialties.

A wide variety of aircraft are on display. Three aircraft are of particular interest: the F-82 Twin Mustang, the Curtiss Jenny and the SR-71 Blackbird. The F-82 is a Korean War era, twin-fuselage variation of the famous P-51 Mustang. The Curtiss Jennys were flown by barnstormers between the World Wars and served as trainers for thousands of pilots. The Blackbird's notoriety stems from its use as a high-speed spyplane (over 2000 mph). A sister plane in early 1990 set the coast-to-coast speed record at 68 minutes.

DIRECTIONS TO MUSEUM: Travel west from San Antonio on Hwy. 90. Exit onto Military Dr. and go south to west main gate of Lackland AFB.

ADMISSION COST: Free.

HOURS OF OPERATION: Open 9am-5:45pm daily. Closed New Year's Day, Easter, Thanksgiving and Christmas.

MUSEUM NOTES: Aircraft are located indoors and outdoors with the majority displayed outdoors. There is a gift shop, but film is not available. There are restaurants near the base.

Display Aircraft

MANUFACTURER	MODEL	POPULAR NAME
Beech	C-45	Expeditor
Beech	T-34	Mentor
Bell	P-63	Kingcobra
Bell	UH-1B	Iroquois "Huey"
Boeing	B-17	Flying Fortress
Boeing	B-52	Stratofortress
Boeing	CIM-10A	Bomarc
Cessna	O-2A	Skymaster
Cessna	T-37	Tweetybird
Cessna	T-41	Mescalero
Consolidated	B-24	Liberator
Convair	F-102	Delta Dagger
Convair	T-29	
Curtiss	JN-4D	"Jenny"
Douglas	B-26	Invader
Douglas	B-66	Destroyer
Douglas	C-47	Skytrain

Douglas	C-118	Liftmaster
Douglas	SM-75	Thor
Fairchild	C-119	Flying Boxcar
Fairchild	C-123	Provider
Grumman	HU-16	Albatross
Lockheed	C-121	Super Constellation
Lockheed	F-80	Shooting Star
Lockheed	F-94	Starfire
Lockheed	F-104	Starfighter
Lockheed	SR-71	Blackbird
Lockheed	T-33	Shooting Star
Martin	RB-57	Canberra
Martin	TM-61	Matador
Martin	TM-76	Mace
McDonnell	F-101	Voodoo
McDonnell	GAM-72	Quail
McDonnell	F-4	Phantom II
North American	B-25	Mitchell
North American	F-82	Twin Mustang
North American	F-86	Sabre
North American	F-100	Super Sabre
North American	P-51	Mustang
North American	T-6	Texan
North American	T-28	Trojan
North American	T-39	Sabreliner
Northrop	F-5	Tiger II
Northrop	F-89	Scorpion
Northrop	T-38	Talon
Republic	F-84	Thunderjet
Republic	F-105	Thunderchief
Republic	JB-2	Loon
Republic	P-47	Thunderbolt

Lone Star Flight Museum
2002 Terminal Drive, Galveston, Texas 77554
(409) 740-7722

The Lone Star Flight Museum is relatively young—they purchased their first plane, a Corsair, in 1985. But judging from the contents of this new museum in Galveston (the museum was formerly located in Houston), the museum staff certainly knows how to acquire, restore and display noteworthy aircraft, as well as return them to flying status.

The museum collection emphasizes airplanes constructed during the late 1930s and 1940s. Military planes make up the bulk of the collection, and among them is a Grumman F3F. The F3Fs were the last carrier-based biplane fighters in service with the Navy. They entered service in 1936 and were removed from front-line squadrons shortly before World War II. The Navy was at first reluctant to switch to the faster monoplane design, prefering the perceived greater strength of the biplane. But the speed disadvantage became too great and biplanes were phased out. Grumman followed the F3F with the F4F Wildcat, the first of Grumman's famous `Cat series of fighters.

Among the exhibits is the Conoco Hall of Power, a display of aircraft engines that includes the jet engine from a World War II Messerschmitt Me 262.

DIRECTIONS TO MUSEUM: The museum is located at Scholes Field Municipal Airport. From I-45 exit onto 61st St. and travel south to Stewart Rd. Turn right onto Stewart and go straight onto Jones Rd. Turn right towards Moody Gardens, then left onto Airport St. Museum is at intersection of Airport and Lockheed Sts.

ADMISSION COST: Adults $5.00; children (under 14 yrs.) and senior citizens $2.50.

HOURS OF OPERATION: Open daily 10am-5pm. Closed New Year's Day, Easter, Thanksgiving and Christmas.

MUSEUM NOTES: Display aircraft are indoors. Film is available in the gift shop.

A brochure is available.

Display Aircraft

MANUFACTURER	MODEL	POPULAR NAME
Beech	B18H	
Beech	D17S	Staggerwing
Beech	T-34	Mentor
Boeing	B-17G	Flying Fortress
Cessna	UC-78	Bobcat
Consolidated	PB4Y-2	Privateer

Fairchild	C-123K	Provider
Grumman	C-1A	Trader
Grumman	F3F	
Grumman	F6F	Hellcat
Grumman	F7F	Tigercat
Grumman	TBM	Avenger
Lockheed	P-38L	Lightning
Noorduyn	UC-64	Norseman
North American	B-25	Mitchell
North American	T-6	Texan, Harvard
Republic	P-47D	Thunderbolt
Spartan	7W	Executive
Stinson	L-5	Sentinel
Temco	TT-1	Pinto

Museum of American Aviation

3119 Growdon Road, San Antonio, Texas 78227
(512) 436-9299

The Museum of American Aviation possess a one-of-a-kind airplane, the XC-99. Constructed by Convair in San Diego, it was the cargo version of the B-36 intercontinental bomber. The only XC-99 built first flew in 1947, entered Air Force service in 1949, and was retired in 1957. Approval has been granted to place the plane on the National Historic Registry, making it one of only two planes on the Registry.

The XC-99's tail, engines, wings and landing gear are the same as those used on the B-36. The plane could carry 400 troops or 100,000 pounds of cargo at a range of 8,100 miles. Maximum speed was approximately 300 miles-per-hour. The XC-99 was the largest land-based, piston-engine aircraft ever built (the Spruce Goose was larger, but it was a seaplane).

At time of publication an offer was being considered by the museum for purchase of the XC-99. Call museum to verify presence of XC-99.

The museum also has a collection of artifacts related to early flight. Particularly interesting are items from flying machines constructed by Jacob Brodbeck. Brodbeck attempted powered flight in the late 1800s using springs for power.

DIRECTIONS TO MUSEUM: The museum is off of Hwy. 90 west of Kelly Air Force Base, which is southwest of San Antonio.

ADMISSION COST: Adults $1.00; children 50¢.

HOURS OF OPERATION: Open Saturday and Sunday 10am-5pm.

MUSEUM NOTES: Display aircraft are inside and outside. Film is available in the gift shop. There are vending machines onsite and a restaurant is nearby.

A brochure is available.

NASA Lyndon B. Johnson Space Center

Public Services Branch, AP4, Houston, Texas 77058
(713) 483-4241

The focal point for the United States' efforts in manned spaceflight is the Johnson Space Center. Carrying out the task of mission control, all manned missions since Gemini 4 have been under the direction of personnel at Johnson. The installation is a research and development facility for NASA with primary responsibility for training astronauts, designing and developing spacecraft and their systems, as well as planning and executing space flights.

The tour of Mission Control Center is the only guided tour. All other tours are self-guided. Tickets for the Mission Control Center tour are passed out on a first-come, first-served basis at the Visitor Center. Many of the buildings open for the tour are occupied during working hours so visitors can observe Space Center personnel at work. However, some buildings may be closed to the public without prior notice.

Saturn V rockets propelled all Apollo lunar missions. Each of the Rocketdyne F-1 engines in the first stage developed 7,650,000 pounds of thrust. The massive power of the five engines was required to lift the 6,423,000-pound Saturn V/Apollo off the launch pad and into space.

On display are space suits, space equipment, spacecraft, rockets and a variety of artifacts including the largest moon rocks presented for public viewing. The spacecraft include modules from the Mercury, Gemini and Apollo missions and the Lunar Module and Lunar Rover.

DIRECTIONS TO MUSEUM: The Space Center is south of Houston. From I-45 exit onto NASA Road 1 and go east approximately three miles to the NASA Visitor Center.

ADMISSION COST: Free.

HOURS OF OPERATION: Open daily 9am-4pm. Closed Christmas.

MUSEUM NOTES: Spacecraft are indoors and outdoors. Film is available in the gift shop. There are vending machines and a cafe onsite. Restaurants are nearby.

A brochure is available.

Display Spacecraft

MANUFACTURER	MODEL
Chrysler	Mercury Redstone
McDonnell	Gemini capsule
McDonnell	Mercury capsule
McDonnell Douglas	Saturn V
North American Rockwell	Apollo command module

Pate Museum of Transportation

P.O. Box 711, Fort Worth, Texas 76101
(817) 396-4305

The Pate Museum of Transportation has on exhibit an impressive collection of automobiles and aircraft, as well as artifacts and memorabilia reflecting transportation in the United States. Begun in 1969, the museum is sponsored by a foundation that provides funds for the expansion and improvement of the museum.

Among the military aircraft on display is a Vought F-8 Crusader. The Crusader was the last fighter developed by Vought. First delivered to the Navy in 1956, Crusaders served with the Navy and Marine Corps until 1986. A Crusader was the first carrier-based aircraft to exceed 1,000 mph, and former Marine pilot and astronaut John Glenn set a transcontinental speed record of 3 hours 23 minutes (average speed 725 mph) in 1957. The unique structural aspect of Crusaders is the variable incidence wing. The wing of a Crusader is located high on its fuselage and the wing is hinged where the rear portion attaches to the fuselage. The wing can pivot upward so the front portion is higher thereby improving slow speed flying characteristics. This mechanism allowed the creation of a high-speed plane while providing the pilot with a good handling plane during a carrier landing.

Originating as the Fairchild C-82 Packet during World War II, the design evolved into the C-119 Flying Boxcar and was flown in the Korean War. The rear of the fuselage splits into clamshell doors allowing entrance for large equipment. Over 1,100 were built. Some flew during Vietnam as AC-119 gunships, deadly planes that would loiter over combat areas and provide fire support with their multiple rapid-firing guns.

The H-21 was orginally designed and manufactured by Piasecki Helicopter Corporation. Piasecki was purchased by Vertol Aircraft, which was subsequently merged with Boeing. Frank Piasecki pioneered the concept of twin rotors. In 1945 he built the PV-3, the predecessor of the H-21. Its distinctive shape resulted in the nickname "Flying Banana."

DIRECTIONS TO MUSEUM: The museum is just north of Cresson on US 377.

ADMISSION COST: Free.

HOURS OF OPERATION: Open 9am-5pm Tuesday-Sunday. Closed Monday and major holidays.

MUSEUM NOTES: Most display aircraft are outdoors. Film is not available onsite. There are no eating facilities onsite or nearby.

A brochure is available.

Display Aircraft

MANUFACTURER	MODEL	POPULAR NAME
Boeing	XF-99	Bomarc
Douglas	C-47D	Skytrain
Driggs	Dart II	
Fairchild	C-119	Flying Boxcar
Grumman	F9F-6	Cougar
Grumman	HU-16B	Albatross
Hiller	OH-23	

Kaman	HH-43	Huskie
Lockheed	T-33	Shooting Star
McDonnell	F-4	Phantom II
McDonnell	F-101B	Voodoo
McDonnell	Mercury capsule (mock-up)	
North American	F-86H	Sabre
North American	T-28	Trojan
North American Rockwell	Apollo capsule (mock-up)	
Piasecki	CH-21B	Workhorse
Republic	F-105	Thunderchief
Republic	RF-84F	Thunderflash
Ryan	Firebee	
Vought	F-8	Crusader

Silent Wings Museum
909 Silent Wings Boulevard, Terrell, Texas 75160
(214) 563-0402

The Silent Wings Museum is an outgrowth of the Military Glider Pilots Association and its desire to commemorate World War II glider pilots. Their accomplishments and involvement in World War II remain largely unknown to the general public and the museum serves as a repository for the artifacts and memorabilia that mark their deeds.

Approximately 5,000 glider pilots earned their wings during World War II, all volunteers. Glider operations were highly hazardous due to the equipment, landing hazards and enemy action. By design, all combat glider missions ended behind enemy lines. Glider pilots experienced a 37 per cent casualty rate during the war while performing missions in Burma, France, Holland, Germany, Italy and the Philippines. In 1952 the glider program was terminated.

An interior view of the Waco CG-4 glider displayed at the Silent Wings Museum. Military gliders were constructed to be light, but rugged. Combat flights were one-way, so all unneccesary material was left out during construction. The airframe was designed for basic flight capability, maximum load capacity and occupant protection during landing.

The Waco CG-4 glider was constructed to be functional, somewhat aerodynamic in shape, and simple to build. Most were towed behind either a Douglas C-47 or Curtiss C-46. Sixteen manufacturers produced the CG-4 during World War II.

The mainstay of the glider program was the Waco CG-4A glider. Although 13,909 were produced, only three examples remain in the country, one of which resides in the Silent Wings Museum. The CG-4A was constructed primarily of wood and fabric with a welded steel tubing fuselage skeleton. The normal load consisted of 13 men plus the pilot and co-pilot, however separate pieces of equipment such as a jeep, bulldozer or 75mm howitzer could be carried. The glider displayed in the museum was reconstructed from components found in California and Pennsylvania.

Also exhibited are training gliders, artifacts and memorabilia which relate to glider and airborne operations.

DIRECTIONS TO MUSEUM: The museum is situated at Terrell Municipal Airport. From I-20 exit onto Hwy. 34 northbound. Proceed to Airport Rd. and follow signs for museum.

ADMISSION COST: Free (donations appreciated).

HOURS OF OPERATION: Open Tuesday-Saturday 10am-5pm; Sunday noon-5pm. Closed Monday. Closed major holidays.

MUSEUM NOTES: Display aircraft are indoors. There is a gift shop, but film is not available. A restaurant is nearby.

A brochure is available.

Display Aircraft

MANUFACTURER	MODEL
Laister-Kauffman	TG-4A
Pratt-Reed	PR-G-1
Schweizer	TG-2A
Schweizer	TG-3A
Waco	CG-4A

Southwest Aerospace Museum

330 N. Spur 341, Fort Worth, Texas 76108
(817) 735-4143

The Southwest Aerospace Museum is adjacent to Carswell Air Force Base. Carswell has long been a part of the Strategic Air Command (SAC) and is now base for a wing of B-52 bombers and a squadron of KC-135 tankers. Across from the air base at the end of Spur 341 is the huge General Dynamics aircraft plant.

Reflecting the role of the Strategic Air Command, the museum possesses three of the bombers instrumental in the implementation of SAC's mission. The B-36 was the first bomber capable of intercontinental bomb delivery and the B-36J on display was the last built. The B-58 was the first supersonic bomber. Both the B-36 and B-58 were built at the former Convair (now General Dynamics) plant adjacent to Carswell AFB. The museum also possesses a B-52, still the mainstay of SAC after over 30 years in service.

Aircraft such as B-52s, F-16s and KC-135s operating from Carswell can be viewed from Spur 341 which parallels Carswell's main runway.

DIRECTIONS TO MUSEUM: From I-30 exit onto Spur 341 (exit 7B). Go north two miles on Spur 341 to museum.

HOURS OF OPERATION: Open Thursday and Friday 10am-3pm; Saturday and Sunday 10am-4pm.

ADMISSION COST: Free.

The massive B-36 was the first intercontinental bomber. The bomber was born during World War II out of fear that Germany might control all of Europe, and a bomber would have to traverse the Atlantic to bomb the enemy. Need for the bomber lessened as World War II came to a close, but the Cold War revived the demand for the bomber. Controversy arose concerning its expense and relatively slow speed compared with the new jet fighters, however, more than 380 were built. The last B-36 was retired from service in 1959.

The North American F-100 (known as "Hun") was the first supersonic fighter in the world. Entering Air Force service in 1953, the Super Sabres flew missions in Vietnam before ending their service with Reserve and Air Guard units in the 70s. The F-100s are probably best known for the red, white and blue color scheme of the Air Force Thunderbird demonstration team. The Thunderbirds flew F-100s before millions of spectators for 13 years beginning in 1956.

MUSEUM NOTES: Display aircraft are out-doors. Film is available in the gift shop. A restaurant is nearby.

A brochure is available.

Display Aircraft

MANUFACTURER	MODEL	POPULAR NAME
Boeing	B-52D	Stratofortress
Boeing	KC-97	Stratofreighter
Convair	B-36J	Peacemaker
Convair	TB-58A	Hustler
Lockheed	T-33A	Shooting Star
LTV	L450F	
North American	F-86L	Sabre
North American	F-100	Super Sabre
Northrop	F-89D	Scorpion
Republic	F-105F	Thunderchief
Sikorsky	UH-34D	Seahorse
Vultee	BT-13A	Valiant

Hill Air Force Base Museum

OO-ALC/XPH, Hill Air Force Base, Utah 84056
(801) 777-6818

Hill Air Force Base has existed as a military air base since 1940. The base currently is a part of the Air Force Logistics Command and serves as a repair and maintenance facility. With over 20,000 military and civilian personnel working at the base, it is Utah's largest employer.

Among the display aircraft is a Sikorsky R-4B helicopter, one of the few remaining. Procured during World War II, the R-4B was the first operational military helicopter. Twenty-seven entered service and were the first step towards the eventual extensive use of helicopters by the military.

Also on display is a Boeing B-29. Hill AFB was a major renovation center during the Korean War as World War II B-29s were readied for combat. Over 4,000 were built from 1943 to 1946 and flew as bombers, search planes, weather planes and air refueling tankers. Their most remembered missions were the dropping of the atomic bombs on Hiroshima and Nagasaki. The Russians were so impressed with the B-29, that after three B-29s landed in Siberia during WWII, the Soviets kept the bombers, copied the construction and built over 1,000 of their own version, designated the Tu-4.

DIRECTIONS TO MUSEUM: Hill Air Force Base is south of Ogden. From I-15 take exit 341 to museum.

ADMISSION COST: Free.

HOURS OF OPERATION: Open Tuesday-Friday 9am-3pm; Saturday 9am-5pm; Sunday 11am-5pm; closed Monday. Closed New Year's Day, Thanksgiving and Christmas.

MUSEUM NOTES: Display aircraft are mainly outdoors. Film can be purchased in the gift shop. There are vending machines onsite and a restaurant is nearby.

A brochure is available.

Display Aircraft

MANUFACTURER	MODEL	POPULAR NAME
Beech	C-45H	Expeditor
Bell	H-13T	Sioux
Boeing	B-17G	Flying Fortress
Boeing	B-29	Superfortress
Cessna	O-2A	Skymaster
Cessna	U-3A	
Convair	C-131B	Samaritan
Convair	F-102A	Delta Dagger
Convair	VC-131D	

Curtiss	P-40	Warhawk
Douglas	C-47B	Skytrain
Fairchild	C-119C	Flying Boxcar
Fairchild	C-123	Provider
Hughes	OH-6A	Cayuse
Kaman	H-43B	Huskie
Lockheed	P-80	Shooting Star
Lockheed	T-33A	Shooting Star
Martin	B-57A	Canberra
McDonnell	F-4C	Phantom II
McDonnell	F-101B	Voodoo
North American	F-86L	Sabre
North American	F-100A	Super Sabre
North American	T-28B	Trojan
Northrop	F-89H	Scorpion
Piasecki	H-21B	Workhorse
Republic	F-84F	Thunderstreak
Republic	F-84G	Thunderjet
Republic	F-105D	Thunderchief
Republic	F-105G	Thunderchief
Sikorsky	H-34J	Choctaw
Sikorsky	R-4B	Hoverfly
Stearman	PT-17	

Air Power Park and Museum

413 West Mercury Boulevard, Hampton, Virginia 23666
(804) 727-1163

Hampton is centered in one of the heaviest concentrations of military bases in the country. Norfolk is home for the Navy's Atlantic Fleet and one of the world's largest navy bases. There is also a wealth of early American history in the area worth investigating.

The Air Power Park and Museum is not far from Langley Air Force Base and artifacts and memorabilia in the museum reflect the history of Langley and local area aviation. Langley AFB is the oldest continuously operated base in the Air Force having been in service since 1917. It is now headquarters for the Tactical Air Command.

One of the country's first military missiles, the Chrysler Jupiter missile was developed at the Army's Redstone Arsenal in Alabama. Due to a governmental change in missile policy, the Jupiter was assigned to the Air Force and designated the SM-78. The Jupiter was capable of carrying a nuclear warhead to a target 1,500 miles away. New missiles resulted in retirement of Jupiters in 1963.

The F-86L was created by modifying the wing and adding engine cooling ducts to D models of the F-86, plus installing upgraded electronic equipment. The D and L models are easily identified by the radome bulb on the nose. Over 2,000 D models were built, of which 981 were modified into L models.

The museum possesses several jet fighters from the decades of 1950 and 1960. Particularly interesting is the British Hawker Kestrel. The Kestrel is capable of vertical takeoff and landing and is the predecessor of the Harrier now serving with the Royal Air Force and U.S. Marine Air Corps.

Also on display is one of the last Lockheed T-33A Shooting Stars to be removed from the Air Force inventory. T-33s served the Air Force as a jet trainer and in a variety of other roles for nearly forty years. Although last manufactured during the 1950s, the airplane remains in service with a number of foreign countries.

DIRECTIONS TO MUSEUM: From I-64 exit onto Mercury Blvd. (exit 64B) and follow Mercury approximately 2 miles to the museum.

ADMISSION COST: Free.

HOURS OF OPERATION: Open daily 9am-5pm. Closed New Year's Day, Thanksgiving and Christmas.

MUSEUM NOTES: Display aircraft are outdoors. There is a gift shop, but film is not available. There are vending machines and a restaurant is nearby.

A brochure is available.

Display Aircraft

MANUFACTURER	MODEL	POPULAR NAME
Bell	UH-1M	Iroquois "Huey"
Boeing	CIM-10A	Bomarc
Chrysler	SM-78	Jupiter
Hawker	P.1127	Kestrel
Hughes	AIM-4	Falcon
Javelin		
Lockheed	A-2	Polaris
Lockheed	F-104C	Starfighter
Lockheed	T-33A	Shooting Star
McDonnell	F-101F	Voodoo
McDonnell	Mercury Capsule	*Little Joe*
North American	F-86L	Sabre
North American	F-100D	Super Sabre
Northrop	F-89J	Scorpion
Republic	F-84F	Thunderstreak
Republic	F-105D	Thunderchief
Western Electric	Nike Ajax	
Western Electric	Nike Hercules	

Flying Circus Aerodrome

P.O. Box 99, Bealeton, Virginia 22712
(703) 439-8661

Here is an opportunity to look at flying examples of wood and fabric biplanes, and watch an airshow. Every Sunday the Flying Circus displays their airplanes and piloting skills.

The group of airplanes consists of several "classic" airplanes. One of the most famous planes in aviation history is the ubiquitous Piper Cub, and the Flying Circus possesses two Cubs. The Cub probably introduced more people to general aviation than any other airplane of its era.

The Flying Circus also flies Stearmans and Tiger Moths. Largely known for their training roles, the Stearman PT-17 was utilized to train thousands of United States pilots while the de Havilland Tiger Moth served as a trainer for a like number of British Commonwealth pilots.

DIRECTIONS TO MUSEUM: From I-95 exit onto US 17 northbound and travel approximately 22 miles to route 644 (a Flying Circus sign stands at the intersection). Turn right onto 644 and travel approximately 3/4 mile to Aerodrome on left.

If traveling from Warrenton, travel south on US 17 to route 644 (watch for Flying Circus sign at intersection). Turn left onto 644 and travel approximately 3/4 mile to Aerodrome on left.

ADMISSION COST (includes air show): Adults (12 yrs. and above) $8.00; children (under 12 yrs.) $3.00.

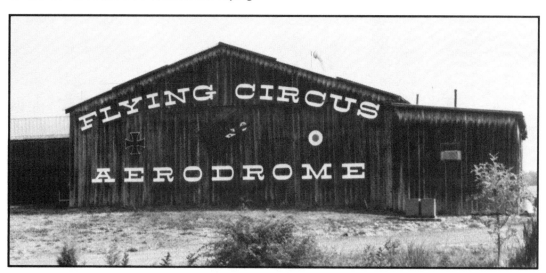

Lettering on the hanger identifies the site as home of the Flying Circus.

HOURS OF OPERATION: Open Sunday 11am-dusk.

MUSEUM NOTES: Display aircraft are indoors and outdoors. Film can be purchased in the gift shop. There is a snack bar on the premises.

A brochure is available.

Display Aircraft

MANUFACTURER	MODEL	POPULAR NAME
Corben	Jr. Ace	
de Havilland	D.H.82	Tiger Moth
Fleet		
Piper	J-3	Cub
Ryan	PT-22	
Stearman	450	
Stearman	PT-17	Kaydet
Waco	UPF-7	

Marine Corps Air/Ground Museum

MCCDC, Quantico, Virginia 22134
(703) 640-2606

The Marines were the first to evaluate and implement the support of ground troops with aircraft. The museum demonstrates air/ground teamwork through exhibits of aircraft, weaponry, equipment and artifacts from the time the airplane was introduced into Marine Corps service.

The collection is comprised primarily of Marine Corps piston-engine airplanes that served during the two world wars and lesser wars. The unique aspect of the museum is in presenting aircraft that were used in the very difficult mission of close air support for ground forces, a facet of military aviation not often addressed by other museums. Close air support requires precise, low-altitude flying to assure the target is struck while reducing the possibility of hitting friendly forces. This type of attack also exposes the aircraft to fire from enemy ground forces.

During the 1920s and 1930s, Boeing was a manufacturer of fighter planes for the American military. In 1927 Boeing delivered to the Navy the FB-5, the first carrier-based fighter plane. Twenty-seven were built and saw service aboard the Navy's first aircraft carrier, the Langley. *The planes later flew in Marine Corps units. The FB-5 was powered by a Packard engine rated at 520 hp.*

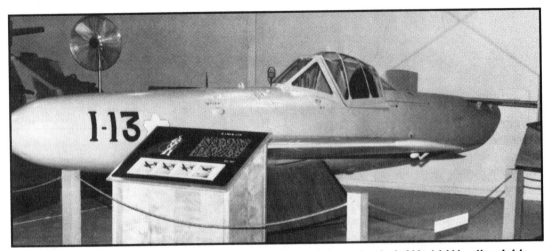

The most sophisticated airplane used by the Japanese in their World War II suicide air attacks was the Kugisho Ohka rocket plane. Nicknamed "Baka", meaning fool, by U.S. personnel, the plane was dropped from a bomber and powered by three solid-fuel rockets. The small size, less than 20-foot wing span, and high speed, over 550 mph, made them difficult targets and highly effective.

DIRECTIONS TO MUSEUM: From I-95 take exit for Quantico Marine Base. Follow signs to base and follow directions provided by guard at gate.

ADMISSION COST: Free.

HOURS OF OPERATION: Open 10am-5pm Tuesday-Sunday from April 1 to November 26. Closed Monday. Closed Easter and Thanksgiving.

MUSEUM NOTES: Display aircraft are indoors and outdoors. No restaurants are nearby.

A brochure is available.

Display Aircraft

MANUFACTURER	MODEL	POPULAR NAME
Beech	JRB-4	Expeditor
Bell	HTL-2	
Boeing	F4B-3	
Boeing	FB-5	
Convair	OY-1/2	Sentinel
Curtiss (replica)	A-2	
de Havilland	DH-4	
Douglas	R4D-6	Skytrain
Douglas	SBD-5	Dauntless
Grumman	F4F-4	Wildcat
Grumman	F6F-3	Hellcat

Grumman	F9F-2	Panther
Grumman (General Motors)	TBM-3	Avenger
Kugisho	Mod 11	Ohka
Mikoyan-Gurevich	MiG-15	"Fagot"
North American	B-25D/PBJ-1	Mitchell
North American	SNJ-5	Texan
Sikorsky	HO3S-1	
Sikorsky	HOS-1	
Sikorsky	HRS-1	
Stearman	N2S-3	
Thomas-Morse	S-4	Scout
Vought	F4U-4	Corsair
Vought (Goodyear)	FG-1D	Corsair

NASA Langley Research Center

Visitor Center, Mail Stop 480, Hampton, Virginia 23665
(804) 864-6000

Langley Field was the birthplace of the United States government's involvement with aeronautics. Construction began in 1917 to house the testing facilities of the National Advisory Committee on Aeronautics (NACA) at Langley, which would become the most important flight research center in the world.

The single most important testing device developed and used at Langley is wind tunnel testing. In a wind tunnel a model is suspended while air moves past the model at the desired speed, which may exceed twice the speed of sound in some wind tunnels. A wind tunnel provides researchers with the means to test aircraft designs without endangering pilots and aircraft, at significantly less cost and time. Several wind tunnels are in use at Langley with the largest 30 feet high by 60 feet wide. A vertical wind tunnel en-

The Apollo XII Command Module Yankee Clipper *was launched on November 14, 1969, and carried Alan Bean, Charles Conrad and Richard Gordon on their lunar mission. The mission inspected the unmanned lunar lander Surveyor 3 that had landed on the moon's surface in 1967. The mission also brought back 75 pounds of lunar material.*

ables researchers to observe the spin characteristics of models before the actual plane undergoes flight testing. Spin testing is perhaps the most dangerous portion of flight testing.

Aided by wind tunnel research, Langley researchers were instrumental in designing airfoils, propellers and airframes, as well as testing equipment that might improve aircraft performance, such as retractable landing gear and engine cooling.

With the advent of space exploration, Langley expanded its efforts towards testing and developing space equipment and astronaut training. The first seven Mercury astronauts were trained at Langley. Projects currently underway at Langley include developing an aerospace plane and the construction of large structures in space.

The museum reflects the history and diverse nature of the research undertaken at Langley. The aeronautics section of the museum addresses such subjects as wind tunnels, computerized flight simulation, structural testing, construction materials and future airplanes. In the space section are exhibits explaining the solar system, space and various related scientific concepts. On display is the Apollo XII Command Module, astronaut David Scott's space suit worn during a moonwalk, a lunar orbiter and a full scale model of the Viking Mars Lander. At the museum entrance is a moon rock.

DIRECTIONS TO MUSEUM: From eastbound I-64 take exit 63 onto Rte. 134 and follow signs to NASA. From westbound I-64 take exit 62-B onto Rte. 17 north and follow signs to NASA. Directions to museum are provided at gate.

ADMISSION COST: Free.

HOURS OF OPERATION: Open Monday-Saturday 8:30am-4:30pm; Sunday noon-4:30pm.

MUSEUM NOTES: Display spacecraft are indoors. Film is available in the gift shop. There are no restaurants on the base, however, a wooded picnic site is next to the museum.

A brochure is available.

NASA Wallops Flight Facility

Visitor Center, Wallops Flight Facility, Wallops Island, Virginia 23337
(804) 824-2298

Wallops Flight Facility is operated by NASA's Goddard Space Flight Center located just outside Washington, D.C. (see also page 135). The Wallops Flight Facility mission is suborbital space research. Special rockets, balloons and aircraft are launched at Wallops to obtain research data for scientific projects focused on the atmosphere and space below orbital altitudes.

Wallops was one of the first rocket launching sites in the world with a launching on July 4, 1945. The facility annually sends from 40 to 45 rockets into the atmosphere. Much of the hardware is reusable and the cost is relatively inexpensive.

Wallops is also the site of the only airport totally controlled by NASA. As such, NASA performs aeronautical testing at Wallops in areas such as noise abatement, flight testing and airport terminal research.

The Visitor Center presents an overview of air and space flight, both manned and unmanned, and the contributions NASA and Wallops have made in aeronautical research. There is a moon rock on display that was brought to Earth on Apollo 17, plus other space-related artifacts. "Hands-on" displays demonstrate Space Shuttle operation. Model rockets are sent skyward on the first Saturday of each month, plus every third Saturday in June, July and August.

Several rockets are exhibited including: Aerobee 150, Astrobee F, Little Joe, Nike-Apache, Scout and Tiamat. Also present is a four-stage reentry vehicle.

DIRECTIONS TO MUSEUM: Wallops is located on the Atlantic Coast of Virginia. From US 13 turn onto Rte. 175 eastbound. The Visitor Center is approximately six miles from US 13.

ADMISSION COST: Free.

HOURS OF OPERATION: Open Monday-Thursday 10am-4pm; open daily in July and August. Closed New Year's Day, Thanksgiving and Christmas.

MUSEUM NOTES: Rockets are indoors and outdoors. There is a gift shop, but film is not available. Vending machines are on the premises.

A brochure is available.

U.S. Army Transportation Museum
Building 300, Besson Hall, Fort Eustis, Virginia 23604
(804) 878-1182

Fort Eustis is home for the Army Transportation Center and School. Army personnel are trained in all aspects of the vast transportation system of the Army including mainte- nance of aircraft, motor vehicles, rail equipment and harborcraft. The museum presents an historical overview of the complex worldwide system used to supply the Army. Over 90 pieces of equipment are on display.

The helicopter has been an important vehicle for supplying frontline units and accom- plishing a wide variety of tasks. The museum has twelve rotorcraft exhibited and one of the more unique is the Sikorsky CH-54, known as the Skycrane. The Skycrane is aptly named as its primary mission is the movement of heavy, awkward objects that re- quire the special capabilities of a helicopter. During the Vietnam War, the CH-54 was used to move unflyable helicopters by means of a sling system beneath the Skycrane.

The Army investigates and tests on an ongoing basis new devices or systems for better transportation of men and materiel. In the course of its research, the Army has ex- plored some exotic ideas. On display is one of only two flying saucers known to have been constructed and flown. Known as an Avro-Car, it was an early attempt at vertical takeoff and landing, but it was only capable of rising four feet off the ground. Equally exotic is the rocket belt on display. Designed for personal transportation and proven in

Is this the future conveyance of Army soldiers? Tried and tested by the Army, this mini-hovercraft didn't progress past the testing stage.

Hanging from the ceiling in the museum's outdoor display is this Piper L-4 Grasshopper, the military version of the civilian Piper Cub. While the L-4 was devoid of firepower, enemy soldiers always took anxious note of its presence. For when an L-4 flew over, often times artillery shells soon followed. During World War II, the German Luftwaffe awarded one point towards a medal if a German pilot shot down an Allied fighter, and two points for shooting down a Grasshopper.

flight, the concept was turned down by the Army. A rocket belt was used for a stunt sequence in one of the James Bond movies.

DIRECTIONS TO MUSEUM: Fort Eustis is adjacent to Newport News. From either US 60 or I-64, exit onto Fort Eustis Blvd. and travel west to Fort Eustis. Directions to the museum will be provided by the guard at the gate.

ADMISSION COST: Free.

HOURS OF OPERATION: Open daily 9am-4:30pm. Closed Easter and all federal holidays.

MUSEUM NOTES: Display aircraft are indoors and outdoors. Film is available in the gift shop.

A brochure is available.

Display Aircraft

MANUFACTURER	MODEL	POPULAR NAME
Avro	Air Car	Mark II
Beech	RUH-D	Seminole
Beech	U-8D	Seminole
Bell	OH-13	Sioux
Bell	SK-5	Hovercraft
Bell	UH-1B	Iroguois "Huey"

Bell Rocket Belt		
Cessna	L-19	Bird Dog
Curtiss-Wright	GEM 2x	
de Havilland	CV-7	Caribou
de Havilland	U-1A	Otter
de Havilland	U-6	Beaver
Delackner	Aero-Cycle	
DOAK	V-TOL	
Grumman	OV-1A	Mohawk
Hiller	OH-23C	Raven
Hughes	OH-6A	Cayuse
Hughes	YAH-64	Apache
Lockheed	AH-56	Cheyenne
Piasecki	CH-21C	Shawnee
Piasecki	UH-25	Mule
Piasecki	VZ-8P-2	Airjeep II
Piper	L-4	Grasshopper
Sikorsky	CH-37B	Mojave
Sikorsky	CH-54	Tarhe (Skycrane)
Sikorsky	UH-19	Chickasaw
Sikorsky	VH-34C	Choctaw

Virginia Aviation Museum

5701 Huntsman Road, Sandston, Virginia 23150
(804) 222-8690

The Virginia Aviation Museum has on display airplanes representing the pre-World War II era, when two wings and fabric were the norm.

Several airplanes in the collection are noteworthy. The SPAD VII World War I fighter is one of only eight remaining. The Curtiss Robin is airworthy and a rare example. The Taylor E-2 Cub was the forerunner of the famous Piper Cub series. The Jungmeister was the premier aerobatic airplane of its day and was used as the advanced trainer for German Luftwaffe pilots. The Fairchild FC-2W2 *Stars and Stripes* participated in Commander Byrd's expedition of 1929 and was the first aircraft to fly over Antarctica. The airplane amassed 187 hours of antarctic flying time.

Curtiss Robins were produced in the late 1920s with an enclosed cockpit as an alternative to the more prevalent open cockpit of the era. Two passengers sat side-by-side behind the pilot who was positioned in the center. Robins derive historical notoriety from the 1938 flight of Douglas "Wrong Way" Corrigan. Corrigan, against the permission of authorities, flew a Robin solo from New York to Dublin, Ireland. Asked what his reason was for proceeding with the prohibited flight, Corrigan replied that he actually intended to fly to the West Coast, but his compass had malfunctioned by 180 degrees.

The Travel Air 2000 is a classic airplane from the 1920s. The trainer of the day, the Curtiss "Jenny," was wearing out and the Travel Air 2000 became a popular replacement. The Travel Air Company was formed by legends of the aircraft industry, Walter Innes, Lloyd Stearman, Clyde Cessna and Walter Beech. The 2000 was powered by the readily available, war surplus Curtiss OX-5 engine.

DIRECTIONS TO MUSEUM: The museum is located adjacent to Richmond International Airport which is east of Richmond. From I-64 take exit 47A,B and follow signs to airport and museum. The museum is situated on Huntsman Rd., which is just off the entrance road to the airport.

ADMISSION COST: Adults $3.00; senior citizens $2.00; children $1.00.

HOURS OF OPERATION: Open Tuesday-Sunday 10am-4pm. Closed Monday.

MUSEUM NOTES: Display aircraft are indoors. There is a gift shop, but film is not available. A restaurant is nearby.

A brochure is available.

Display Aircraft

MANUFACTURER	MODEL	POPULAR NAME
Aeronca	C-2N	
Bellanca	CH-400	Skyrocket
Bücker	Bu 133c	Jungmeister

Fairchild	24G	
Fairchild	FC-2W2	*Stars and Stripes*
Heath	Super Parasol	
Monocoupe	110 Special	*Little Butch*
Pietenpol	Air Camper	
Piper	J-3	Cub
Pitcairn	PA-5	Mailwing
SPAD	VII	
Standard	E-1	
Stinson	SR-10G	Reliant
Taylor	E-2	Cub
Travel Air	2000	
Travel Air	D-4000	
Vultee	V1-A	

Fairchild Heritage Museum

92nd Combat Support Group/CCEM, Fairchild Air Force Base, Washington 99011
(509) 247-2100

The Fairchild Heritage Museum is located on Fairchild Air Force Base. The Strategic Air Command is the controlling command for units at Fairchild, which hosts a wing of B-52 Stratofortresses and an air refueling wing.

The museum comprises a variety of military artifacts reflecting both United States and local military history. German and Japanese artifacts are also on display. A library containing historical and military oriented subjects is located in the museum.

An air park adjacent to the museum is the display area for the six aircraft making up the museum's exhibit. The museum's B-52 Stratofortress was the first B-52 to down a MiG fighter, the action occurring during the Vietnam War. Of 774 B-52s built, approximately 250 remain in service. Designed as a deliverer of nuclear weapons, only two B-52s have dropped live nuclear bombs. Those flights were part of atomic testing. During the Vietnam War they dropped massive loads of conventional iron bombs, and in a program of continuous modification, now carry cruise missiles.

DIRECTIONS TO MUSEUM: The museum is located on Fairchild AFB, which is west of Spokane on US 2. Directions will be provided at the Visitors Center at the base entrance.

ADMISSION COST: Free.

HOURS OF OPERATION: Open Monday, Wednesday, Friday and Saturday 10am-2pm.

MUSEUM NOTES: All display aircraft are located outside. Film is available in the gift shop. Restaurants are nearby.

A brochure is available.

Display Aircraft

MANUFACTURER	MODEL	POPULAR NAME
Boeing	B-52D	Stratofortress
Douglas	C-47D	Skytrain
Lockheed	T-33	Shooting Star
McDonnell	F-101C	Voodoo
North American	F-86D	Sabre
Republic	F-105G	Thunderchief

McChord Air Museum
62 MAW/CVM, McChord Air Force Base, Washington 98438
(206) 984-2485

McChord Air Force Base is a component of the Military Airlift Command. Operating Lockheed C-141 Starlifters, McChord is a major airport for transport to Pacific destinations.

McChord was conceived as a bomber base before World War II. In the museum's collection is a Douglas B-18A Bolo. At the outbreak of war, there were more B-18s than any other bomber in the Air Corps. Outmoded by then current standards, the airplanes were relegated to training and coastal defense missions. The Bolo reflects the pre-war bombing concept before the strategic bombing philosophy evolved. The B-23 on display demonstrates the attempt by Douglas to update the B-18 with more powerful engines and fuselage changes. However, the B-23 did not inspire the military and only 38 were manufactured.

Also in the collection is the last T-33A Shooting Star built for the Air Force. Lockheed built it in 1948. Thousands of Air Force pilots were first introduced to jet aircraft while undergoing training in a T-33. After phasing out as trainers, many T-33s served as squadron "hacks" performing utility flights and building flight time.

DIRECTIONS TO MUSEUM: McChord AFB is just south of Tacoma. From I-5 exit onto Bridgeport Ave. and follow signs to McChord AFB. Bridgeport ends at main gate for McChord. Directions to museum will provided at main gate.

ADMISSION COST: Free.

HOURS OF OPERATION: Open Tuesday-Sunday noon-4pm. Closed Monday. Closed major holidays.

MUSEUM NOTES: Display aircraft are outdoors. There is a gift shop, but film is not available. A restaurant is nearby.

A brochure is available.

Display Aircraft

MANUFACTURER	MODEL	POPULAR NAME
Douglas	B-18A	Bolo
Douglas	B-23	
Douglas	C-47	Skytrain
Douglas	C-124	Globemaster II
Fairchild	C-82	Packet
Lockheed	T-33A	Shooting Star

Museum of Flight

9404 East Marginal Way South, Seattle, Washington 98108
(206) 764-5700

The Museum of Flight presents a broad-based view of aviation history. The museum is situated in Seattle where Boeing Aircraft Company is the prominent employer in the region. The well-being of Boeing directly affects Seattle as reflected by the historical artifacts found in the museum that trace Boeing's history. Anyone familiar with aviation recognizes Boeing's presence in military and civilian aviation history, from the huge bombers to the jet airliners.

Unlike most museums which are situated in refurbished hangers or cavernous, dark buildings, the Museum of Flight is enclosed by an airy glass and steel structure. Several aircraft are suspended from the ceiling as if in flight. An interesting view is from one of the upper levels.

In the foreground of this view of the museum is a Boeing 80A. The plane was restored after finding it on a garbage heap in Anchorage, Alaska. Air travel on the Model 80 was a step up with such amenities as hot and cold running water and leather seats. Besides manufacturing airplanes, Boeing also operated Boeing Air Transport, which eventually merged with four other air transport companies to become United Airlines in 1931.

Unique among the museum's aircraft is an Aerocar III that can be converted from car to airplane in ten minutes, a 1929 Boeing 80A-1 trimotor, the first Boeing airplane, a Stearman C-3B, a Swallow mailplane and a Curtiss Robin. The aircraft on display encompass aviation history from first flight to the modern era.

Of particular interest is the "Red Barn." Dating back to the earliest days of the Boeing Company, and listed on the National Historic Register, the Red Barn was the manufacturing facility for the wood era aircraft. Originally situated near the bay, it was moved to its present site, then restored. Artifacts and exhibits in the Red Barn outline Boeing's history and demonstrate to the visitor the craftsmanship necessary to produce wood and fabric airplanes.

The museum is located adjacent to the taxiways and runways of King County International Airport (Boeing Field), which ranks among the fifteen busiest airports in the country. Airplanes using the airport range from small planes to massive airliners, providing an interesting flying show during peak operating hours.

DIRECTIONS TO MUSEUM: From I-5 take exit 158 then turn right onto East Marginal Way. Follow signs to museum.

HOURS OF OPERATION: Open daily 10am-5pm, until 9pm Thursday and Friday. Closed Christmas.

ADMISSION COST: Adults $4.00; teenagers (13-18 yrs.) $3.00; children (6-12 yrs.) $2.00.

MUSEUM NOTES: Display aircraft are indoors and outdoors. Film is available at the gift shop. There is a restaurant nearby.

A brochure is available.

Display Aircraft

MANUFACTURER	MODEL	POPULAR NAME
"B&W" (replica)	C	
Aerocar III		
Aeronca	C-2	
Aeronca	L-3B	
Beech	18	
Bensen	B-8M	
Boeing	80A-1	
Boeing	B-17F	Flying Fortress
Boeing	P-12	
Boeing	WB-47E	Stratojet
Bowers	Fly Baby	
Curtiss	JN-4D	"Jenny"
Curtiss	Robin	
Dornier	DO.27	
Douglas	A-4F	Skyhawk
Douglas	DC-3	

Douglas	DC-3	
Durand	Mark V	
Eipper	Cumulus	
Fairchild	24W	
Fournier	RF-4D	
Grumman	F9F-8	Cougar
Gyrodyne	QH-50C	
Hiller	12E	
Kasperwing	180B	
Let	LF-107	Lunak
Lilienthal Glider (replica)		
McAllister	Yakima Clipper	
McDonnell	Mercury Spacecraft (replica)	
North American Rockwell	Apollo Command Module	
Northrop	YF-5A	Freedom Fighter
Piasecki	H-21B	Workhorse
Rutan	Quickie	
Rutan	VariEze	
Stearman	C-3B	
Stearman	PT-13A	Kaydet
Stinson	SR	Reliant
Swallow		
Taylorcraft	A	
Wickham	B	
Wright Glider (replica)		

Pearson Air Museum

1105 E. 5th Street, Vancouver, Washington 98661
(206) 694-7026

The museum is situated on Pearson Airpark, the oldest operating airfield in the United States. Operations at the field date from the landing of a dirigible in 1905. Airplane use began in 1911 and the site was an important terminal for civilian and military flying in the Northwest during aviation's early years. The Pearson Air Museum serves to preserve the heritage of flying at the field.

The airplane collection is extensive and focuses on planes of World War II or earlier vintage, although there is an Apollo spacecraft simulator as well. The airplanes are privately owned and flyable, so some airplanes may not be present at all times.

On display is a Cessna Airmaster. The Airmaster was designed by Dwane Wallace, nephew of Clyde Cessna, founder of Cessna Aircraft Company. Sales of the Airmaster kept the company afloat during the lean Depression years. Clyde Cessna retired in 1936 and Wallace succeeded him as president until his retirement in 1983.

DIRECTIONS TO MUSEUM: From I-5 exit onto Mill Plain Blvd. and travel east to Ft. Vancouver Way. Turn right onto Ft. Vancouver Way then turn left onto 5th St. and follow to museum.

ADMISSION COST: Adults $2.00; children $1.00.

HOURS OF OPERATION: Open Wednesday-Sunday 10am-5pm during summer months. Open Wednesday-Sunday noon-5pm during winter months. Closed Monday and Tuesday all year.

MUSEUM NOTES: Display aircraft are indoors. There is a gift shop, but film is not available. There is a restaurant nearby.

A brochure is available.

Display Aircraft

MANUFACTURER	MODEL	POPULAR NAME
American Eagle	Eaglet	
Bellanca	Pacemaker	
Cessna	Airmaster	
Cessna	T-50	Bobcat
Curtiss	JN-4	"Jenny"
de Havilland	D.H.82	Tiger Moth
Fleet	2	
Hawker	Hurricane	
Meyers	OTW	
Naval Aircraft Factory	N3N-3	

North American	AT-6	Texan
Ryan	ST	
Starduster II		
Stearman	PT-13	Kaydet
Travel Air	4000	
Waco	ASO	
Wolf	"Samson"	

EAA Air Adventure Museum

EAA Aviation Center, Oshkosh, Wisconsin 54903
(414) 426-4800

The Air Adventure Museum is an outgrowth of the Experimental Aircraft Association (EAA) and serves to educate visitors as well as commemorate aviation's pioneers and significant aircraft. The museum is situated on the grounds of EAA headquarters.

Organized by Paul Poberezny in 1953, the EAA presently lists 121,000 members in 700 chapters around the world. The EAA is primarily concerned with sport and recreational aviation. Particular emphasis is placed on providing the "little guy" with the help and means to enter and stay in aviation. The association works with the government in protecting the rights of the recreational pilot and lightplane owner.

The museum has on display prototypes of several experimental aircraft and kitplanes as well as replicas of the Wright Flyer, the Rutan Voyager and the Ryan *Spirit of St. Louis*. Located behind the museum, Pioneer Airport is active during the summer with antique and classic airplanes often flying. Opened recently, the Eagle Hanger houses warbirds of the World War II era.

Every summer the EAA conducts the world's largest fly-in at Wittman Field, which is adjacent to the EAA grounds. The fly-in is a week-long event drawing several thousand aircraft and hundreds of thousands of people. Wittman Field becomes the busiest air-

Nearly 6,000 Nakajima Ki-43 fighters were produced during World War II, second only to the Zero in Japanese aircraft production. Smaller and cheaper than the Zero, the Ki-43 was superior to early Allied fighter planes, but, like the Zero, failure to upgrade the design led to high losses as Allied fighters improved.

The Super Solution *was built by Emil M. "Matty" Laird, a self-taught airplane constructor and businessman. In 1930 B.F. Goodrich decided to enter the Thompson race and contacted Laird, four weeks before the race. Laird built the race-winning* Solution *(the name was a retort to a previous winning plane's name,* Mystery*). In 1931 Jimmy Doolittle, famed air racer and military leader, piloted the modified* Solution, *now the* Super Solution, *to first place in the Bendix cross-country air race. Rather than stopping at the race's finish point, Cleveland, Doolittle continued on to Newark, New Jersey, and chopped over one hour off the coast-to-coast record.*

port in the world for one week. Attend if you can, but be forewarned that motels in the area are usually full.

DIRECTIONS TO MUSEUM: From US 41 exit onto Hwy. 44. Turn right at the first traffic light east of Hwy. 41 onto Poberezny Rd. EAA is on the left.

ADMISSION COST: Adults $5.00; senior citizens and children (8-17 yrs.) $4.00.

HOURS OF OPERATION: Open Monday-Saturday 8:30am-5pm; Sunday 11am-5pm. Closed New Year's Day, Easter, Thanksgiving and Christmas.

MUSEUM NOTES: Display aircraft are located indoors and outdoors. Film is available at the gift shop. There are vending machines onsite and restaurants are nearby.

A brochure is available.

The cutaway of the Acro Sport I reveals its internal construction. Designed by Paul Poberezny, over 1,000 sets of plans have been sold. Using a Lycoming O-290 engine (125 hp) the plane's maximum speed is 135 mph. The plane is capable of performing competitive aerobatic maneuvers.

Display Aircraft

MANUFACTURER	MODEL	POPULAR NAME
Acro Sport I (cutaway)		
Aeronca	C-2N	Scout
Aeronca	C-3	Master 500
Aeronca	LC	
Bates	Tractor	
Bede	BD-5	
Benson	Gyrocopter	
Boeing	B-17	Flying Fortress
Boeing (Hughes) Super Stearman		
Brock	KB-2	
Bücker	Bu 133	Jungmeister
Cessna	AW	
Cessna	CG-2	
Chanute glider (replica)		
Church Midwing		
Columbia	J2F-6	Duck
Corben	Baby Ace	

The Lockheed Vega displayed in the EAA Museum is painted in the scheme of the famous Winnie Mae, flown by record-setting pilot Wiley Post. Vegas were the first aircraft with both a monocoque fuselage and cantilever wing. A monocoque fuselage utilizes the skin of the fuselage to carry load and distribute stress, thereby reducing the size of the internal framework. The skin of a Vega was constructed by forming a three-layer wood shell in a mold, then fastening the two shells together. The cantilever wing incorporates all structural members within the wing, doing away with all the speed-reducing external wires and braces. Vega construction prompted the name "plywood bullet."

Cricket	MC-12	
Culver	PQ-14	
Curtiss	E-8-7S	Pusher
Curtiss	JN-4D	"Jenny"
de Havilland	Mk B.35	Mosquito
de Havilland	DHC1	Super Chipmunk
Douglas	A-1	Skyraider
EAA Biplane		
Eipper	MX-1	Quicksilver
Elmendorf Jackrabbit		
Erco	Ercoupe	
Fairchild	FC-2W	

The Mosquito was designed during 1938 by de Havilland as an unarmed, daylight bomber, but was initially turned down by Britain's Royal Air Force (RAF). The RAF reconsidered and ordered production after redefining the plane's mission as reconnaissance. To save the use of critical metal, the plane was built of wood. Over 7,000 Mosquitos were built in Britain, Canada and Austrailia in variations that included reconnaissance, bomber, fighter, torpedo and trainer.

Fokker (replica)	Dr.I	Triplane
Glasair		
Grumman	F8F-2	Bearcat
Heath	LNA-40 Super Parasol	
Heath	Super Parasol	
Laird (replica)	"Super Solution"	
Lancair	200	
Langley (replica)	Aerodrome	
Lockheed	5C	Vega
Lockheed	F-80	Shooting Star
Lockheed	P-38J	Lightning
Lockheed	T-33	Shooting Star
Long	LA1	Midget
Luscumbe	Phantom 1	
Meyer	Little Toot	
Monocoupe	113	
Nakajima	Ki-43-II	Hayabusa "Oscar"
North American	F-86	Sabre
North American	F-100	Super Sabre
North American	XP-51	Mustang
Northrop	F-89	Scorpion

Parker	American Special	
Payne	Knight Twister	
Pereira	Osprey II	
Pitts	S-2	
Pober	P-9 Pixie	
Pober	Sport P-5	
Republic	F-84	Thunderjet
Republic	F-84F	Thunderstreak
Rotorway	Scorpion	
Royal Aircraft Factory (replica)	S.E.5	
Rutan	Quickie	
Rutan	VariEze	
Ryan	SCW-145	
Ryan (replica)	NYP	*Spirit of St. Louis*
Schempp-Hirth	Nimbus	
Smith	DSA-1 Miniplane	
Smyth	Sidewinder	
Stinson	L-5	Sentinel
Stits	*Baby Bird*	
Stits	SA-2A	*Sky Baby*
Stolp	SA-300	*Starduster Too*
Taylorcraft	BF-50	
Thorp	T-18	
Wittman	D-12	*Bonzo*
Wright Flyer (replica)		

Air Shows

Each year, millions of people travel to airfields to watch skillful pilots demonstrate their piloting prowess and the capabilities of their aircraft. From the first days of ballooning, aircraft have been attractions.

In the early 1900s, just the sight or anticipated presence of an airplane would draw a sizeable crowd. A gathering of airplanes became an event. As piloting skills and airplane construction improved, the flying event became a spectacle with a circus atmosphere, one-upmanship was the credo of the air show performer. But accidents ensued and the government clamped down on the "death-defying" acts, resulting in more responsible promotions. World War II, Korea and Viet Nam brought military airpower to the attention of the public, which wanted to see the planes they had built, paid for, read about and seen in the media. Today's air shows provide the spectator with a blend of highly polished civilian performers and impressive military demonstrations, plus acres of aircraft on display.

But air shows are not just grandiose, act-a-minute spectaculars performed at metropolitan airports, there's also the air shows conducted at smaller rural airfields. These smaller events may present only one "big-name" act, but the occasion provides a friendly, relaxed atmosphere to watch and discuss airplanes. For those who are interested in seeing particular types, models or brands of aircraft, there are fly-ins promoted by special-interest clubs and associations. These organizations pick an airport as a congregating point and fly-in for a weekend. The emphasis may be as broad as including all biplanes, or con-fined to a particular make or model airplane, such as Beech Staggerwings. The admission price, if any, is usually minimal and the pilot/owner generally likes to talk about his or her pride and joy.

Obtaining information on local air shows depends on the local media. Large events are usually covered, but information on small events and air shows elsewhere in the country may be unavailable, or hard to obtain. Most aviation magazines have event calendars that list the major air shows, but for more detailed listings, aviation tabloids are better sources. Two very good newspapers are *Atlantic Flyer* and *Pacific Flyer* (the papers divide the country roughly at the Mississippi River). Each monthly issue provides listings for several months. Keep in mind that any event is subject to last-minute postponement or cancellation. Contact the *Flyers* at the following addresses and phone numbers:

Atlantic Flyer
Civil Air Terminal
Hanscom Field
Bedford, MA 01730
(617) 274-7208

Pacific Flyer
3355 Mission Ave.
Suite 213
Oceanside, CA 92054
(619) 439-4466

An additional source of air show information is the International Council of Air Shows (ICAS). This organization sponsors the Flight Line Club. Membership in the club provides a newsletter with air show schedules, stories about performers and

Air Force Thunderbirds

industry news. Contact ICAS at the following address and phone number:

ICAS
Flight Line Club
1931 Horton Rd., Ste. 7
Jackson, MI 49203
(517) 782-4466

There are many outstanding air show performers. The two top attractions are the Air Force Thunderbirds and the Navy Blue Angels.

The Air Force Thunderbirds

Organized during the infancy of the jet age, the United States Air Force Thunderbirds have demonstrated their flying skills before more than 245 million amazed spectators around the world. The Thunder-

birds have performed for presidents, potentates and fans in 53 countries. An appearance by the `Birds makes any air show a major attraction. In 1987 the "Ambassadors in Blue" flew before their largest single-day crowd when 2,250,000 people followed their smoke trails above Coney Island, New York.

The Thunderbirds were established at Luke Air Force Base in 1953 and took to the air in F-84G Thunderjets, later changing to the swept-wing F-84F version. The unit was originally named the "Stardusters," but the name didn't catch on and the legendary bird of Indian lore was chosen. In 1956 the team moved to its present home at Nellis Air Force Base on the outskirts of Las Vegas, Nevada. That same year the team transitioned to the F-100 Super Sabre, their demo plane for the next 13 years, the longest they would perform in any plane model. During sub-sequent years the Thunderbirds flew the F-105 Thunderchief, F-4 Phantom II, T-38 Talon and F-16 Fighting Falcon, the current team airplane.

The Thunderbirds are comprised of not only the pilots, but also officers and enlisted personnel who volunteer to be members of the elite team. Positions with the team are highly sought and prestigious, but the price is grueling hours to meet the team's demanding schedule. Also take note of the Thunderbird ground personnel. Just like the pilots, they are the best in the Air Force at their specialty.

The Thunderbirds are listed on USAF organizational charts as the 3600th Air Demonstration Team. Although the Thunderbirds exist to demonstrate their prowess in the air, they are officially attached to a regular Air Force unit. The Thunderbird team must be capable, should a military emergency arise, to repaint and configure the airplanes for combat within 72 hours.

Presently, the `Birds are flying the General Dynamics F-16 Fighting Falcon. The plane uses a "fly-by-wire" control system as opposed to earlier hydro-mechanical systems, thereby earning it the nickname "electric jet." F-16s are capable of flying at twice the speed of sound (Mach 2), but the plane is flown at subsonic speeds during a Thunderbird show.

A guided tour of the Thunderbirds' home base is available on Tuesday and Thursday afternoons at 2 pm. Visitors must notify the guard at the main gate of Nellis AFB that they wish to take the tour. Nellis is situated northeast of Las Vegas near Hwy. 604 or Nellis Blvd.

Contact the Thunderbirds at the following address:

Thunderbirds
USAF Air Demonstration Squadron
Box 9733
Nellis AFB, NV 89191

The Navy Blue Angels

Since 1946 over 230 million people have witnessed the aerobatic flying routine of the Navy's Blue Angels flight demonstration team. The Blue Angels characterize the professionalism, capability and pride of personnel serving in Navy and Marine Corps aviation units.

The Blue Angels flew their first show in June 1946 at their original home base of Jacksonville Naval Air Station. They first flew in Grumman F6F Hellcats, but two months later the Grumman F8F Bearcat became the team's airplane. With the Bearcats also came the "diamond" formation as an expression of the Blue Angels prowess at precision flying. The traditional blue and gold color scheme was introduced in 1949 as well as the team's first jet, the Grumman F9F-2 Panther. The team was disbanded in 1950, but reorganized in 1951 at Corpus Christi Naval Air Station. A later version of the Panther was flown until 1955 when the Angels were relocated to their present home, Pensacola Naval Air Station, and the Grumman F9F-8 Cougar became the team's plane. Subsequent seasons were flown in Grumman F11F Tigers, McDonnell Douglas F-4J Phantoms, McDonnell Douglas A-4F Skyhawks and McDonnell Douglas F/A-18 Hornets. The Angels flew the A-4 Skyhawks for the longest period, 12 years.

Navy Blue Angels

Each year approximately fifty Navy and Marine Corps aviators are selected to undergo the interview process needed to select members for future openings. From the candidates, the Angels will pick two or three new flying members for next year's team. The squadron commander, also the formation flight leader, or Number 1, is selected by the Navy. There are over 100 personnel in the unit and selection for the non-flying positions, enlisted as well as officers, is considered recognition of outstanding performance.

The diamond formation is the centerpiece for the Angels' air routine. Traditionally, the Number 2 position—on the right wing of the leader—is filled by a Marine Corps pilot. The Number 4, or rear plane, is flown by an Angel from the previous year's team. This places an experienced team member in a position to look over the formation and survey the other planes for potential trouble.

Attending, and often participating in the show, is *Fat Albert*, a Lockheed C-130 Hercules. *Fat Albert* is a flying workshop and supply plane for the maintenance and ground crews. The air and ground crews for the C-130 are selected from the Marine Corps with the same criteria established for the remainder of the Angels team. *Fat Albert* is equipped for jet-assisted takeoff (JATO) with rockets installed on each side of the fuselage. Firing the rockets during takeoff boosts the plane into the air at a 45-degree climbout while using less than 1,500 feet of the runway—an impressive sight.

During the year, the Blue Angels will normally travel approximately 140,000 miles. In addition to the time spent flying and preparing for air shows, members of the Angels also spend any available time performing public service and recruiting duties. Officers and enlisted personnel visit schools, hospitals and local functions and as ambassadors for the Navy and Marine Corps.

The Angels currently fly the McDonnell Douglas F/A-18 Hornet. The Hornet is a multi-mission, high performance tactical aircraft that was designed to perform both fighter and attack missions. Although all of the Angel's maneuvers are flown at subsonic speeds, the F/A-18 is capable of a maximum speed of 1,190 mph. Hornets are "state-of-the-art" and should serve as front-line aircraft into the next century.

Contact the Blue Angels at the following address:

Blue Angels
Public Affairs Office
U.S. Navy Flight Demonstration Squadron
Pensacola Naval Air Station, FL 32508

Aircraft Locator

Bibliography

Anderton, David A., *The History of the U.S. Air Force*. Crescent Books, New York, 1981.

Angelucci, Enzo, and Bowers, Peter. *The American Fighter*. Orion Books, New York, 1985.

Angelucci, Enzo. *World Encyclopedia of Civil Aircraft*. Crown Publishers, New York, 1981.

Boyne, Walter J. *The Aircraft Treasures of Silver Hill*. Rawson Associates, New York, 1982.

Christy, Joe. *The Illustrated Handbook of Aviation and Aerospace Facts*. TAB Books, Blue Ridge Summit, PA, 1984.

Epic of Flight, The, a series. Time-Life Books, Alexandria, VA, 1980-1983.

Fahey, James C. *U.S. Army Aircraft 1908-1946*. Ships and Aircraft, New York, 1946.

Fahey, James C. *USAF Aircraft 1947-1956*. Air Force Museum Foundation, Wright-Patterson AFB, OH, 1978.

Gunston, Bill, and Spick, Mike. *Modern Fighting Helicopters*. Crescent Books, New York, 1986.

Gunston, Bill, ed. *The Encyclopedia of World Air Power*. Crescent Books, New York, 1986.

Gunston, Bill. *The Illustrated Directory of Fighting Aircraft of World War II*. Prentice Hall, New York, 1988.

Larkins, William T. *U.S. Navy Aircraft 1921-1941/U.S. Marine Corps Aircraft 1914-1959*. Orion Books, New York, 1988.

Montgomery, M.R., and Foster, Gerald. *A Field Guide to Airplanes*. Houghton Mifflin, Boston, 1984.

Roberts, Michael. *The Illustrated Directory of the United States Air Force*. Crescent Books, New York, 1989.

Terzibaschitsch, Stefan. *Aircraft Carriers of the U.S. Navy*, 2nd ed. Naval Institute Press, Annapolis, MD, 1989.

Wagner, Ray. *American Combat Planes*, 3rd ed. Doubleday, Garden City, NY, 1982.

Wood, Derek. *Jane's World Aircraft Recognition Handbook*, 4th ed. Jane's Information Group, Alexandria, VA, 1989.

Yenne, Bill. *The Encyclopedia of US Spacecraft*. Exeter Books, New York, 1985.

Index

See also Aircraft Locator starting on page 291 for listing of aircraft on display in museums and air parks.

Doug Brendel
"The Outsidah"

Ipswich in Stitches

THE OUTSIDAH'S GREATEST HITS SO FAR

Front cover design: Kristina Brendel
Inspiration: The People of Ipswich, Massachusetts
Back cover photography: Oleg Yarovenko

ISBN 978-1-67803-364-4

www.DougBrendel.com

Printed in the United States of America

CONTENTS

Welcome to Ipswich!................................1

Silly idea, isn't it? Yes, mostly

Stop reading.

Stop, I said.

Why are you still reading?

It's amazing, in a way, that you're still reading.

Some 300 times over the course of nearly a decade, I have elbowed my way into the consciousness of unsuspecting readers as "The Outsidah."

Yeah, 300 newspaper columns and online posts. Sheesh.

I came up in Chicago in the days when great newspapers — the *Tribune*, the *Sun-Times*, the *Daily News* (R.I.P.) — featured famous columnists: Mike Royko, Irv Kupcinet, Siskel & Ebert, the complicated Bob Greene. People on the train would say, "Did you see what Royko said today?" I wanted to be Royko! I still do. Of course, he wrote 7,500 columns in his lifetime, which puts me some 7,200 behind him. If you haven't stopped reading yet, something tells me you're not going to last another 7,200 rounds of this stuff.

But let us pause and consider who, or what, "The Outsidah" really is.

In theory, each of my 300 columns has offered something approximating commentary on life in small-town New England from the standpoint of a newcomer.

In reality, I've basically just sat in my bathrobe in my house in Ipswich, Massachusetts, and said whatever came to mind.

This endless slow-motion fiasco began with Dan MacAlpine, editor of what was at that time the *Ipswich Chronicle* newspaper. He only asked for 500 words at a time, and only once a month; but it all got out of hand. It takes me 500 words just to clear my throat. And after my lifetime in big cities like Chicago and Phoenix, I found life in Ipswich so entertaining, "The Outsidah" could have been daily. Maybe hourly. Sue me; I'm loquacious.

When the *Chronicle* merged with two other papers to become the *Chronicle & Transcript*, one unintended side-effect was that now, six towns instead of just one were subjected to the Outsidah's nonsense. This gave me a vast swath of the North Shore to comment on, which was almost certain to go badly. Instead of only a few thousand Ipswich residents squirming as, for example, I considered the Ipswich train station and proffered a proposal on porta-potty potential (which I still say is a grand idea), now there were housewives in Hamilton, widows in Wenham, and various readers in Boxford, Topsfield, and Middleton, all at risk of being rankled, or simply bewildered, by the Outsidah's odd opinions.

Then a new Ipswich paper, the *Ipswich Local News*, got going, and it comes straight into your mailbox whether you want it to or not, and since editor John Muldoon runs the Outsidah too (at least the columns that talk about Ipswich), now even more people are at risk.

Anyway, for me, it's been a hoot.

For my readers, eh, maybe not so much.

My wife Kristina — who is an honors student in Literature at the University of Massachusetts, so she should know — observes that my first 300 columns have really been just four columns ceaselessly regurgitated. There's (1) the column about local traffic, (2) the column about local weather, (3) the column about local wildlife, and (4) the column reflecting what former Ipswich Town Manager Robin Crosbie called my "morbid fascination with local government."

I don't prefer to think of The Outsidah in such irksome terms. I would say The Outsidah's record is 300 brilliantly variegated essays which have just happened to clump around four utterly captivating themes. With varying results.

For example, in the first 300 columns:

- I have interviewed a cigarette-smoking deer, a mosquito on vacation, and a grieving chipmunk widow, and eavesdropped on a squirrel-couple's domestic dispute.
- I've insulted both Rowley and Saugus so often, it's become a contest, with prizes, and a parade.
- I've been flamed (more than once) for my wisdom about right-of-way on North Shore thoroughfares.
- I've publicly accused a Town Manager of stealing my garbage can. (Charges were later dropped.)
- I've offered major public-service reporting, like my exposé on feral chickens.

And so on. You can see how I've contributed to the quality of life around here, right?

It feels strange, in a way, to have 300 columns behind me. "The Outsidah" has outlasted the Little Neck controversy (during which I patiently taught non-local readers how to pronounce "Foeffees"), the perchlorate crisis (also featuring a pronunciation lesson), the endless "almost finished" construction of Ipswich's High Street bridge (which was good for, I don't know, three or four dozen columns), and the appearance of a bear in someone's backyard. I've commented on and survived countless nor'easters, potholes, and lawn-watering bans — and weathered multiple local elections and Town Meetings — all, I'm happy to say, without losing more than a couple hundred friends. The

Outsidah has had something to say about New Hampshire drivers, cell phones in church, the vending machine at Ipswich Town Hall, and dog poop.

Where else could you get all this valuable stuff?

Yes, I know, it's been mostly silliness. There are far more important things in life than whether Topsfield wins the Chowderfest competition. So I'm going to try to have it both ways: celebrating 300 "Outsidah" columns AND doing something meaningful. Here's how:

This book, *Ipswich in Stitches: The Outsidah's Greatest Hits So Far*, is a compilation of — if not the funniest columns, then at least the least lackluster columns, of the first 300. And **all profits from the sale of this book will go to NewThing.net**, the humanitarian charity that my wife and I lead in the former USSR. See how we're turning this into something meaningful?

NewThing.net provides practical care and support for orphans, abused and abandoned children, children in foster care, the homeless, the disabled, the elderly, hospital patients, and many others in the Republic of Belarus. And because we're all-volunteer on the U.S. side, every penny donated to NewThing.net actually goes into Belarus.

This is deeply rewarding work — and it's *important*. Way more important than this "Outsidah" baloney. Check NewThing.net. You can even sign up for free photo reports, and visit the former Soviet Union without ever leaving home!

Questions, comments, complaints, hate mail, and/or snarky rejoinders will be happily received; just email Unconventional @DougBrendel.com. Also feel free to send up to 7,200 ideas for new columns.

Okay, *now* you can stop reading. I'm done for the day.

Doug Brendel
Linebrook Road
Ipswich, Massachusetts

4

Traffic Is the Best Part

I can't help myself. I keep writing about Ipswich traffic. Rowley drivers. New Hampshire commuters. Right-of-way and left-turn signals and that funky green and white double line along the outer edges of Linebrook Road. What a fantastic world we live in!

I spend most of my life in the confines of my antique house; I may spend fewer hours per month driving than just about anyone in town — and yet my moments behind the wheel so completely consume my internal hard drive that when it comes time to write "The Outsidah," traffic is often all I can think of. Every time I write about something other than traffic, it's the result of a superhuman act of the will.

Okay, turn on your right blinker and let's get going.

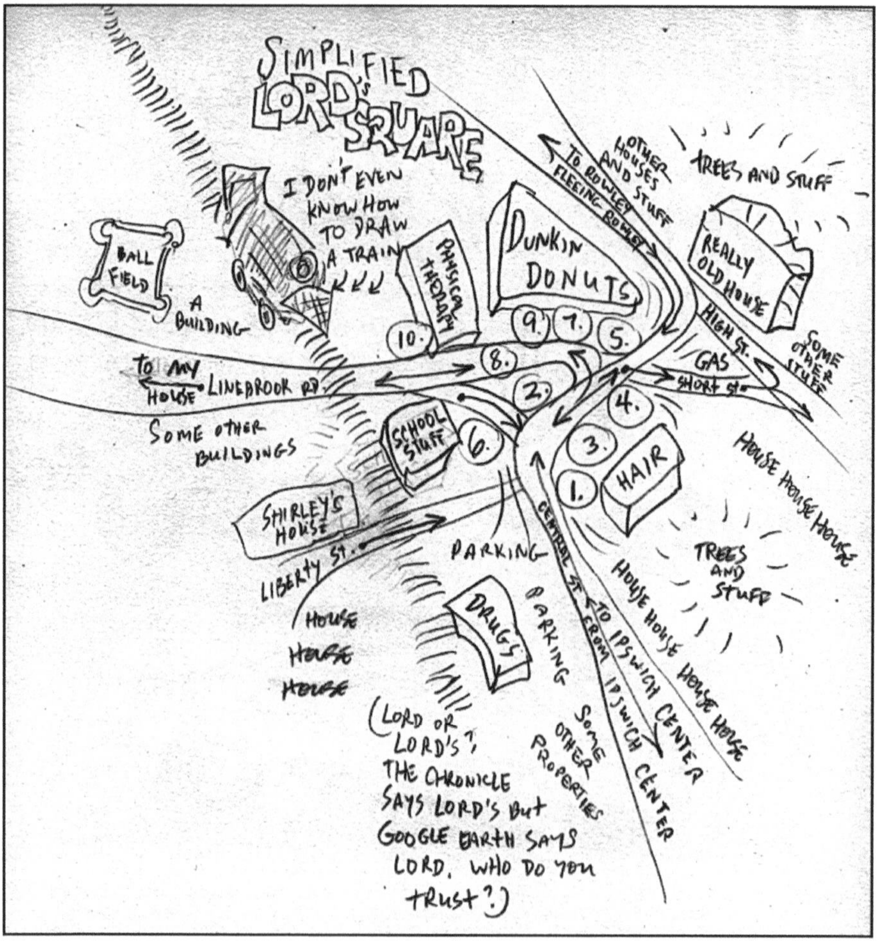
SIMPLIFIED LORD'S SQUARE
I DON'T EVEN KNOW HOW TO DRAW A TRAIN
BALL FIELD
A BUILDING
PHYSICAL THERAPY
DUNKIN DONUTS
OTHER HOUSES AND STUFF
TO ROWLEY
FLEEING ROWLEY
TREES AND STUFF
REALLY OLD HOUSE
HIGH ST.
SOME OTHER STUFF
GAS
SHORT ST.
TO MY HOUSE
LINEBROOK RD
SOME OTHER BUILDINGS
SCHOOL STUFF
HAIR
HOUSE HOUSE HOUSE
SHIRLEY'S HOUSE
LIBERTY ST.
PARKING
CENTRAL ST TO IPSWICH CENTER
FROM IPSWICH CENTER
HOUSE HOUSE HOUSE HOUSE
TREES AND STUFF
DRUGS
PARKING
HOUSE HOUSE HOUSE
SOME OTHER PROPERTIES
(LORD OR LORD'S?, THE CHRONICLE SAYS LORD'S but GOOGLE EARTH SAYS LORD. WHO DO YOU trust?)

February 10th, 2011

How to Get to My House

I'm new to Ipswich. Forgive me.

I adore this town. I chose it. But now that I've lived here about 18 months, I confess – as a hopeless former non-New Englander – there are some details that confuse me.

Like Lord's Square, for example. Dunkin Donuts, Rite-Aid.

I remember the first time I drove into Ipswich center from the north. I remember my first encounter with Lord's Square. I didn't realize then, of course, that it's called Lord's Square. Today, an 1872 map of the town hangs in my living room, and you can see why it's called "Lord's" — because the Lord family seems to have owned just about everything in the neighborhood back then.

But my first time passing through, I wasn't calling it "Lord's Square." What I was saying at that moment was more along the lines of "Whoa! What am I— Where does this—?"

Lord's Square is where Ipswich jerks you around.

The dependable State Route 133, going by the noble name of High Street, has been rolling pleasantly along toward town, steady as you please, when suddenly it veers to the right — as if it saw something terrifying just ahead on Short Street. Then it careens to the left — to avoid becoming Linebrook Road, I guess — and by the time it passes Rite-Aid, it's all straight and calm again, and calling itself Central Street.

To a newcomer, it's like a video game. Except if you die, you don't get to play again.

And it's even more confusing for the uninitiated coming back the other way.

The day came when, for the first time, I needed to give an out-of-towner directions from Ipswich center to my place on Linebrook. It's simple — Central to Linebrook. Simple, except for Lord's Square.

OK, imagine this: you'll head west on Central until the road bends to the right. But at that very moment, you are going to want to turn left. Yes, you're going right because the road goes to the right, but you want to go left. Just trust me, Larry.

So as you're going to the right, put your left turn signal on! Yes, you heard me. You're turning right, and you signal left. Then — you stop. No, there's no stop sign. No signal. But you need to stop — because now that you've turned to the right, it's time to go left. And there's a stream of traffic coming at you. Traffic veering to avoid Short Street. How do I know why they're avoiding Short Street? They just are!

Now pay attention, Larry. You're going to turn left, toward the laundromat. But don't go to the laundromat. Keep turning left. Yes, it's sort of a U-turn. It's Lord's Square. No, it's not actually a square. It's sort of a triangle. But not exactly. *Just be quiet and do what I say!*

OK, now that you've turned right, and left, and left ... I have good news. You're on Linebrook Road.

But watch out for trains. The first sign you see on Linebrook Road is important: NO TRAIN HORN.

If you make it across the tracks, you will probably survive the trip to my house. You've done the hard part. You've navigated Lord's Square.

Larry? Are you still there?

March 10th, 2011

Pushing 40

It doesn't take long, after you move to Ipswich, to understand that this town has a pace all its own.

About 40.

That's 40 miles per hour.

No, it doesn't matter that you're on the 25 mph section of Linebrook Road. People there zip past my house doing ... eh, let me check my radar ... about 40.

It also doesn't matter that you're on that taut little north-south slingshot of Route 1 that slices across the western extremity of Ipswich, where the speed limit is 50. You can be in a great big hurry, but you're stuck behind someone going ... oh, I would say ... about 40.

When you move to Ipswich, they sneak in while you're asleep and embed a chip in your brain; the very next morning, you're not capable of driving any other speed. The sign says 25? Aw, maybe 40 will be OK. The sign says 50? They can't be serious. I'm driving 40! Yeah, 40: the sensible speed.

Oh yes, as you're approaching Ipswich center, you touch the brake. Why? Because the sign tells you to slow down? No. You touch the brake because an elderly fellow is hobbling across Central Street to Marcorelle's, and you will send him careening to the pavement if you hit him, and if you hit him, you will have to stop and get out of your car for the whole police report thing, and you will wind up on the police log page of next week's *Chronicle*. All of which will really, really undermine your speed advantage. And until now — since you've been driving in Ipswich, after all — you've been doing about 40.

Sure, there are parts of town where you don't drive 40 ... places where you drive about 40 the first time, but then you learn not to. Washington Street, for example. Town Meeting debates aside, it's not really about whether to narrow it or widen it or make it a pedestrian parkway. It's about potholes. The first time you take Washington Street — where the official limit is 30 — you go about 40. You do that once. Then, after you get your car out of the shop, with your alignment adjusted and your axles welded back into place and your vertebrae re-sequenced, you pick your way along Washington Street like a land mine tester.

But basically, here in Ipswich, we do about 40.

As a new resident, I learned this first. I learned this before I learned about the Clam Box, or realized the truth about the Feoffees. Before I ever tried to get on the beach without a sticker in my window. Before I attempted to debate selectman Ray Morley about the value of

labor unions. I learned this before all of that: we, here in Ipswich, drive about 40.

Hello, officer, what seems to be the problem?

Well, do you know how fast you were going?

Yes sir, I was doing about 40.

And do you know what the speed limit is?

Yes sir. I'm an Ipswicher. We go 40.

Oh. OK, then. Move along.

June 23rd, 2011

Five-Way Stop

They tried to warn me.

When you've lived in Arizona for most of two and a half decades, and you tell a friend that you're moving to Massachusetts, first their face snaps around to see if you're joking, then they frown because the look on your face tells them that you're not joking, and then their mouth opens — a look which I now recognize as cod. ("Close your mouth, Michael," Mary Poppins said; "we are not a codfish.")

And then, after a certain amount of stuttering, your friend typically starts in with the warnings.

They warn you about the Massachusetts weather. The politics. High taxes and liberal churches and — horror of horrors — universal health care.

But most of all, they warn you about the traffic.

They hear "Massachusetts" and they think "Boston." Boston traffic! Shoot me now!

And of course, they're somewhat correct. Boston traffic is, shall we say, intense. I have a very small car, yet somehow, when I drive in Boston, I manage to be in everyone's way. They honk at me, they yell at me. I am a nuisance to them. When they're driving 80 mph in a 35 mph zone, and I'm doing my best to keep up with them, they still hate me. On the other hand, when I'm standing stock-still, or barely inching along in the colossal crush of cars — someone still finds a way to be upset by the lane I've chosen, or insulted by my decision to switch lanes, or disgusted by the fact that I simply exist at all, because apparently I've taken the space that someone worthier could have been occupying.

However, my friends "back west" are wrong to generalize about Massachusetts traffic on the basis of their few rare experiences with Boston traffic. This is not Boston. This is Ipswich. We live by a much different code. We are a town. We are human.

So we have decided to overdo it in the opposite direction.

You come to a stop at an intersection in Ipswich, and you look to see if there's anyone you can possibly let go before you. If there's any question whatsoever, you wave to them, to signal them that you would very much like them to go first. If there's a line of cars behind you, it doesn't matter. If you have the right of way, and it's enormously confusing to the person you're signaling to, that doesn't matter either.

At "Five Corners" in Ipswich Center, trying to turn from Market Street onto Central, I have had 20-minute conversations with the drivers on Central, entirely in hand signals. A partial transcript:

(Wave.) "Go ahead."

(Double wave.) "No, please, you go."

(Flitting fingers.) "No, by all means, go ahead."

(Hand swooping.) "You have the right of way."

(Hand swirling.) "Yes, I know, but I'm nice. This is Ipswich. Please go ahead."

(Triple wave.) "Actually, you have more traffic backed up behind you than I have backed up behind me; so please, go ahead and turn."

(Fingers spread, pushing motion.) "No, I can't; I have invested heavily in this conversation, and if I go ahead, it will somehow communicate to the people waiting behind me that I was a fool for entering into this hand-signaling traffic-law-distorting exercise in the first place; please go ahead; I need you to go ahead; my honor is at stake."

At this point, I finally go ahead and pull out. I don't care who has the right-of-way. The law no longer matters. Here in Ipswich, we are human beings. Traffic laws are for primitive places. Like Boston.

July 29th, 2011

You Can't Get There From Here

My brother-in-law visited from Dallas recently, and boy was he confused.

He was trying to find his way around by taking note of the numbers on houses. He had this idea that somehow the house number relates to the distance you've already driven from the center of town. Ha! Doesn't he know this is Ipswich? You cannot lay down a scientific grid here — twelve houses per block, eight blocks per mile; forget about it. We're one of the oldest communities in America (after Masconomet's folks, that is), and nobody back then was thinking about master-planning a house-numbering system. They were just trying to coax enough food out of the ground to survive. (Colonial boy: "Please, Mama! No more clams for dinner, or I'm going to sign on with Masconomet!")

You can no more gauge distance in Ipswich using house numbers than you can tell what direction you're going by what street you're on. We're a classic 376-year-old colonial town; our streets are laid out along the precision routes originally established by skittish deer and wandering cows. If you're going SOUTH on NORTH Main Street, you turn LEFT to get onto SOUTH Main Street. That cow had been drinking.

I sympathize with my desperately confused brother-in-law. I grew up on the grid. On the South Side of Chicago, the streets have romantic names like East 59th Street. Then I moved to Phoenix, where they went Chicago one better. Instead of just one-half of the city being numbered, the entire metropolitan area is numbered. I lived at 15261 North 92nd Place. There is also a 92nd Street, a 92nd Avenue, and a 92nd Drive. If you flunked math, you gotta have GPS just to get to the Dairy Queen.

But in those master-planned cities, with their quadrants and their right-angled street corners, you do have a feel for distances. If you're on the 15200 block, you know you're a mile from the 16000 block — eight blocks to a mile. You're driving along, glancing at house numbers, and your brain goes click-click-click-click-click, continuously calculating your position. In Ipswich, we have a somewhat different situation. You don't look at house numbers to calculate distance. You don't calculate distance at all. You calculate time. How far is it? About 20 minutes. Everything in Ipswich is about 20 minutes.

House numbers will do you no good. If he stayed more than a few days, my brother-in-law would have a stroke. In my neighborhood, for example, 3 Charlotte Road is next door to 3 Randall Road. How could I explain this to my brother-in-law? I had no words. "Just look away," I said. I think he was beginning to twitch.

Linebrook Road, the longest street in town, is also the most extreme example of colonial-era house-numbering. The first guy to build a house on Linebrook called it #1. The first guy to build a house on the other side of the road called it #2. It made sense. You build a house, you look at your neighbor's number, you take the next number. Houses on the north side of the street get the odd numbers, houses on the south side get the even numbers. New England rationality! But three-and-three-quarters centuries later, more folks built houses on the north side than on the south side. So my house is in the 400s, and my neighbor across the street is stuck back in the 300s.

And my brother-in-law is still craning his neck, squinting at house numbers, trying to get to Logan.

March 1st, 2012

Checkpoint Clammie

I propose checkpoints.

At the town line, on every major artery, you have to clear the checkpoint.

It's like the guardhouse at Crane Beach, only it's not just for beachgoers. It's for everybody passing through our town.

If you're an Ipswich resident, you don't have to stop. You can sail on through the checkpoint with a little Ipswich resident sticker in your windshield, or a beach sticker will do. Or we'll have a little Mark of the Ipswich Beast, an invisible clam-shaped insignia laser-etched into your palm or your forehead — a little device at the checkpoint will read your insignia and cheerfully wave you on into our fine town.

The others, however, must pull over, to a special parking space, and stop.

Then, you non-Ipswich intruder, you'll have to roll down your window, and the checkpoint guard comes over to you, and subjects you to The Ipswich Driving Quiz:

1. Are you an Ipswich resident, who simply happens to be out driving around without your sticker or the Mark of the Beast? (Yes? On your way. Don't let it happen again.)

2. Have you heard of Five Corners?

3. How many corners does Five Corners actually have? (Correct answer: seven.)

4. Who has the right of way at Five Corners — Central and South Main Street drivers, North Main Street drivers, or Market Street drivers? (Deceptively simple truth: Central and South Main Street drivers always have the right of way.)

(Topsfield residents only:) 5a. What will you do after Topsfield Road turns into Market Street and you come to the stop sign at Ipswich Center? (Answer: Wait until there's an opening in traffic, then pull out.) 5b. Will you nose out into crossing traffic in an attempt to shame someone, or intimidate someone, into letting you cut in? (Correct answer: No, sir, no way, I would never do such a thing.)

6. Have you ever heard of Lord's Square?

7. Is Lord's Square really a square? (Correct answer: No, it's sort of a triangle on Quaaludes.)

8. Approaching Lord's Square from either High Street or Central Street, where are you supposed to come to a stop? (Answer: You don't stop.)

9. As you approach Lord's Square, when it feels like you should stop, what will you do? When you desperately want to stop at the first sharp curve, and then it feels like you *really* ought to stop at the second sharp curve, what will you do? (Correct answer: keep driving.)

10. What is likely to happen if you give in to that overpowering urge, and you stop at one of the sharp curves at Lord's Square? (Correct answer: Multiple vehicles behind me will plow into my rear end, and I will deserve it, because there are no stop signs for drivers passing through Lord's Square. There are no traffic signals. There are not even any "Slow down or you'll roll that Grand Cherokee" signs. If I stop at Lord's Square, I am committing an outrageous offense against the people of Ipswich, because I am making up a whole new traffic rule

entirely on my own, and risking my life, and the lives of others, and the others are probably Ipswich residents, whose taxes are urgently needed. So no, officer, I will not stop at Lord's Square.)

Those who pass the Ipswich Driving Quiz can then continue through the checkpoint and proceed through town — unless they have New Hampshire plates. I've followed New Hampshire plates through town. In my opinion, they'll need a personal escort.

I understand these checkpoints will cost money. I am willing to fund them personally. I understand these checkpoints will require staffing. I am willing to volunteer. I understand the checkpoint guards will be loathed. I am willing to arm myself.

For the cause.

March 22nd, 2012

Give Me Liberty or Give Me Anything Else

I've had quite a lot of unpleasant feedback to my March 1st column, suggesting that out-of-town drivers arriving at our borders should be subjected to a simple 10-question quiz before being allowed to pass through Ipswich driving enormous death-machines on wheels, otherwise known as Chevrolets, Jeeps, and BMWs.

Not that Ipswichers have questioned the wisdom of my plan. No. I have been hailed as a veritable genius, with a certain future in municipal traffic planning. Heaven knows our interim Town Manager won't be contributing to this issue; he's thrown us over in favor of Swampscott.

No, the great body of complaints about my March 1st driver-interrogation plan has come from residents of Liberty Street. They feel I haven't given *them* enough attention.

Some of these folks have not left Liberty Street since it was made a one-way.

They are still trapped there, trying to get out onto Lord's Square.

A few have escaped by turning right onto Central — 4 a.m. seems to be the best time for darting out into the flow of traffic on 133 and 1A — but those who need to cross traffic to join the northbound hordes heading toward Rowley are, for the most part, still stuck on Liberty Street.

And this is not just about turning left or right. Heaven forbid you should need to get from Liberty to Short Street, to fill your gas tank at the Prime station or get a haircut at Detangles. Cutting across both lanes of traffic is like — well, let's just say it's a good thing that the Whittier-Porter Funeral Home is only one hard right turn and a half-mile up High Street.

Children have been born and raised on Liberty Street, have celebrated their high school graduations on Liberty Street, at grand balls thrown in their homes on Liberty Street, and are still waiting — hoping and praying — that someone will turn off of Washington Street and park in front of their house and come inside and meet them and fall in love with them and take them away to a better life.

But it never happens. Because you can't get off of Liberty Street. It's one-way.

Does anybody else find it ironic that a street called "Liberty" is the most traffic-constricted in the entire town? I dread the day someone in Ipswich town government decides that the street I live on should be renamed "Freedom Boulevard"; that's the day the Marini Farm tractors will queue up and begin an endless 20-mile-per-hour trek up and down the road formerly known as Linebrook. The Parade of Zombies.

(Shocking fact: You can calculate, simply on the basis of mathematical statistics, how long you have lived in Ipswich. The formula is simple: $A \times 3.177 = B$, where A = the number of times you've been trapped behind a farm vehicle on Linebrook Road. The value of B, then, is your years-lived-in-Ipswich quotient.)

Please understand: I have no complaints. I love Ipswich, and I am content to leave the residents of Liberty Street trapped there. It is an opportunity for compassion. When I drop by Rite-Aid for a refill on a certain essential commodity — hearing aid batteries, perhaps, or stool softener tablets — I may take an extra few moments (if the weather is decent) to wander across the parking lot, and check in on our friends there. Our friends who are "on Liberty" but, unfortunately, not "at liberty."

"Hello, friends! How are you doing?"

And of course, they respond graciously, by honking their horns. Because they're sitting in their cars. Trying to get off of Liberty Street.

June 14th, 2012

Showdown at the
O.K. Depot Square

Last week, I was on Depot Square, trying to turn left onto Market Street. Sure, it can take a little while to get an opening in the traffic streaming up from Topsfield Road, especially when the train has just disgorged its commuters. But the practical reality is, eventually you will indeed make your left onto Market. A second seems like a minute, and a minute like an hour; but the truth is, the wait for a vehicle at the Depot Square stop sign is really very, very short. You do not need someone coming northbound to notice your plight and stop, completely busting the most basic of traffic laws, to wave you out — so that now *you* get to do something illegal and unsafe too!

Yet there I was, in my very small car, waiting patiently for a break in traffic, when some good-hearted soul did exactly this. It almost seems that some folks drive around town quivering with anticipation, hoping against hope that they'll find someone to be nice to. And here was one of them. The driver slowed, then stopped dead, giving me a warm smile and an array of hand signals, clearly urging me to embrace the innate kindness of Ipswich's drivers. Or maybe just wanting to play Pretend Traffic Cop.

I might have gone ahead and taken the left, except that at almost exactly the same moment, a southbound driver was approaching this same intersection from the north. This new vehicle was, of course, the very death-machine that right-of-way traffic laws were designed to help you avoid. If I had obeyed the Pretend Traffic Cop in the northbound car, I might have been clobbered by the southbound car.

But instead, the driver in the southbound car noticed the driver in the northbound car, and they decided to have a niceness contest. The southbound car stopped in traffic, the driver began waving his hands even more passionately, and smiling even more warmly, than the northbound driver had — while Market Street gradually clogged with vehicles.

I should have been grateful. It was a lovely moment. Neighborliness in action.

But somehow, in the face of such effusive friendliness — I snapped.

No, I growled to myself, I am not going to pull out and make my left turn. It's wrong. They can't make me do it.

21

And I sat there.

It was not just a niceness contest; it was the Niceness Olympics. The two Good Samaritans kept gesturing, more and more vigorously, their smiles melting into scowls, and soon giving way to what surely appeared to be profanity.

But I refused to budge.

I wasn't really fighting them. I didn't make any of the gestures that came to mind in response to their finger-waggling and palm-swiping and forearm-jerking. In fact, I didn't even really look either one of them in the eye. Instead, I decided to let them learn this lesson at their own pace. I just kept sitting there. At the stop sign. Stopped. Waiting for traffic to glide by. The way it's supposed to.

I took to blithely looking around at random things — Did you realize there are 16 steps in the stone staircase on the property directly across the street? Hey, the fourth button on my radio isn't tuned to any station. Oh man, the things you learn if you look into your rearview mirror — my eyebrows really could use a trim.

What happened next still astonishes me.

I realize now that Ipswich drivers, once they've committed to suspending traffic laws in order to prove how polite they are, will not back down. They will force-feed you their goodness or kill you trying — unless they die first. This must be the same spirit that broke the back of the British Empire.

On that amazing morning, under no circumstances would either driver make the first move. I have no doubt that we might still be sitting there today, with the frustrated drivers behind them cutting new makeshift commuter routes through the Institution for Savings drive-through and the alley beside Green Grocer.

Finally, I was the one who blinked.

In a spasm of frustration and wonder, I gunned it, squealing out into the intersection and wheeling left onto Market. And feeling like a fool, of course, with dozens of drivers staring as I passed them. I, after all, was the moron who had been holding up traffic.

Hey, buddy, their glares seemed to say, *don't you know how to drive in Ipswich?*

February 13th, 2014

Please Pull Forward

I hear there are plans for a drive-through at the Dunkin' Donuts on Lord's Square. Of course such a plan would have to be approved by various committees, subcommittees, departments, officials, Town Meetings, state regulatory agencies, the Church of England, and God.

Please, God: Vote yes.

In the matter of whether Dunkin' should be allowed to build a drive-through, my own personal preference is no secret. On the one hand, on a bright, beautiful Ipswich winter's morning, I can stay seated in my car, casually lower my window, calmly speak to a disembodied voice, and confidently place my order from the comfort of my well-heated vehicle, with Steely Dan in the CD player. On the other hand, I can wangle a parking space, wobble across the ice to the doorway, and stand in line for some number of minutes with people who apparently didn't realize before they left the house that other human beings would be subjected to what they look like so early in the morning.

I think it's crucial for the Dunkin' drive-through to gain approval, if only because of the precedent it will set. After Dunkin', there will be no end to the proliferation of drive-throughs in Ipswich, and life in our grand little town will be even more grand. For example:

- We could have a drive-through at Town Hall. You pull up to the Treasurer's Office, take your auto registration from your glove compartment, flash it at Ann Wright, she takes your $20, hands you your beach sticker, and you're on your way.
- Upstairs, I recommend a Monday evening drive-through for Selectmen's meetings: You pull up, pitch your citizen's query, get your answer, and hit the gas. No need to park, walk up two flights of steps, and fight for a seat among all those concerned citizens.
- I suggest a drive-through at Rite-Aid for flu shots. Roll down your window, roll up your sleeve, *wham!*
- The Clam Box needs a drive-through, but based on the length of the line out front in summer, their drive-through should probably be a tunnel. Otherwise, High Street will be log-jammed halfway to Rowley.
- At my church, I'll be recommending a drive-through Eucharist. You get the liturgy on your car radio while you're waiting in line, and the priest's benediction recedes pleasantly into the background as you pull away.
- And finally, regarding Town Meeting. It's not feasible to have a drive-through, but we could set up a good old-fashioned drive-in. Pull your car into a space on the parking lot, dial up the audio, and there on the big screen appears a 40-foot-tall version of Town Moderator Tom Murphy. How to vote from your car? Simple. Honk if you love the amendment.

March 6th, 2014

Caution: Paid Pedestrian Crossing

If you're sitting at Five Corners, needing to turn left onto Central Street, you're doomed.

Well, maybe not technically "doomed." But you are probably going to sit there for a long, long time. Long enough to ponder complicated questions like "Am I technically 'doomed'?" Or, "What are the mathematical odds of my getting out there onto Central Street without causing an accident?" In fact, you'll have enough time to figure those odds with a pencil and paper. Using long division. Or using an abacus, if you happen to have an abacus in your cup holder.

In any event, you're going to be there awhile.

However, there is hope. You do have allies in this situation. They're called "pedestrians."

People on foot have enormous power in the Commonwealth of Massachusetts. They can stop Mack trucks in their tracks. Since pedestrians have the right of way — and something like super-powered right of way in designated crosswalks — they can stop traffic without a gesture, without a badge, without even a lawyer.

So your most realistic hope for pulling out into the intersection at Five Corners may be a pedestrian who happens be crossing the street. If you're sitting on Market Street hoping against hope to turn left onto Central, your best friend is the woozy housewife stumbling out of the Pub after a few midday beers and crossing South Main to get a massage at Slight of Hand. The moment she sets foot on asphalt, traffic moving toward Five Corners from all six possible directions comes to a nervous halt. This is how 18.7% of all drivers in Ipswich get across Five Corners.

Which means, what we need, to alleviate traffic congestion at Five Corners, is street-crossers. (Not street-walkers. Not cross-dressers. Please read carefully.) Here's how the program works. When you subscribe, you get a little transponder to affix to your windshield, just behind your rear-view mirror, next to your EZ-Pass box. As you approach one of the accursed stop signs at Five Corners, your transponder sends a signal to one of the street-crossers I have hired for your convenience. They'll be stationed at the ten corners we so fondly refer to as Five Corners. Each of them will have a little unit that lights up and vibrates, like the thingy you get from the hostess at a tacky chain restaurant when you have to wait for a table. The moment the street-crosser gets the signal, he or she will start crossing the street. Traffic will grind to a halt. You'll be able to ease your vehicle forward, and by the time my street-crosser has street-crossed, you'll be too far out into the intersection to be denied a place in the stream of traffic.

Proceed, with snickering.

If the subscription program is successful, we'll add kiosks at certain points leading toward Five Corners, where non-subscribers can get in on the fun. For example, as you drive toward Ipswich Center on Central Street, when you come to Mineral, there will be station where you can pull to the curb, pay $5 (cash, please), then immediately proceed to Five Corners. There, a street-crosser will ensure your smooth passage by walking right in front of that Congregationalist SUV trying to sneak across from North Main Street after a chili cook-off at First Church.

As a public service, I intend to hire young people, hard-hit in the current economy, as street-crossers. Young people are also the bravest demographic group, and this is, after all, a stepping-out-into-traffic sort of job. After the business is well established — and assuming no young people have been mowed down by inattentive Hummer-drivers, leading to colossal lawsuits and legal fees — we will begin hiring senior citizens. I'm thinking a senior citizen with a particularly problematic hip could be a hero in this scenario. You not only get through Five Corners yourself, but you make all the other cars wait a really, really long time. This could be the basis of a Premium Club membership option.

Please join.

P.S. Special note to Liberty Street residents: Before you ask, the answer is yes. We do hope to bring our service to Lord's Square.

March 20th, 2014

Take the Ipswich Pothole Quiz

Sure, you think you know Ipswich potholes. But now we'll find out just how *much* you know.

Truth or Myth?

1. The Essex County Cartographers' Society is developing a map of Ipswich which differentiates between potholes, sinkholes, craters, cavities, caverns, caves, chasms, canyons, dips, depressions, basins, bowls, holes, hollows, indentations, ravines, rifts, gorges, gaps, gullies, and gulches. (This is a myth. Such a map could be created, but there is no Essex County Cartographers' Society.)

2. A pothole officially becomes a sinkhole when something sinks into it. (Myth. To become a sinkhole, the pothole must swallow something worth $250 or more, and appear on YouTube.)

3. Potholes can be avoided by driving more slowly. (This is truth. However, many potholes are obscured by puddles, so you also have to avoid puddles. Also, if there are simply too many potholes and

puddles for the wheels of your vehicle to avoid them all, go for the puddles, thereby decreasing your chances of injury to vehicle or vertebrae. After all, not every puddle hides a pothole. Thank heaven.)

4. Potholes are formed by water seeping through cracks in the asphalt, then expanding as it freezes, which enlarges the gaps and weakens the pavement. (This is truth elsewhere, but a myth in our town. Ipswich potholes are actually dug out in the middle of the night by people from Newbury who are desperately short of Plum Island landfill.)

5. The potholes in this town are a nefarious plot by chiropractors and car repair people, perhaps inspired by the nuns at the end of *The Sound of Music* sabotaging the Nazi vehicles. (Myth. We already know who digs our potholes. See #4.)

6. There's a pothole on Linebrook Road you can see on Google Earth. (This is a myth. It's on Randall.)

7. Our pothole guys, exhausted and despairing after this endless winter of thawing and refreezing, have given up and gone to Florida. (This is a myth. According to the Town website last week, the Department of Public Works "is currently in the process of performing pothole repairs throughout Town. We will be focusing our efforts on the main roads and working our way back to local roads.")

   (Bonus item: Our potholes are being left in place deliberately, because of a twisted public-policy decision. This is a myth. DPW Director Rick Clarke did not wake up one morning toward the end of autumn and say to himself, "Hey! Great idea! We could make Ipswich like Beverly!")

8. You can report potholes to DPW through the Town website, or by emailing DPW Clerk Michele Young via micheley@ipswich-ma.gov. (Truth.)

9. Michele Young's inbox is full. (Myth.)

10. If two cars approach each other on Mile Lane where potholes on both sides leave only a single vehicle width available for driving, the car approaching from the north has the right of way. (This is a myth. The right of way belongs to whichever driver has more nerve, and/or better insurance.)

11. The pothole guys are working as fast as they can. (This is the truth. There are only so many pothole guys, and only so much pothole-repair equipment, because there is only so much money in the pothole-repair budget. If we had twice as many pothole guys deploying twice as much pothole-repair equipment, our potholes would be filled twice as fast. Of course this would require twice the budget. Perhaps an override? As John Adams or someone almost certainly said, "Let all complain about potholes except those who complain about taxes.")

12. A nine-year-old in full Pee Wee football gear disappeared into a very large pothole on High Street. (Myth. It was a Volkswagen.)

August 4th, 2014

If I Can Make It There

It was my understanding, upon moving to Ipswich, that I could "go all the way." By train, that is. To New York City, I mean.

This seemed too good to be true, however; and indeed, I found that it wasn't quite as simple as getting on a train and going all the way to New York. This fact became clear shortly after I finally found the website of the Massachusetts Bay Transportation Authority, generally referred to as the "MBTA." (For several months I didn't understand what "MBTA" was; I thought perhaps people were saying a French word, *embitiez*, except that *embitiez* isn't French for anything.)

I quickly discovered that, here in coastal Massachusetts, the train is not necessarily "the train." The MBTA website has "Rider Tools," including a "Trip Planner," which will help you navigate between commuter rail, subway, bus, and *boat*. Boat! I've never lived close to the ocean before, but I am pretty sure that a boat is not a train.

The MBTA website is where I learned that Ipswich is on something called the Newburyport/Rockport Line, and if you catch the commuter rail at Ipswich Station heading toward Boston, you've made a good start. But you can't just stay on the train and get off at New York. You can only stay on the train till you get barely inside Boston. At North Station, they make you get off. Unfortunately, the train that goes on to New York does not leave from North Station. It leaves from South Station. So you need to get from North Station to South Station.

These two stations are less than *seventy-four hundred feet* from each other — so it should be simple. Less than a mile and a half. According to Google Earth, you can walk. Take Canal Street down to Federal Street, cut across to Congress Street, past City Hall, past (ironically) the First National Bank of Ipswich (at State Street, on your right), past Jayne's Flower Shop (at Franklin, on your left; promotional fee paid), passing a total of 14 Starbucks and 96 Dunkin' Donuts, and 25 minutes later, you're there.

But no, I was on a quest. I wanted to stay on the train. *Come on, gimme the train that runs from North Station to South Station.* Imagine my surprise, then, encountering the shocking truth: In 384 years of existence, with one of the oldest railway systems in America, and 394 miles of rail lines, the City of Boston has never put in the 7,392 feet of track it would take to connect North Station directly to South Station.

The solution, for travelers like me, turns out to be the subway, the beloved "T." In my studies, I discovered that the T is not necessarily simple, but it does come in a number of pleasant colors: the northerly-southwesterly Orange Line, the southerly-northwesterly Red Line, the dashing easterly Silver Line, the northeasterly Blue Line (which I want to take simply because it winds up at a place called "Wonderland"), and the venerable granddaddy of the system, the westerly Green Line.

To get from North Station to South Station? No problem. You have choices. You can take the Orange Line to Downtown Crossing, then change to the Red Line for South Station. Or you can take the Green Line to Park Street, then change to the Red Line. (Amtrak officially recommends, if you have luggage or children in tow, just forget the train thing and take a taxi. When a *railroad* service warns you against taking the train, you gotta pay heed.)

Finally, however, by some means or another, you are likely to wind up at South Station, where you can get on a train bound for New York City, and in something like four hours, you're supposed to be there.

So, last week, this was my plan. I arranged to be dropped off at Ipswich Station, and my adventure began. (Ipswich Station is a joy in and of itself, a visually exciting ridged metal roof suspended at a daring angle over a series of artsy benches mounted on world-class concrete.)

The train came.

I climbed on. It was something of a thrill, I confess.

I found a seat. I looked out the window with a deep-down sense of satisfaction.

Soon the conductor was calling out the next stop.

"Rowley!"

How curious.

I have not lived in Ipswich long, but I could have sworn that Rowley was north of Ipswich, as opposed to, say, New York, which is, for example, south of Ipswich.

The most important lesson I learned on this trip is that when you're waiting for a train at Ipswich Station, you're facing west. So if you want to get from Ipswich to New York by train, you have to get on a train that goes from right to left. Not left to right. The train going left to right is going to Newburyport. By way of Rowley.

The second most important lesson I learned on this trip is that it takes 14 minutes to get to Newburyport, and once you're there, it takes 16 minutes for the train to start back again. And another 14 minutes to get back to Ipswich.

In other words, it takes 44 minutes to go nowhere.

October 23rd, 2014

Cashless Ipswich

Great news, Ipswich. Our money troubles are over.

Let me explain.

Have you driven into Boston lately? It's a whole new world. Forget about stopping to pay a toll on the Tobin Bridge, crossing the Mystic River on 1A into the city. The Bridge is alive, apparently. And it has an accounting degree! It will calculate what you owe — and bill you!

If you've equipped your vehicle with an EZ-Pass transponder, you pay $2.50 — electronically, automatically — to get into Boston on the Tobin. (To get your transponder, Google "MassDot" and you'll probably see an EZ-Pass link. Or use the "Highway" tab on the MassDot website.)

On the other hand, if you don't have a transponder stuck to the windshield behind your rearview mirror, you pay $3. How? Here's how. The bridge's cameras take a photo of your license plate as you wheel through, then they mail you a bill. If you don't pay, something bad happens. I don't think it's actually SWAT teams in Registry of Motor Vehicles jumpsuits converging on you with AK-47s, but it's bad. Don't do it. Pay your bill.

So the technology for cashless collections is totally available. Here in Ipswich, it can change everything for us. I suggest we offer a transponder designed to look like a clam, and it would sit like a bobble-head doll on your dashboard. (When you drive beyond New England on vacation, people in parking lots walking in front of your car will say, "How cute.")

At key points all over Ipswich, your Dash-Clam™ will auto-collect fees. Its work will be silent, instantaneous, and painfully apt.

For example: No more pleading with voters for school money: As you drive through a school zone, if you voted "yes," you sail through free of charge. If you voted "no," you get a bill for $500.

Ipswich drivers will be charged the price of an ice cream cone as they pass White Farms heading toward Rowley — because we know, if you don't stop at White Farms, you're heading to Down River.

Drivers leaving the downtown area via Lord's Square have to pay $250 if they stop at High Street. (The first government employee to erect a "DO NOT STOP / KEEP GOING / NO STOP HERE" sign at that intersection gets a night out on the town with the Outsidah, all expenses paid.)

The Town will collect a total of $10,000 a day from drivers who, when the light turns green, make a left turn against oncoming traffic. If you're the only one who commits this grievous violation of the right-of-way, you pay the whole $10,000 for the day. If you're one of two, you each pay $5,000. But on a typical day in Ipswich, you can count on getting a bill for something in the neighborhood of five bucks.

And finally, if you go past my house at 45 mph, even though the posted speed limit has been 25 mph for nearly a mile, your Dash-Clam sends you a bill for $1.2 million.

November 27, 2014

Going, Going, Gone

"Hamilton-Wenham! Next stop, Ipswich!"

Ladies and gentlemen, as our Hamilton-Wenham passengers step daintily off the train — (Oops! Excuse me. Didn't mean to get in the way of your jodhpurs!) — I want to take this opportunity to thank you all for utilizing the Newburyport arm of the Newburyport-Rockport Line of the MBTA's commuter rail service. We trust you've had a comfortable ride up from North Station, or Salem, or one of those other towns down there.

I'd like to speak briefly to our Ipswich-bound passengers in particular. I hope you remaining Rowley and Newburyport passengers will bear with me for just a moment. This is really a message for folks planning to get off the train at our next stop, which is Ipswich Station.

As a service to you, our highly valued Ipswich-bound passengers, we want to be sure we provide all the information you need in order to arrive comfortably in Ipswich. Here's the main thing: We recommend that you use the restroom here on the train, before we get there. The point being: There are no public restrooms at Ipswich Station.

In fact, Ipswich Station is not really much of a "station" at all. Like the train stations in many North Shore towns, it's actually a simple slab of concrete alongside the tracks — with a big rain-roof standing on poles, a few hard benches, and a newspaper vending machine or two. There is no enclosed structure, you understand. (Which certainly means no public restroom facility. If they're not going to build an enclosed train station, they're sure as heck not going to build an enclosed restroom; I mean, that's just logical, right?)

Certainly we hope you will feel free to take full advantage of our lovely and spacious *free* restrooms right here on your friendly MBTA train. You'll actually find that restrooms are a beautiful feature of any and all of our MBTA commuter rail cars, provided the rail car was built in 1987, 1988, 2005, or 2012. If you happen to find yourself in a car built in other years, we apologize for any incontinence — er, uh, inconvenience. (Sorry for the no-bathroom train cars; I guess that's just how the politics were, in those years when train-restroom funds were being appropriated, or vetoed, or filibustered, or perhaps traded away for votes on other, more important bills, like the ban on tattoos, or Sunday liquor sales before noon.)

Your friends here at the MBTA recognize that some passengers may prefer not to use the restrooms on the train, because of — in the case of our male passengers — the inevitable jostling of the train during the actual, uh, release function; and/or perhaps, regardless of your gender, you feel queasy about the whole idea of doing your business in a metal cubicle where similar business has already been done by thousands of strangers on similar train trips; plus, afterward, you can't help but wonder where your business goes post-flush, and when, and how (since, after all, you're moving, rather rapidly, over train tracks), and you can't stop thinking about it.

So, dear Ipswich-bound passengers, as we approach Ipswich Station, if you still need to go to the bathroom but you've decided to wait, we here at the MBTA would like to give you a few helpful pointers, to keep in mind after you de-train at Ipswich Station:

1. Public urination is illegal.

2. Just because there is no public restroom facility at Ipswich Station, you should *not* get your hopes up for a porta-potty. There are no porta-potties at, adjacent to, near, or within a kidney stone's throw of, Ipswich Station. There could be — it doesn't cost much to hire a porta-potty company to put a porta-potty anywhere — construction companies do it all the time. But the Town of Ipswich has wisely determined that if you got off the commuter rail line at Ipswich Station and saw a line of porta-potties, you would be horrified by the tackiness. Unless, of course, they were historically accurate porta-potties. The kind of porta-potties they used in the early 1700s. In that case, it would be OK.

(Plus, to be fair, they've tried porta-potties in the past, with tragic results. Porta-potties in Ipswich have been set on fire, and tossed in the river, not necessarily in that order, and not as part of Ipswich Illuminated. It seems that porta-potties somehow bring out the worst in the Ipswich Vandals & Hooligans demographic. Repeatedly replacing porta-potties? Pricey.)

3. When you leave the train at Ipswich Station, you will naturally head down Market Street. Please note that most of these businesses do not offer public restrooms. If you visit an eating or drinking establishment, you will likely find a restroom available. But if you're buying insurance, having your eyes examined, or purchasing a clever Ipswich-themed fridge magnet, you may just have to hold it.

4. There is a free public restroom inside the Visitor Center, which you can use without eating, drinking, or buying anything anywhere in the Town of Ipswich. The Visitor Center is only a quarter-mile from the train station, the first 80% of which is downhill. If you happen to have brought your bicycle on the train with you today, you'll have no trouble gliding down to Five Corners; keep your momentum up, hang a right at the Pub, coast up over the Choate Bridge. You'll find the Visitor Center — and sweet relief — on your left.

You'll also be happy to know that the MBTA hopes to announce, very soon, a lending program which will make skateboards available to our commuter rail passengers leaving the train at Ipswich Station. We couldn't afford bicycles, but we trust that your skateboard will get you, just as quickly, to where you need to go. So to speak.

Please note that the Ipswich Visitor Center restroom is often overwhelmed, sometimes better attended than the art shows in the next room. So we would ask that you please be patient with the others in line. It is not technically against the law, but it is regarded as somewhat vulgar, to offer cash to the people ahead of you.

What? Oh, excuse me, I'm sorry, I didn't realize. Ladies and gentlemen, let me correct myself. The Ipswich Visitor Center is closed for the season.

"Ipswich! Next stop, Rowley!"

Thank you for your attention, and good luck.

PART II

Ipswich Is Wild Life!

Animals have co-existed with humans since the human Adam gave the animals their names. It apparently took him quite a long time and he was having a bad day when he got to hippopotamus.

In my previous habitats, which were largely urban, I didn't have near as much interaction with the animal kingdom as I have here in Ipswich. So the fauna have inevitably made their way into a number of Outsidah columns.

We're about to begin our safari, folks. Please keep your hands inside the vehicle.

April 19th, 2012

Crow Tableau

It's clear to me that folks who have lived in Ipswich their entire lives — about 13,000 of you, it seems to me — are totally OK with the crows.

I lived in Chicago for decades. We didn't have crows in Chicago. We had pigeons. Millions of pigeons. It was pigeon paradise.

In that city's vast public plazas — sprawling rectangles of concrete punctuated by enormous, puzzling sculptures, places where you were supposed to saunter about, or make out on park benches, or eat your sack lunch on a sunny day — pigeons, by their sheer numbers, made all of these options impossible. It was the early bird version of Occupy Wall Street. There was an immense, warbling ash-colored carpet of feathers and beaks and googly eyes, a covering so thick you could hardly walk. If you could get space on a park bench, one look at where you'd be sitting and you didn't feel like eating your lunch — Chicago is one enormous pigeon toilet — and even less like smooching your sweetie. It was pointless to wave the pigeons away: a thousand fat gray birds would erupt, flapping and gurgling and bumping into each other, only to settle back down dopily right in front of you again.

From time to time, the city fathers would proclaim a pigeon purge, but these were generally halfhearted gestures. This was Chicago, after all, which means most of those pigeons were on the rolls as Democrats, and essential on Election Day.

I lived in Phoenix for decades, too. We didn't have crows in Phoenix, either. We had roadrunners — just like the cartoon, except that in real life they're even sillier-looking. Roadrunners are incapable of walking. They can stand still, or they can jet. When they want to go somewhere, they lean forward and explode into a high-speed Groucho walk. But without the cigar. And without the mustache. Or the eyebrows, or the glasses. But other than that, it's just like Groucho.

But when I arrived in Ipswich, I didn't find multitudinous masses of pigeons, or the zigzag vapor trails of roadrunners. I did, however, find crows.

This is no measly blackbird. This is no little birdcage-sized birdie. This is a major animal. I would never want to be guilty of exaggerating, but it looks to me like a crow could easily fly off with your schnauzer. My neighbor Tanya is a black belt, but I've had crows in my backyard that I would never bet against in a round of kickboxing against her.

These are formidable fellows. They strike fear in the heart of the uninitiated. I can be in my backyard, minding my own business, when a sinister shadow falls over the land, a shadow like a 737. Then another, then another. The crows are coming. I shiver. Once they're on the ground, they survey the grounds and begin their caustic commentary. You don't have to speak crow to know what they're saying — in spite of their apparent partial deafness.

"What?" "What kind of place is this?" "What's to eat?" "What?" "I hate it here!" "So do I!" "What?" "What in the world are we wasting our time here for?" "What?" "Look at that moron!" "What?" "With the beard!" "What?" "Let's hate him!" "What?"

They stalk about the yard, glowering at the world with such disapproval, I almost feel obligated to do something different, just to seek their favor. Maybe somehow arrange a better menu for them? I normally toss out stale Meow Mix the cat refuses to eat; perhaps the crow-gods require better. Premium chipmunk cadaver-snacks? Pâté de fish guts?

To live in Ipswich, one must learn to co-exist with the crows. I am learning. I am a crow-ed student.

September 6th, 2012

Deer, Me

So I said to the deer, in my backyard, "You OK?"

It was only a courtesy, on my part. She looked entirely OK to me.
Like all the other deer who frequent my backyard. Well fed. They eat

the hostas in my garden. There seem to be enough hostas in my garden to supply the entire outer Linebrook deer population on an annual basis. The hostas keep coming up, the deer keep eating them, and I have yet to find a deer dead of malnutrition in my backyard.

This deer seemed comfortable. Not nervous at all. I think they know by now that I won't take action against them, even though they don't legally have any claim to my property. (At one point I tried to take a doe to court to share a portion of my tax burden, but her clever lawyer used that weepy "Bambi defense," and I didn't have a chance with the jury.)

So I tried to be casual, and friendly, to this deer. She was lounging at my backyard pub table, under my umbrella. Sitting on one of my bar stools, with one of her hooves propped up on the next stool. Her fat, hosta-stuffed belly was protruding unpleasantly. But was I going to comment on this? No. I'm trying to be a good neighbor.

"You OK?" I asked her.

She looked at me with that look. You know, that look that deer give you. I don't mean that "deer in the headlights" look, because this was about 5 p.m. so it wasn't even dark. No. She was giving me that other look. It's the look that deer give you when you encounter them in broad daylight. They sort of lower their eyelids and seem to give you a sneer. They look at you as if to say, "What are *you* doing here? You're a nuisance. Your very presence forces me to put my annoying hair-trigger nervous system on alert. Why don't you just go away?"

You know this look. If you have a teenage daughter, you certainly know this look.

"You OK?" I asked the deer.

She leaned back sullenly on the bar stool, tapping her cigarette into an ashtray on my pub table.

"Don't like that sign," she muttered.

"What sign?" I asked.

She cocked her head toward Lillian Drive.

"Deer Crossing," she rasped, and took a drag on her Virginia Slim.

I know the sign well. Yellow, diamond-shaped. Silhouette of a deer jumping across Linebrook Road.

"You have a problem with the sign?" I asked her.

She sighed heavily and took another swig of her Budweiser.

"I don't like where they make us cross," she finally grumbled.

I didn't know what to say.

"Why do you think cars keep hitting deer?" she demanded. "Because they make us cross at the worst possible places." She crushed her butt. "I've lost three cousins on Linebrook Road alone. Every one of them was crossing legally, right at the sign."

She looked away.

I took a breath. "I think they put the signs up where the deer *want* to cross," I ventured weakly.

The doe snorted. "Sure they do," she grunted. "You think I don't want to cross at the light? But no. Ipswich has me crossing in the kill zone. Thanks." She drained her Bud. "Thanks a lot."

I gulped.

"This town is hell for deer," she murmured.

She swung her leg down and stood up from the chair. "Gotta go," she said, heading toward the road without looking back. "Rush hour. Wish me luck."

August 8th, 2013

Banished

That rattling in the ceiling?

That's squirrels, skittering about in the attic of my antique house, living up there without even offering to pay rent or do any of the household chores.

I wonder how they got in there, until I notice a gaping hole chewed in one corner of my roof. A ragged aperture, and growing. Where once there was a beautiful angle, the roof pleasingly connecting to the exterior wall in the style of the era — now the point of connection is ragged, an open scab on my beloved 1817 Federal Period house. *Hee hee!* the squirrels seem to snicker. *We've bitten a hole in your history!*

What alarms me most is that they've put in a doorway without a single Town of Ipswich permit. This could mean penalties — serious fines — possibly loss of membership in the Assistant Building Inspector's fan club. These wretched rodents could ruin my finances *and* my social life — on top of the ugly cavity they've gnawed.

How to fight back? I am helpless. My primary experience with squirrels is *tsk-tsk*ing as I drive by their squashed carcasses on Linebrook Road. ("Too bad," my heathen side mutters. Then my religious side takes over: "Give rest, Lord, to the soul of Your servant [insert squirrel's name here] who has fallen asleep, where there is no pain, sorrow or suffering. In Your goodness and love for all, pardon all the sins he [she] has committed in thought word or deed, for there is no [squirrel] who lives and sins not. Amen.")

In my besieged home, I need help. My squirrel-squatters are eating my mortgaged wood; they have apparently failed to qualify for food stamps. My domicile is being decimated, nibble by nibble. I need a pest professional. A varmint vanquisher.

The uniformed professional who pulls into my driveway is nonchalant. He shrugs. He has fought this evil before, and prevailed. He is armed not with a gun or a poison, but with a small, squirrel-sized door. He climbs up a very tall ladder and affixes the door over the dreadful defect. If I didn't have trouble with the Ipswich building inspector before, I am sure to now.

But this is no ordinary door. This door only opens one way: *out*. A squirrel can leave the comfy confines of my attic, but when he tries to return....

"Honey, I'm home!"

(Skittering and scratching sounds from inside.)

"Honey, it's locked!"

(More squirrel sounds.)

"Honey, come on. Open up."

"Harold? Is that you?"

"What do you mean, 'Harold, is that you'? Do you normally have guys coming to visit you when I'm not home?"

"Harold, why are you outside? Come in the house!"

"I'm trying to tell you, woman! I'm locked out!"

"Oh, for Pete's sake. I didn't lock the door."

"Will you please just open it?"

"It opened just fine when you left for work this morning."

"I know that! But it doesn't seem to be working now!"

(Skittering sounds. The door swings open. She steps out.)

"Look. It works perfectly. You are so squirrelly."

"Thanks a lot. I love you too."

(The door slams behind her.)

"Oh, great. Bang on the door. The kids can let us in."

"The kids went to the park."

(They stare at each other for a long moment.)

"This is how it went for Adam and Eve too, isn't it."

"I hate moving."

August 15th, 2013

Greenheads Are People Too

Two greenheads are dressing in the women's locker room after a long day at Crane Beach.

"Good summer?"

"Nah, not that great."

"Me neither."

"Took a chunk out of Brenda McCarthy today. No big deal."

"I got Heidi Bartlett last week."

"Don Francis in Week 1. Shoulda heard him howl!"

"But such a rainy summer. One day I had to fly all the way to Mitchell Road to find an exposed neck. Got some farmer lady in an orchard."

"Just doesn't seem to be as much fun as it was when we were young."

"Yeah."

"I remember that first summer on the marsh, as a little larva. Almost 200 of us. Starving! Mucking through the mud and the thatch, hungry for anything."

"I found an earthworm that summer."

"I ate my brother."

"You do what you have to do, I guess."

"Gotta bulk up to form that pupa, so you can hunker down for that first winter."

"It is New England, after all."

"But then — wow! Busting out of that pupa in the spring — *kapow!* Hormones!"

"I know, right? I was like, Where's Mr. Right? Aw, heck, you'll do!"

(A sigh.) "It was good, that first time."

"Yeah, but then *wham!* You're pregnant! And then *wham!* You're delivering. And delivering, and delivering."

"I guess it just goes with being a *Tabanus nigrovittatus*. I had 192 larvae my first time out."

"And then, the moment they wheel you into recovery, *kaboom!* The hunger pangs! Out of nowhere! You've never had a drop of blood in your life, but for some reason, all of a sudden, you can't think of anything but the red stuff."

"That summer, there was nobody, I mean *nobody* on the beach."

"I just started going house to house. I bit Mr. Wasserman."

"Good for you."

"But this year has been the worst. So many good flies disappearing into those black boxes."

"I try to tell them, 'Don't do it! It's a trap!' But they're all like, 'It's big and dark like a horse or something, and *I'm starving!*' And zip! They're gone."

"It's sad. I lost almost a thousand of my closest girlfriends in a single hour last month."

"I swear, I've thought about just throwing in the towel. Shoot into a black box, hang up the ol' bra, call it a day."

"Ginny! No!"

"I'm tellin' ya, I've had 857 kids this summer, and I'm tired."

"You'll feel better soon. I'm sure of it. Our life cycle isn't that long."

"I'm sick of this! The men don't go out and hunt for blood. The men don't plop down in the mucky marsh and pop out 150 babies at a time. The men don't have to dodge flyswatters and bite horse skin and have their dinner punctuated by shrieking children. For the men, it's just sex and veggies, sex and veggies. Nectar! Fruit juice! They have no need for blood protein! They live on carbs! I hate them!"

"Ginny, come on. Hey. I love that green eye shadow."

"Don't try to make me feel better. You're always so cheery. 'Ipswich! We get to live in Ipswich!' Like a world-class beach somehow makes it OK that you have 857 kids."

"Well, you don't exactly have to take care of them all. I mean, look, you're not a mother duck."

"The greenhead life is a drag, Doris. It's all strategy, strategy, strategy. I got Penny Bernard by waiting under the top of her boat. I got Valda Winsloe on the river. But it's getting harder and harder. Chuck Kollars doesn't even roll down the windows of his PT Cruiser during most of July. I got all the way to Jim Engel's place on outer Linebrook, looked around, and I was the only fly around. It was embarrassing."

"I know, honey. Things will get better."

"I'm tired of being written up on Wicked Local. I'm tired of landing on a slathering of Skin So Soft and spending the next hour licking it off. *Glecch!*"

"Come on, let's go get something to drink. There's a Catholic family having a backyard barbecue this evening. A bloody Mary will do you good."

May 29th, 2014

Ant Can't Rant

    Those large black ants? The solitary ones you've seen in your kitchen this spring, marching alone across the counter from the fridge to the sink?

    Those are carpenter ants.

Let me assure you, they're not called carpenters because they "measure twice and cut once."

These guys infest anything wooden — say, your First Period house, or your newly installed Home Depot tool shed. They like to hollow out great cavernous "galleries," and extensive tunnels to get there, in your wooden structure, especially where there's moisture. Like under your window. Or under your deck, your porch, the eaves of your roof. They don't eat the moist, chewy wood, like a termite. They just bite off the wood, tiny-little-ant-sized-mouthful by tiny-little-ant-sized-mouthful, and spit it out, and then do it again. And again. Until one day, your house groans lugubriously and caves in on itself.

What carpenter ants *do* eat is gross: They feed mostly on dead insects. (One favorite snack: sucking the bodily fluids out of a dead bug head.) But they send out scouts to find these tasty morsels, and if the scout's route happens to take him through your kitchen, you may soon have a caravan of carpenters climbing your coffee pot.

"Hold on a minute," I said to one the other day.

"What?" the ant shot back, barely pausing between the knife rack and the Cuisinart. "I'm busy."

"Do you realize this is my house you're in?"

"Eh, I'm just a scout," the ant replied with a sneer. "I'm not stealing your precious Lucky Charms."

"Yeah, but you're casing the joint for your accomplices!"

The ant sat down grumpily on his bulbous posterior metasoma and crossed two of his legs. "Look. It's a job. I bring them the information, and what they do with it is their business. I can't take responsibility for the actions of every ant in the colony. Do you check the politics of your car mechanic?"

He pulled a single strand of tobacco out of his tiny backpack. "Got a light?"

"No smoking. House rule," I muttered. "My wife would kill you."

"Your wife would kill me anyway," the ant sniggered. "Come on, gimme a light. Haven't you ever heard of the 'one last cigarette' tradition?"

I didn't like the way he kept changing the subject.

"You realize what thin ice you're skating on, don't you?" I demanded. "If we see you, we squish you. You're not a very fast species."

"Yeah, I put in for rollerblades, but...." He rolled his eyes. "Budget cuts, ya know."

I snorted. Then I was embarrassed and pulled out a handkerchief and tried to pretend to be blowing my nose.

"Look," the ant continued, "I'm union. I do what I'm told. The contract we negotiated is very fair, in my opinion. I use biochemical pheromones to mark the shortest path from the nest to the food source. Which in your case is from just under the southwest corner of your screen porch — to that bag of tortilla chips you accidentally tore too far down the side."

I choked. Then I was embarrassed and tried to pretend it was a simple cough.

"Once we get the foraging trail established," the ant went on, pausing to yawn a tiny yawn, "my work is done. I move to the next house on my job list."

He pulled out a tiny iPad and perused the screen.

"Chris and Tammy. Three small kids. *Plenty* of food sources."

I summoned my shame and rage in an effort to get back on the offensive.

"But you're not the only one at risk, cutting through my kitchen like this," I growled. "We have another house rule, here at the Brendels': When we kill a carpenter ant, we count. If we get up to seven in a single day, we call the exterminator. Once he comes in, your whole gang goes down."

The ant shrugged four of his shoulders. "You think we don't know all this?" He shook his clypeus with a glare of contempt. "We know your house rule. We can hear, ya know. 'Seven in a day.'" He grunted with derision. "Have you gotten up to seven yet?"

"Well, no."

"Of course not, dummy." He smugly folded his antennae together. "Because we only send out six scouts a day."

I had no retort for this.

So I squished him with my thumb.

"Honey," I called to my wife, "phone the bug guys."

July 31st, 2014

Three Bugs Walk Into a Bar

[A mosquito, a tick, and a midge are sitting in the hotel bar on the first evening of the annual Ipswich Pest Convention.]

BARTENDER: What'll ya have?

MOSQUITO: Bloody Mary.

TICK: Bloody Mary.

MIDGE: Bloody Mary. [turning to the others, chewing her gum] So how was you gals'es year?

MOSQUITO: [wiping her proboscis primly with her napkin] Mine was quite terrible, actually. A deplorable year, by any reasonable measure. It's not just people with their *psssht! psssht!* spray cans. Now it's the state. The Commonwealth — of Massachusetts! They're flying airplanes over the marshes, creating pesticide clouds. Honestly! When I first heard about it, I said to myself, 'What is this? Syria?'

Every other week in the *Chronicle*, it's West Nile, West Nile, West Nile! And these liberals, dear me — with all their direct-mail solicitations from humanitarian charities in Africa — they're fixated on malaria. Waterborne diseases! From mosquitoes! I look at my husband and children, and I find myself asking, What are we? Monsters? We don't carry diseases. We come from a long line of respectable New England mosquitoes.

[She smooths her skirt over three of her knees.] My great-great-grandmother bit Kitty Dukakis. All she left was a red welt and an itch. That was all. Truly. It was gone in a day or two. Our family always does things properly.

MIDGE: [after a long, hard look at the mosquito] Kitty Dukakis? Really? That's the best you got?

MOSQUITO: [slightly deflated] My aunt was once swatted by Mitt Romney.

[A long pause.]

MOSQUITO: But that was at a lake in New Hampshire.

MIDGE: [turning to the tick] OK, good-lookin', whatchou been up to this year?

TICK: [checking her lipstick] Well, my year's been pretty good, in spite of the bad press. You know how it is. Sure, Lyme is bad. But the P.R. is terrible. Just terrible. People panic. Just like with anything, you know? The Dunkin' drive-through? I was totally for that. [She snaps her compact shut.] So everybody's like, Ticks! Lyme disease! Yes, of course, some ticks carry Lyme disease. But please. My boyfriend was complaining about the bug spray — I told him, "Larry! It's the *generalizations* that are killing us!" I don't have Lyme. I keep myself clean. Larry and I only dine in respectable places. Those ticks west of Route 1, where people don't even realize it's still Ipswich, they're the worst.

MIDGE: There's Ipswich west of Route 1?

TICK: [rolling her eyes] I'm trying to be serious here. This is my point: People think us adult ticks are causing the Lyme problem. They don't understand that this is a juvenile problem, and we in the tick community are working on it with our youth. We just need time to change our system, ya know? It's politics. The tick community doesn't welcome change. We're *still* trying to get a skate park for our nymphs. God, I wish it could still be like it was when I was a kid, out around Hood Pond. When I was a larva, Hood Pond was heaven.

[The tick takes a long, soulful draw on her Bloody Mary. She turns to the midge.] So how was your year?

MIDGE: [with a broad smile, revealing a missing tooth] I thought you'd never ask! Best year ever! I sympathize with you plus-size chicks. You can't get through the screens. Ha! Yeah! They're makin' the screens tighter and tighter! Me? *Zip!* I'm in there.

[She scratches her belly.] I love them upstairs windows. These antique houses, no central A/C. They have to leave the windows open to survive the summer nights. Humans! Yeah! I love the fat ones while they're sleeping. They don't even notice. [She slurps her drink.] Last week I got a guy on outer Linebrook about eight times, all around his hairline. By the time I flew away, he looked like a tacky red light-up Statue of Liberty souvenir.

MOSQUITO: [sniffing] Oh, please. I don't appreciate subterfuge. It's hypocrisy. I go in the open, as the sun begins to sink — the most beautiful time of the day. I focus on a lovely expanse of human flesh — the females are best, with their sleeveless sundresses — especially during a backyard cocktail party, with plenty of music and laughter. I settle onto that lovely epidermis, just above the clamshell bracelet. From this point, it's a matter of surgical-precision timing: *In! Suction! Eyes up!* I'm watching for her other hand to come sailing in — here it comes — and at the last possible moment — *Nose up! Fly away!*

[She sighs.] I love the sound of her slapping her own arm as I'm buzzing off. It's proof that the system is working. I made a human smack herself. Again! All is right with the world.

MIDGE: That's sick. But I love it.

MOSQUITO: [slumping a bit] My only worry is, the older I get, the harder it is to fly off with such a big belly full of hemoglobin. Perhaps I should think about settling down at our place on the swamp, up in

Byfield. Let my children take care of me. But if I'm entirely honest with myself, there is still the thrill of the kill. [She glances at the others.] Am I a beast?

[A greenhead walks in and sits at the bar. The mosquito, the tick, and the midge all silently turn away.]

MOSQUITO: [under her breath] Drinking problem.

TICK: [muttering] Floozy.

MIDGE: [quietly] Two hundred eggs every time she takes a drink.

BARTENDER: [to the greenhead] What'll ya have, lady?

GREENHEAD: Bloody Mary.

October 9th, 2014

O Death! Where Is Thy Rodent?

I probably should not have attended. Just because you feel badly about the "dear departed" does not necessarily mean it's appropriate for you to show up at the funeral. For example, if you happen to have some measure of responsibility for the dear departed's departure.

Which in this case, I guess I did.

I did not personally assassinate the chipmunk. My cat did the deed. My cat, Hercules Frank Brendel, is a skilled hunter, but a gentle giant: too much of an innocent to kill what he catches. He faithfully patrols our 200-year-old house, inside and out, with an unswerving devotion to a single, simple mission: Any uninvited creature must be chased and caught, then dropped, chased and caught again, then dropped again — over and over, until, inevitably, the weary little critter gets away for good.

Herc's sister, Queen Anne, is in charge of insect invaders. She's too classy to swat at anything bigger than a dragonfly. But Hercules is fiercely efficient at scaring off *Mammalia*, *Reptilia*, and those feathered, winged, egg-laying vertebrates. He does not murder the mice. He does not slaughter the snakes. He does not finish off the finches. He just pummels them, like a feline Rocky Stallone, until they decide to go somewhere else.

It's a shame, in a way. Herc has the cool of a hit man. He could make it as a killer, if only he had the instincts to take it all the way. (He seems to have a particular contempt for voles — which doesn't bother me, because so do I.) He bounds into the meadow behind our house and emerges with a furry, squirming mouthful. He marches to the part of our backyard that he has designated as his own private Roman Coliseum, and he proceeds to play with his prey. I must say, as a city boy, there's something deeply pleasing about knowing that the rodent being smacked like a soccer ball this afternoon won't be crunching the cashews in my kitchen cabinet tonight.

But this week, Hercules made a little error. He was off his game a bit. He momentarily lost his light touch. Perhaps as he prepared to carry his latest victim out of the meadow and into the backyard, he somehow tripped in the tall grass, or stumbled over a stone. Maybe he was a bit hung over, after staying out too late the night before with the cat from across the street, slurping Sam Adams empties tossed out by rude drivers on Randall Road.

Whatever the reason, Hercules did something unfortunate.

He chomped a chipmunk.

Bit a bit too hard. Crunched a crunch too crunchy. Snapped something in that little guy's anatomy that wasn't designed to snap.

So when Hercules dropped it in the backyard, it went thunk.

I've been accused of heartlessness when it comes to wildlife, but this was not an easy moment for me. Chipmunks are cute. Everyone agrees that chipmunks are cute. Whoever thought up "Alvin" was brilliant. So when Hercules marched out of the meadow to the Coliseum with a chipmunk in his teeth, I already felt a bit of a catch in my throat.

But when I realized the chipmunk had already passed over into that great burrow in the sky ... when I realized that this little guy had stuffed his cheeks with goodies from my garden for the last time ... when I realized that my cat had snuffed out a universally beloved, iconic, cartoonish, delightful symbol of playfulness, cheer, and happy-go-lucky nonchalance...

Well, I had no choice. I had to go to the funeral.

It was a small affair — I mean, the attendees were small. It was a big affair in terms of number of attendees. Clearly the deceased was greatly loved. There in a circle around the grave were his five children from the summer litter; four slightly larger children from the spring litter; ten adult children from last year's litters; nine more from the litters of the year before last; and of course, one very weary widow. There were lots of little sniffles, and plenty of moist, red-rimmed little eyes, as the little chipmunk clergyman squeaked out some tiny Scriptures.

I stayed well off in the background. I didn't care to be seen at all. Unfortunately, however, just as the service ended — right after the eight little chipmunk pallbearers had lowered the little chipmunk coffin into the ice cream carton-sized hole in the ground — the grieving widow caught a glimpse of me. She never looked away. She turned her steely little eyes on me and marched all the way up to me in her tiny black dress, her tiny black veil quivering with each step of her tiny black Diego di Lucca heels.

"You have some nerve," she rasped.

"I'm sorry," I replied quietly.

"It's too late for apologies," she answered sharply. "You let your cat out. To commit murder."

"I don't think it was technically murder. Murder is intentional. I think this might have only been——" I gulped. "—chipmunkslaughter."

"Uh huh," she grunted. "Once a cat, always a cat."

She turned and stalked away. For a moment, I didn't move. Then, suddenly, I heard the whirr of sleek feathers cutting through the air. A beautiful blue-gray Cooper's hawk swooped out of nowhere, grasped the chipmunk widow in its talons, and lifted her into the sky without so much as a pause.

The widow shrieked at me as they disappeared together: "I suppose this is your bird, too!"

April 11th, 2016

Would You Like Me to Tell You About Our Specials?

Finally, no more snow in the 10-day forecast, so I put the pub table back up in the backyard, with the crank-operated umbrella planted in the middle of it, and the sturdy plastic-and-metal outdoor bar stools standing all around it like attentive soldiers.

It didn't take long for her to show up. She wasn't intimidated a bit by the soldiers. I stepped out my back door to enjoy the tentative warmth of a breezy spring day, and there she was. Lounging in one of my pub chairs, as if she owned the place. The doe, the one who frequents my backyard with whatever relatives she happens to have in tow.

"Mild winter," she rasped, in that sneery way of hers. "That's what I hear."

"Well," I replied uneasily, not wanting an argument, "it did seem to be."

"Humans," she exhaled, pushing the last of her cigarette into the glass top of my pub table. "You should live outdoors, like we do. *Then* you wouldn't call it mild."

I didn't know what to say.

"I see you had no interest in helping us out," she went on, bumping another Virginia Slim out of its box.

"What do you mean?" I asked.

She tossed the box on the table and pulled a fancy gold lighter out of her purse. "That nice new garden you planted last year."

I didn't know where the doe was going with this. The deer hated our garden? "Uh, that was my wife," I replied quietly. "She planted the garden." Then I immediately felt guilty for throwing my wife under the bus.

The deer lit her cigarette. "Plenty of kale in that garden," she sighed, then took a long draw, breathing out the smoke through her narrow black nostrils. "God, I hate kale."

It was true. We planted kale last year. (It did great! And it stayed green all winter! We were thrilled.)

I gulped. "It's a fad," I offered weakly. "It's in all the recipes these days."

"Yeah," she snorted. "And I see it doesn't *die*. The winter was so *mild*, lucky you, the kale stayed green right straight through. You must be so *happy*." She glowered at me, those big doe-eyes burning hot and black. "Did you plant any azaleas? Any tasty rhododendrons? A few roses? A little delicious dogwood? Do I see any lilacs to lick my lips over? Crocuses? Daylilies? Anything out here a deer might enjoy? No. Kale! You planted kale!"

I shifted my weight to the other leg and tried to look nonchalant. "Actually, I don't think it's our responsibility to feed—"

"You go *feast* like a Roman emperor in your precious Salt Kitchen & Rum Bar," she murmured. "You're so happy huddling over your beer at the new Brewer's Table."

"Actually, I don't drink beer."

"Whatever." She tossed her butt into the grass. "You pull food off the shelves at Market Basket all winter long. We're stuck out here, having to make do, in this overgrown backyard you call your 'meadow.' And we got *what*, here? A few miserable apple trees. The shoots of a baby white pine. Have you ever tried chewing on a white pine?"

"Uh, no."

"It's like eating toothpicks, only the minty ones," the deer snarled.

"We have hostas," I answered weakly. "All around the house. Lots of hostas. Deer eat hostas."

"I'M SICK OF HOSTAS, OK?" she cried, pounding her hoof on the table.

Finally she sat back. She took a deep breath. She gave me a long, lugubrious look. "Kale," she intoned. "How do you stand that stuff? It's like spinach, but without the redeeming humor of the Popeye cartoons."

Finally she leaned on the pub table and reached for her Ipswich Ale. She took a deep gulp, then set the bottle down and stared at it. Her rage was silently building.

"I'm sick of you people trying to starve us out," she said, her teeth grinding, "planting marigolds and irises, stuff that would gag a moose. We won't touch holly, you know that. Or blackberries. Oregano is like poison to us. And if I see any more mint, I'm going to scream."

I cleared my throat. "I don't think anybody is actually planting blackberries," I offered. "They just happen."

The deer looked at me with that look that deer give you. Not the paralyzed, panicky deer-in-the-headlights look. I mean the other look. When they see you in broad daylight, and their eyes say, "What are you staring at, moron? Can't you see you're disturbing my perfectly placid presence?" It's something like the look you get from your manager at work, when your manager is 30 years younger than you.

"Blackberries just happen," she repeated. "Sure. Tell me another story."

She let herself down off the bar stool, and the four empties jiggled on the table.

"*God* plants blackberries," she grumbled, stuffing her things into her purse. "It isn't random. He does it on purpose. Because he's on your side. He created you *last*. Somehow that makes you *special*."

She started walking, a little unsteadily, in the direction of Linebrook Road. Then she turned back. "They don't let us into Salt Kitchen," she said, stifling a belch. She waved a hoof at the backyard. "This is all we got."

She turned again to go.

"Kale," she snorted as she trotted off toward the Deer Crossing sign. "Geez, we don't *need* to get hit by cars," she muttered. "We have *kale*."

August 3rd, 2017

At First, It Was Only a Couple of Sunflower Seeds

Ever since a horrific coyote assault last year, we keep our surviving cats indoors. As a side-effect, the animal kingdom has expanded its territory. The mice, the voles, the chipmunks, the squirrels, the bunnies, the birdies, and the snakes — all the species once fiercely targeted by our felines — have returned to the premises. They now hop, skitter, twitter, frolic, and slither about the property. They peck, graze, scrounge, and otherwise feed off the land as if God intended it this way. Which I guess he did, at least until he created cats.

We have a fine-looking bird feeder in the backyard, a shingle-roofed little house with see-through walls, hanging from a shepherd's-crook pole. Back in the days when we still had a backyard Cat Patrol, I felt a little guilty about putting birdseed in the little house. It was like luring

62

our innocent, fine-feathered friends into the Carnival of Death: "Step right up, take your chance, peck the sunflower seed and win a prize!"

Now, however, we can fill the feeder guiltlessly. Our backyard is idyllic, a safe haven for rodents, reptiles, robin red-breasts and their ilk. Our cats sit trapped on the screen porch restlessly observing the wildlife. It's Torture TV. They meow and lick their lips, tails twitching with primal longing, till they eventually trudge inside the house, throwing me a spiteful glance on the way to their food bowl, where they crabbily crunch their dry, brown Meow Mix.

I felt good about the full feeder until it became a major budget item. I was soon spending more money on birdseed than gasoline. We could fill the little house to the brim on Monday, and by Tuesday it was empty. This didn't seem possible. There aren't enough birds in our backyard to eat that much seed in a week. If the birds were actually consuming that much birdseed, they would be too fat to fly. We should see a literal "round robin" waddling across the grass. We should have house wrens the size of actual houses. But no. All the birds seemed normal-sized.

Squirrels, maybe? Squirrels love birdseed. But we have a big metal cuff, shaped like an upside-down funnel, underneath the bird feeder, designed to deter squirrels; and as far as I can tell, it works. We have plenty of squirrels, but they have no engineering sense. None seem to have figured out how to prop up a ladder, or shoot a guywire from the nearby maple tree, or stack pairs of fallen branches in a criss-cross pattern, or otherwise employ the laws of physics to get to the coveted delicacies.

So where was all the darn birdseed going?

Yesterday I was sitting on my screen porch, tapping my laptop keys, when the mystery was solved. I looked up to see a doe standing at the bird feeder with her tongue sticking out. Not at me — it was extended into the bird feeder's little bird-sized door. Her head was cocked awkwardly to one side in order to get absolutely as much of her tongue as possible into the little house. She was slurping birdseed into her mouth as fast as she could.

I slapped my laptop shut, set it aside, and stood up, knowing that the sudden activity would send the startled animal scampering away. I was wrong. The doe stopped slurping for a moment, eyeing me wearily, then went back to her task.

"Hey! Cut it out!" I barked at her.

She kept an eye on me, but didn't break stride — er, uh, slurp.

I advanced toward the porch door, attempting to appear menacing. Appearing menacing is apparently not my forté. The deer kept at it.

"What the heck!" I exclaimed, stepping outside. I knew she'd run now. I walked up to her. She only slurped faster.

"Get away from my bird feeder!" I yelled, waving my arms.

Finally she pulled her tongue back into her head and straightened up.

"I can quit whenever I want," she said evenly. Then she stuck her tongue back out and started in again.

I burned with shame. I never realized that birdseed is deer crack. I was providing the drug — pound after pound of it, day after day — to the addict.

"You have to stop," I said.

"I'm not hurting anyone," she replied between gulps.

"I can't afford it," I answered.

"I knew you'd turn on me," she sneered. "You did this to me. Now you loathe me."

"It was an accident! I didn't know!"

"Is that my problem?" she shrieked.

"You don't need more birdseed!" I cried. "You need help!"

The doe took another slurp. "I'll get help later. Just not right now."

I placed a hand gently on her shoulder. "Listen to yourself," I pleaded.

The doe paused. She backed her nose away from the birdfeeder and peered inside, frowning. It was empty.

She swung her face toward me, and blinked her enormous eyes.

"Got any more?" she asked.

April 21st, 2018

Undertaker to the Squirrels

I was sitting in a local bar, which shall remain nameless, and the guy on the stool next to me was a squirrel. Not an ordinary squirrel, it seemed to me. More like a hard-bitten squirrel, world-weary, hunched over his tiny whisky, staring into the alcohol in an unfocused way, tapping the end of his tiny cigarette on the bar.

"You know you can't smoke in here," the bartender said.

The squirrel didn't look up.

"What do I look like, an immigrant? I live here, I know the law."

He sighed heavily, or at least as heavily as a squirrel can sigh, with its tiny squirrel lungs.

"I blame Clinton. Bill, not Hillary. You could smoke just about anywhere before him. The ultimate hypocrisy, if you ask me. The faker who claims he 'didn't inhale' goes on this huge self-righteous no-smoking campaign."

The squirrel glanced at me, but I didn't say anything. He looked back into his tiny squirrel whisky.

"It's like Jimmy Carter," he finally continued, "forcing us all to turn down our thermostats during that oil crisis. Carter! A Southerner! Of course his people wouldn't mind turning down their thermostats. It's warm all year round in Georgia! Sheesh. Here in New England, we were freezing our asses off."

This, I realized, was a very knowledgeable squirrel.

He fell silent, except for the tiny thumping sounds of his tiny squirrel cigarette on the bar. He didn't seem self-conscious at all, even sitting on a tower of folded cloth napkins stacked up on the stool to get him to bar height. I guess if a place is classy enough for cloth napkins, you don't make judgments about a customer being short, or a rodent.

It began to feel uncomfortably quiet at the bar, like it was my turn to speak, but I didn't have anything to say. Finally I cleared my throat and asked, "What do you do for a living?"

He shrugged a tiny squirrel shrug.

"I'm an undertaker."

My face must have given me away.

"Ah, I know," he said. "'You don't seem like the undertaker type.' I get that all the time."

He took a swig of whisky from his tiny squirrel glass.

"The way undertakers are at funerals, you think they're always that way? No, we're normal guys. We stop off at the bar, we snicker at

Trump, we fight with our wives, we hide acorns. That sad, official face on funeral day, that's acting. It's just the job."

I found myself being sort of astonished by all this.

"How did you get started, uh, undertaking?" I asked.

The squirrel shrugged again. "I needed money, I looked around for opportunities. What do you see all over the roads in Ipswich? Dead squirrels. Sure, sometimes a possum, or a cat. Maybe a raccoon, or even a deer. But nothing close to the numbers we get in squirrels."

He shrugged his signature shrug.

"It's a volume business."

I thought about it. "Yes, I guess I do see a lot of dead squirrels on the roads."

"You don't see the half of them," he sneered. "I got my teams out there scraping them off the pavement as fast as we can. We contact the family, offer a beautiful memorial service, proper burial, the works. I'm known as the 'Undertaker to the Squirrels.' Get it? 'Undertaker to the Stars' — "Undertaker to the Squirrels'?"

I had nothing to say to that. He snorted a tiny squirrel-snort.

"Anyway," he went on, "if you see a dead squirrel on an Ipswich road, it's only because my teams haven't gotten there yet. If you see the same dead squirrel two days in a row, it's only because their family was too cheap. Sleazy, if you ask me."

"Huh?"

"What decent family wouldn't fork over a few bucks for even a basic funeral and burial?" he growled. "We get to the deceased, we're ready for action, let the family start healing — that's my line, 'start the healing process' — but then the family says no!"

"Well, if they can't afford it," I began.

"It's not the money," he shot back. "I'll tell you what happens. The mom says to the teenager, again and again: 'Don't run across the road. Use the power lines. Avoid the street.' But the kid, he thinks he knows everything. He thinks he's invincible. He runs across the road. Kaboom."

The squirrel shook his head and glared into his glass.

"And that's my business," he sighed.

We sat in silence for a few moments. Then he swiveled his little squirrel face toward me and sort of squinted.

"It's ironic, isn't it? A squirrel spends his life burying nuts in the ground; then in the end, he's the nut who gets buried in the ground."

"Wow," I said, "that's pretty cold."

"Aw, I never say this kind of stuff in front of the family," he replied, lifting his tiny squirrel chin and waving a tiny squirrel claw at the bartender. "It's all 'Your loved one' and 'the dearly departed' and blah blah blah. But still—"

He tapped his empty little squirrel glass; the bartender nodded.

"Ya gotta admit," the squirrel continued, "it is pretty ironic, right?"

May 1st, 2019

Siri, What's My Turkey Gobbling?

Thanks to an awesome new app, which instantly auto-translates the speech of any species into the language of the user, we can now — finally, thankfully — understand what the wild turkeys are saying as they strut across Linebrook Road, holding up traffic, keeping people from getting work on time, and seemingly oblivious to the serious dent they're making in our economy.

The app, eGobbler, works for a number of animal types, but it's called eGobbler because it was initially developed by geeks in small towns plagued by wild turkeys crossing roads when human drivers urgently needed to be using the roads instead of waiting for wild turkeys. But it was quickly adapted to towns with non-turkey problems, making the eGobbler app name an anachronism. (It doesn't take much to become an anachronism these days.) A village in Uganda actually had a breakthrough with their monkey problem. Some towns in Burundi, I hear, now have select boards made up of equal numbers of humans and giraffes, all thanks to eGobbler. Some better educated mammals misinterpret eGobbler as eGabler, wrongly believing it's an app for interpreting Henrik Ibsen scripts.

The software developers who created eGobbler hoped the app would become a communication tool, perhaps even a negotiation tool, to unclog the rural roads.

Alas. It appears that this dream was not meant to come true.

Here's a recent sample transcript — picked up by Siri on the phone of an unsuspecting driver attempting to pass through Ipswich, a gentleman who had rolled down his windows way before it was really warm enough to roll down your windows, but it was May, and he was just stubborn enough to say, if it's May, I'm rolling down my damn windows.

Turkey 1: Look.

Turkey 2: What?

Turkey 1: Windows.

Turkey 2: Huh?

Turkey 3: He's got his windows down.

Turkey 1: Moron.

Turkey 2: He should look at the thermometer.

Turkey 3: It's well known that the human species can't function effectively in this kind of weather, at least not without layering. But there he is. No sweater!

Turkey 1: Moron. As I said.

Turkey 2: So.

Turkey 3: So what?

Turkey 2: So, should we cross on over?

Turkey 1: Well, we are in the middle of the road.

Turkey 3: The guy without a sweater is sitting there looking at us.

Turkey 2: Yeah, so?

Turkey 3: So.

Turkey 1: So?

Turkey 3: So.

Turkey 2: Guys, please. I'm totally okay with sitting here, in the middle of Linebrook Road. It's comfortable. The price is right. And the cars on either side of us are entertaining. I love to see how they glide to a stop when they realize we're here.

Turkey 1: Truly.

Turkey 2: It's like we're royalty.

Turkey 1: Truly.

Turkey 2: And I love to see the constellation of consternation on their faces as they calculate their options.

Turkey 3: Yes. *Do we run them over? Will they get out of the way? Etc.,* etc.

Turkey 1: I have a question for you guys. Why don't we get signs?

Turkey 2: Signs?

Turkey 3: What do you mean, signs?

Turkey 1: I mean signs like the deer get.

Turkey 2: The deer?

Turkey 1: Yeah, the deer. You know, the large mammals that traipse through Ipswich eating the hostas. Not to mention the berries, the fruits, and grains. And, oh yeah, the acorns and other nuts. And the bark. Oh, and the mushrooms. And—

Turkey 3: Okay, I get it. But you're talking about signs.

Turkey 1: Signs! Along the roadway. They put up yellow diamond-shaped signs, with pictures of deer.

Turkey 2: What? You want a picture of a turkey instead?

Turkey 1: Yes. We should get selective turkey crossing areas too, if the deer do.

Turkey 3: Uh, okay, but, uh, you know, uh, the deer don't use those signs, right?

Turkey: 1: Huh?

Turkey 2: You realize that deer keep getting splattered all over the pavement, right?

Turkey 3: In spite of the signs. Because they don't read the signs. They just cross wherever they want.

Turkey 1: *(after a thoughtful pause)* We read the signs.

Turkey 2: Huh?

Turkey 3: We do?

Turkey 1: We should.

Turkey 2: But we can't read.

Turkey 3: The signs are in English. We can't read English.

Turkey 1: We can learn.

Turkey 2: We can?

Turkey 1: We can at least look at a picture of a turkey and say, *Whoa! Turkey crossing! This is the place to cross safely!*

Turkey 3: *(after another pause)* Okay. Who goes first?

Turkey 2: Wait! Look! He's rolling up his windows.

Turkey 1: It's too cold for him. He's turning around.

Turkey 3: Let's decide this next week.

PART III

Meet Me in St. Ipswich

Sometimes over the years, the Outsidah has had the nerve to sit in the front row at Town Meeting and sketch what he sees. The results, due to the Outsidah's distinct lack of artistic talent, have been mixed.

May 17th, 2012

Town Meeting Sketches

In May of 2012, I was still learning to spell people's names....

75

September 13th, 2012

Might as Well Face It,
You're Addicted to Meeting

I'm ready. Bring it on, baby. Town Meeting, here I come.

Tom Murphy, our very fine Town Moderator, has recently advised us, in these pages, that Town Meeting is coming, and we should get ready for it, and I'm telling you, I am so ready. My heart rejoiceth. Oh, this venerable tradition, unchanged for centuries, yet ever-shifting, ever-new! Oh, this link to our past, by which we lay claim to our future! Oh, this inspiration for overwrought poetry!

Of course, I'm new around here, so I understand I don't get all the nuances. I realize not everyone in Ipswich was happy with the suggestions for Town Meeting that I previously offered in these pages. Some felt it was disrespectful to consider selling Town Meeting survival gear: seat cushions, neck pillows, megaphones, ear plugs. I'm afraid these same folks are probably not going to like my new idea: a kiosk in the lobby offering cake, candles, and pointy hats for those who grow a year older before the meeting is over.

Certainly there are people who feel Town Meeting is fine as it is. I respect this. Some of these folks have lived here since 1633. Think of the cumulative total number of years they've spent in Town Meetings, and you must agree that they deserve to have their say. I admire them. I am a big fan of Town Meeting. It is a venerable and valuable tradition. I think every Ipswich citizen should attend. In fact, I think we should return to the 1643 by-law imposing a one-shilling fine on non-attenders. Of course shillings are hard to come by these days; so as a courtesy, I'd like to have a booth out on the parking lot, where you can buy a shilling for five bucks.

Or maybe we should offer a carrot rather than a stick. Instead of the one-shilling fine, let's set up a cash bar in the lobby. Plus, the YMCA can have a "wellness booth" where they offer energy bars for the weary. And sedatives for the obstreperous.

Town Meeting is worth tinkering with because there will always be Town Meetings. As Moderator Murphy explained in his recent column, an annual Town Meeting is required by state law. I guess if you don't hold one, you get kicked out of the Commonwealth. Perhaps some folks really hate Town Meetings, but they attend faithfully just to keep Ipswich from being deported to New Hampshire. It's one thing to spend six hours of your life stuck in Town Meeting; it's quite another to spend the other 364 days and 18 hours in New Hampshire.

On the other hand, I suspect there are some folks who love Town Meeting too much. While our Ipswich by-laws require the state-mandated annual Town Meeting to be held on the second Tuesday in May, adding a second "special" Town Meeting in October may actually be enabling people who are struggling with a tragic Town Meeting addiction. These are people who keep their rectangular Day-Glo Town Meeting ballots as mementoes. These are people who download the video from ICAM and keep all the Town Meetings in their personal DVD collection. They don't need another Town Meeting. They need help. Maybe we could give them a step-down meeting. Maybe a seat on the Government Study Committee.

But until we vote them the help they need — which of course will require more Warrants, and Articles, and other stuff I'll need the Murpherator to explain to me — I'm going to be there. Front row. Every Town Meeting. No matter how many we have. Meet monthly, I don't care. Bring it. I'm there. Kept my Day-Glo ballot from the last Town Meeting. I'm ready to vote.

October 18, 2012

Live, From Town Meeting
(The "Special" One)

The May Town Meeting is required by law. The October Town Meeting is optional. But we always do it.

I sat in the front row again, with my pencil and sketchpad. Names withheld to protect the, uh, innocent....

17000 6
30000 10
43560 14

G'NIGHT!

May 23rd, 2013

Town Meeting Portraits

How many faces can you identify?

May 22nd, 2014

Town Meeting Sketches

Learning to Draw the Celebrities

It's not easy being untalented, but I do it with gusto, and repeatedly. Citizens of prominence during the Outsidah's first-300-column era have been subjected to frequent artistic abuse, as I struggled to capture them in pencil. My sincere apologies, haha.

(Learning to Draw Robin Crosbie)

(Learning to Draw Tom Murphy)

(Learning to Draw Ray Morley)

(*Learning to Draw Pat McNally*)

(Learning to Draw Bill Craft)

(Learning to Draw Charlie Surpitski)

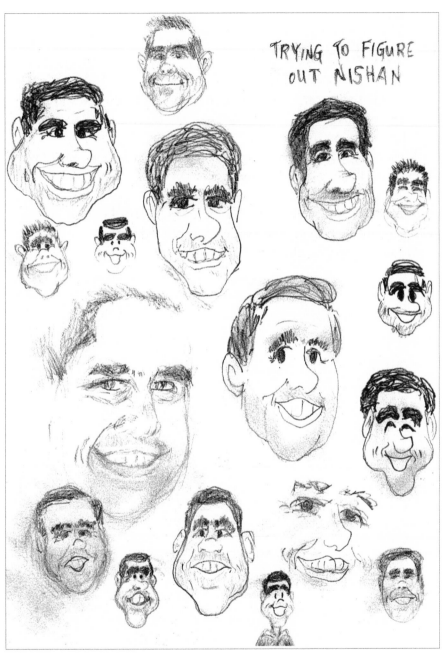

(Learning to Draw Nishan Mootafian)

PART IV

What Else?

My wife is so wrong. She says all my columns fit into four tidy categories (see page 1).

Uh, nooooooo.

Most of my columns, as it turns out, would actually get filed under M, for Miscellaneous. Or Mediocre.

So there.

What follows may be the Guinness World Record biggest miscellaneous section of any book ever published.

Good luck wading through this stuff....

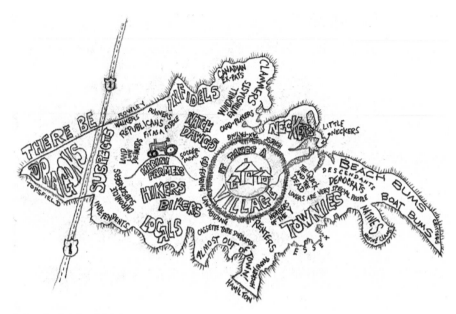

March 16th, 2011

What's in a Name?

This is simple, really. Let's not make it complicated.

It's two syllables, they share a single vowel; these are all sounds common to our language.

"Ipswich."

Say it out loud.

You have no problem saying it. You live around here.

But for people in the Midwest, it's somehow difficult. For people in the South, it's befuddling. For people in the West, it's nigh unto impossible.

I'm on the phone with someone. Where do you live, they ask? "Ipswich," I answer.

But this is an answer that can only be replied to with another question. Choose from the following menu:

"Huh?"

"What?"

"Say that again?"

"Are you kidding?"

Even people who keep their cool and intend to ask "How do you spell that?" seem to be incapable of simply asking the question. They have to precede it with a grunt or a snort or a chortle-swallowing yelp. I say "Ipswich" and I immediately hear the telltale "Arp!" — after which they try to recover: "Uh... how do you spell that?"

Only my cousin in Chicago was able to resist asking a question. Upon hearing the name of my new town, she barked, "Oh, for cryin' out loud!"

It's Ipswich, folks.

People have been living in places called Ipswich since at least the year 1200, when King John granted the English town its first charter — before that, it was "Gyppeswick"; we should be grateful for "Ipswich"!

Chaucer made fun of Ipswich for the conniving greed of its merchants (no connection to our own Ipswich Merchants Association, I assure you), but he didn't seem to find the pronunciation of the town's name funny at all.

In the 1520s and 30s, Ipswich was where Protestants went to be burned at the stake — I suspect this is why John Winthrop sent John Jr. to set up a new Protestant town and call it Ipswich: payback! See? He wasn't trying to be funny at all.

And yet, people hear I live in "Ipswich" and they can't seem to leave it alone. They never had a big overblown reaction when I lived in Griffith, or Springfield, or Scottsdale. I got no chuckles or cackles from Chicago or even Naperville. But now I live in Ipswich. Which makes people giggle uncomfortably.

Of course, in order for the Midwesterners, the Southerners, or the Westerners to "hear" it properly in a phone conversation, you have to spell it. This disturbs them even more. Nothing in their universe begins with the letter I followed immediately by the letter P. Nothing starts with "Ip." There's a visceral craving for a consonant there: they want it to be "Hip" or "Sip" or "Nip."

No, it's "Ip." It starts with the letter I. If Indiana and Illinois can start with I, why can't Ipswich?

Then there's the matter of the missing T. How often do you receive mail addressed to your place in Ipswitch? People desperately want there to be a switch or a witch in there somewhere. Certainly down through history we've had our share of witches — perhaps we still do; I'm not going there — but in the spelling of our name, there's no switch, there's no witch, there's no itch. It's Ipswich. The T is in Boston.

"Ipswich." Say it out loud. And no smirking.

May 19th, 2011

Antiquated

That creaking you hear? That's Ipswich. More antique houses here than just about anywhere in the country. In other places, when houses got old, people tore them down and built new ones. Not in Ipswich. I guess tearing something down and replacing it with something else might require a huge Town Meeting debate, and nobody could stand the thought. Not that! Anything but that! Let's just pound in a few more nails and hold this old place together for another year.

Of course, to those of us who have come here from newer parts of the country — which, come to think of it, would include just about everywhere — antique houses are a major charm factor. A house with a classic white Ipswich Historical Society plaque on the front is desirable. When I began house-hunting, I couldn't understand why anyone would want something built after Calvin Coolidge — not if you could get a Martin Van Buren! Better yet, in Ipswich you can buy a house that's been lived in since long before anybody had ever even heard of a "president," and the British were still the good guys.

Certainly there are other types of houses here. For example, normal modern houses. These are not for people who cling to the past like I do. These people are normal.

And then there are AINOs — Antique In Name Only. Houses that still have their original "bones," but go through the door and wham! It's the 21st century. Where the woman of the house once sat softly singing hymns in her lace bonnet and baking bread in a brick fireplace, now there's a Wii.

But there is another type of Ipswich house. My house. Antique inside and out. Heroically preserved by the previous owner, but still, let's face it: really, really old. Someone took a barn from before George Washington and, just after the War of 1812, added a standard colonial to one end of it. The front of the house leans a bit to the west; the back leans to the east. Or is it the other way around? No two windows hang exactly the same distance from the ceiling. Don't drop anything on the wide pine floors of the kitchen, or whatever you dropped will roll to Boxford.

We made the mistake of inviting an antique-house expert to tour the place. In the dirt-floor basement — which could pass for a dungeon in a low-budget movie — he gestured toward the odd assortment of support beams: some wooden, some metal, some actually straight. "This," he announced, "is 200 years of lazy husbands."

But I adore this house. It's not a "First Period," also known as "Colonial" — and it isn't certifiably a "Second Period," or "Georgian" —

I guess our house is merely a "Third Period," or "Federal." But this is still better, in my opinion, than, say, a "Fourteenth Period," which is "Tedford's." I also prefer it to "Fifteenth Period," also known as "Condo."

I know I'm something of a fanatic. We have retained the squeaking stairs and the jittery banisters and the floorboards that groan when you step on them. We've only updated what we felt we had to — a metal stove in one of the fireplaces, new bricks where old ones were crumbling — but I allowed it reluctantly, and I still feel badly about it.

The ghost of the man who built my house came up from the cemetery down the street and visited me one late night not long ago. He floated around awhile, checking out what we'd done to the place.

"This place is creepy," he shuddered.

June 16th, 2011

If You Said What I Heard You Say

I hear you.

I don't mean I'm tuned in to you spiritually or anything like that.

I mean I hear you. On the street. Outside my window.

When I moved to Ipswich from modern America, I was not only delighted by the number of old houses in this town, but also shocked by how close they sit to the street.

In the old days, building a house far from the road would have seemed crazy, I guess. If you don't have a Toyota to get you from the house to the street, and you don't have a snowplow service to magically clear a mile of driveway, why wouldn't you simplify your life by plopping your house down right at the edge of the road? Besides, there was no *Colonial Idol* on TV to entertain you, and no sitting in front of ye olde compewter on Ye Olde Facebooke: so you *wanted* to hear the clip-clop of an approaching horse. Visitors! Something new and interesting!

My house, for example, reflects these priorities. There was a small barn, built about the time George Washington retired, a reasonable distance from the road. But then, about the time James Madison retired, the owner decided to attach a new house to the barn. Hm, where shall we put the new house? Which side of the barn should it go on? By Jove, I've got it! We'll squeeze it in between the barn and the road! So when you step out of the front door, you're in the southbound lane dodging Harleys!

My wife has gently, lovingly suggested that I sometimes exaggerate in this column, so let me assure you, I don't mean to exaggerate about the proximity of our house to our street. Let me simply say that our front yard is the width of a garden hose. You could unspool a roll of Charmin and conceal our front yard completely.

So no wonder I hear you.

On beautiful Massachusetts evenings, when the weather is so lovely, I want to open my windows, leave them open overnight. And on beautiful Massachusetts mornings, when the sun is up so early, you want to get out, get some exercise. So I don't need to set an alarm for the morning. I have you. Outside my window.

Runners tend to be solo, and all you hear is their feet: *thup thup thup thup thup thup thup thup*. Bicyclists come in pairs, usually men, moving fast — and THEY YELL AT EACH OTHER! So early in the morning, I hear extremely quick, amazingly loud snippets of stories as the bicyclists zip by:

"...HER, MAN! SHE'S GONNA SHAFT YOU..."

"...GET CAUGHT, BUT HE WAS CRAZED..."

"...DEAL WITH THE PROSTATE THING, SO..."

But best of all are the walkers. They're more often women, and they chatter — they're up at dawn, after all, and full of energy — and they think these historic houses they're walking past are museums; the idea that people actually live here, and might be sleeping at this ungodly hour of the morning, never crosses their mind.

Plus, because they're moving so much more slowly than the bicyclists, they spend significantly more time within earshot — which means I get way, way more information than I want:

"...ridiculous! So something had to give. Finally I just told him, this is not right. If I don't get this baby weaned I'm going to scream! What in the..."

"...don't know if it's love. I like him. He's really nice to me. But I like Paul too. Actually I like Paul better. Or maybe it was the margaritas, I don't know. How..."

Really slow walkers — the ones who aren't serious about exercise — offer the longest monologues:

"...said stop! He wouldn't stop. I grabbed his arm, I said stop it! He was like, what, are you gonna call the cops? I said, give it to me. I had to grab it out of his hand! I said this is not right! This is not the yellow I chose for this room! I actually threw the paintbrush at him. I couldn't believe he was actually..."

Some early morning, groggy and half-awake, I'll hear something really incriminating. Or something really threatening. And I'll have to take action. I'll have to intervene. I'll have to roll out of bed, lean out my window, and sound the alarm:

"Hey! I heard that!"

June 22nd, 2011

Sludge Report

It's clear to me now: I arrived in Ipswich ignorant. Topographically, I mean.

When I moved here, after a lifetime in other regions of the country, I had the Donald Rumsfeld problem: I didn't know what I didn't know.

Yes, I knew there was a beach. Then, after I actually saw it, I said, "Wow. Nice beach."

I knew there was a river. Then, after I stood on the Choate Bridge and actually looked at the river, I said, "Wow. Nice river."

I knew there were trees, plenty of trees. Moving here from the Arizona desert, I was especially looking forward to the trees. And sure enough, when I got here, there were trees. Oak and maple, linden and honey locust, spruce and basswood. (I learned these names from a local. I still don't know what they mean. Usually I just look out my window and say, "Wow. Nice trees.")

I also had a handle on special Ipswich features like Castle Hill. A hill, as I understand it, is a particularly elevated place. Having put in 20-plus years in Chicago, I had little experience with these things called hills. When I first visited the Crane estate up there on Castle Hill, I was properly impressed. "Wow," I said. "Nice hill."

But there is one significant topographical feature of Ipswich for which I was utterly unprepared. The marshes.

Shopping on real estate websites for a home in Ipswich — something which became an all-consuming obsession for my wife and me for the last three years before our move — I kept coming across property listings which included this feature: "Marsh views."

And I scratched my head. "This is a *feature?*" I asked myself. "From your window, you can see a *swamp?*"

We had no marshes in Arizona; we had sand and rock. We had no marshes in Chicago; we had pavement. A marsh, as far as I knew, was a strange and dangerous place. A marsh was a reedy bog where anacondas lie coiled and concealed, waiting for an unsuspecting city slicker to make a misstep. A marsh was a quagmire of mud, seething with microbes, and the kind of insects they feature in close-ups on National Geographic specials, giving small children nightmares. ("Daddy, can I sleep with you and Mommy? I can't stop imagining the *Culex tarsalis!*") A marsh was a vast pit of silent, deadly, dark brown Silly Putty, with centuries of skeletal remains gradually sinking in the muck. There Be Dragons.

But then I arrived in Ipswich. For the first time in my life, I saw a marsh. "Wow," I said. "Nice marsh."

This was not at all what I expected. This did not appear to be a sprawling expanse of jungle mire, with the occasional wildebeest snorting and braying while being sucked down to his doom. The marsh, in fact, was peaceful. And breathtakingly beautiful. A magnificent work of art.

(Learning to Draw Dorothy)

Soon I had the good fortune to meet Dorothy Monnelly, a longtime Ipswich school teacher who retired to an equally brilliant career in photography — specializing in fabulous, enormous black-and-white photographs of — marshes! She takes something that's already lovely, and turns it into an even more exquisite thing of wonder. Along with other area artists who reflect the beauty of our marshes in photos and paintings, Dorothy helped to transform my heart, to turn my old scorn for the marshes into appreciation, even esteem.

And then, as chance would have it, my little daughter was part of a Girl Scouts event at the home of one of her friends; and I found myself visiting one of those houses I had looked at online, long before. One of those houses with "marsh views." One of those houses I had so ignorantly waved off. There, at the edge of the backyard, was a vast reedy sea, stretching gorgeously to the horizon.

I was late; the event was already under way. The four little girls and the troop leaders were out in the marsh, on a wooden bridge. As I headed out to join them, carefully picking my way along the path, one of the little girls was coming toward me. She had forgotten something, and she was heading back to the house.

She had almost reached me — I was about to say "Hi!" — when she happened to step off the path.

Splup!

The troop has an opening now. Thanks to the marsh.

December 1st, 2011

Raking Lesson

November is done. It was somewhat confusing to me. This was not like the Novembers we had when I lived in Scottsdale, Arizona.

First of all, I noticed that the trees here in Ipswich had leaves on them. I was not really familiar with leaves in Arizona. Yes, we did have things like trees — spindly, Dr. Seuss-like things sticking up out of the crags, writhing in ultra-slow motion, stretching their thorny fingers toward the brutal sun god, pleading in vain for mercy. These tree-like creatures did not have leaves. They had spines. Spikes. Nasty little pointy things.

But then, as if this were not confusing enough, the leaves here in Ipswich proceeded to change color. Well, at least, I thought they changed color. Long-time New Englanders moaned interminably in November: "The leaves hardly changed!" To which I can only reply: Hey, New Englanders, you don't know from "hardly changed." If you want to experience "hardly changed," go to Arizona. Things don't change color in the desert. Unless you count the difference between beige and taupe.

And then — most confusing of all — the trees began flinging their leaves to the ground. Where I come from, the spiny prickly pointy things have worked so hard just to grind out an existence, just to draw a few meager droplets of acrid moisture from the sand, there is no way they are going to give anything up. But here in Ipswich, the lindens and honey locusts and pin oaks and sugar maples nod smugly at one another, nonchalantly shrug their branches, and mumble: "Eh, it's November. We don't need these garish old leaves. We'll make fresh green ones — but first, perhaps a winter nap."

End result: a lot of leaves on the ground. By observing my neighbors, I have come to understand that you respond to this situation with something called "raking." I purchased a rake, and I tried this activity. It's quite a bit of work, isn't it! You're actually dragging these increasingly heavy groups of leaves across the grass, and making piles. Good exercise.

But unnecessary. After a bit of experimenting, I have come to the conclusion that the secret to dealing with fallen leaves is not really raking *per se*. (It's also not about making your teenage son do it. He will be even grumpier than usual.) The secret to dealing with fallen leaves is to wait for a windy day. This being New England, it won't take long. Then you hold the rake with a very light grip, stroke the leaves toward you, lift gently, and sort of flick the rake a bit to release the leaves. If you do it right, your leaves will fly directly into the Buchanans' yard. I wish you were here with me right now, so I could show you in person; it would be so much easier than describing it: *Stroke, lift, flick. Stroke, lift, flick.* Get in the proper rhythm, with the wind at 12 mph or more, and you can move an acre of fallen leaves across the street in less than an hour. Two Saturdays ago I inadvertently buried Stella, the neighbors' Jack Russell terrier. I could still hear her yipping, but all you could see was the leaf pile quivering.

I think this might work even better with a leaf blower. Can't wait for next November!

January 26th, 2012

The Ipswich-Rowley War

Rowley invaded Ipswich.

It was perhaps inevitable. People in Ipswich, myself included, have been known to make Rowley the butt of various jokes. This is shameful behavior on our part, probably. Rowley is actually a fine town, and we need them, because we don't have a McDonald's. But still, somehow, Rowley seems to have a somewhat humorous quality. Maybe it's the name. I mention Rowley to out-of-towners and in many cases they chuckle. Isn't there just a vaguely odd, roly-poly, puppy-clowny sound to the name "Rowley"?

I felt more or less badly about having this opinion — after all, someone whose name really was Rowley must have founded Rowley — until I learned that Rowley wasn't founded by Mr. Rowley at all. It was founded by Mr. Rogers. Not *that* Mr. Rogers. But see how humor seems to dog this town?

History tells us that Rowley was in fact founded by a certain Rev. Ezekiel Rogers, who arrived on a ship called the *John*. I think it would have been more fitting for the *John* to land at Crane Beach, which was destined to be named for a millionaire toilet-maker. But no. Rev. Rogers and his gang of 20 families got off the *John* and came to Rowley.

If you're going to start a new town, but for some reason you don't want to name it after yourself, you might decide to name it after a place you have fond memories of. Rev. Rogers, however, decided to name this new town after the place back in England that he'd gotten kicked out of. A place called, uh, Rowley.

But now, long-lost historical records, recently uncovered, seem to indicate that residents of Rowley, Massachusetts, at some point got fed up with being chuckled at. A mob, scruffy and surly, assembled at Agawam Diner with clubs and torches. Eyewitnesses claim they were muttering threatening remarks, including "They've chuckled at us for the last time" and "We're really annoyed." The rabble milled around on the Agawam parking lot for a long time, but there was still no seating available. Finally they moved down Route 1, pausing only briefly to re-supply at Winfrey's. Well stocked with penuche walnut-creams and almond buttercrunch, they proceeded to the traffic light at Linebrook Road.

Their strategy was diabolically simple. They planned to seize Linebrook and effectively cut the town in two. Once they had taken control of Marini Farm, they would threaten to withhold the strawberry harvest, at which point they knew the people of Ipswich would cave in and agree to express only the highest esteem for their neighbors to the north. Rowley would finally be chuckle-free.

It might have worked, but they made the mistake of attacking on a blustery Thursday, which is garbage collection day on Linebrook Road. It was very windy, and the invaders found it impossible to advance due to a large number of rolling garbage cans in the street, and no small amount of spilled garbage blowing around. One especially strong gust sent the lid of a Rubbermaid Roughneck 20-gallon sailing like a Frisbee. It struck a Rowley woman who had just popped a Winfrey's turtlette into her mouth, causing her to swallow the entire thing without chewing. Deeply disappointed, she turned around and headed toward home — which discouraged her fellow combatants, and set in motion a general retreat. Most residents of Ipswich were unaware that an invasion had been attempted.

If these historical records are to be believed, Ipswich could be at risk of another attack. So it would be probably be prudent to knock off the Rowley jokes, people.

Come on, if I can resist, so can you.

April 12th, 2012

Welcome to the Talking House

My house in Arizona was so new, so 90s, so George H.W. Bush, so quiet. All square and fitted and plastic.

My house in Ipswich is not George Bush. It's not even Grover Cleveland. It's Adams and Monroe. Half of it was a small barn, built in 1797, the year John Adams became president. The other half is a "Federalist," built in 1817, the year James Madison retired and James Monroe took over. In each half, there's an upstairs and a downstairs, an Upper and a Lower. ("Honey, where are you?" "Upper Monroe!")

An Adams-and-Monroe house is old, sure, but of course not very old at all by the standards of some people in this town. People who live in 1685 houses on High Street drive past my cobbled-together antique-and-a-cow-pen and snort with derision at the white plaque hanging next to my front door. "1817! New construction! Pretender!"

My house is, however, old enough to talk. Literally. You walk through it, and it speaks to you. It creaks or grunts or giggles, depending on the condition of the wood under your feet or the threshold you're crossing. No sneaking around here. And no sleeping in, either: If someone is up and around, you hear them.

There's actually an advantage to this talkative old place: I can save money on utilities, because I don't really need *lights*. Even in the dark, the house tells you, step by step, where you are.

Let's start out back, at the breezeway door. You push, it refuses to open, you put your shoulder into it, it still refuses to open, you bang your shoulder into it, it finally gives way with a *Whump!* You step into the mudroom, and close the door behind you: *Thomp.* You rub your shoulder.

Two steps to the right — the floor says "Tecka, tecka." You pull on the kitchen door, a thin thing salvaged from the 1600s. "Weeep!" it squeaks as you open it. But then, as you close it behind you, it squeaks a different way: "Tew!"

Now you're in the kitchen, Lower Adams. The wide pine floor says *tum tum tum tum.* Turn left, and the floorboards warn you you're heading toward 1817: "Erp! Erp!" In the little walkway where Adams and Monroe meet, the floor says "Ack, ack." You know you're in the Lower Monroe living room when you hear the floor cry out like a movie damsel: "Eek!" If you have a cruel streak, you can actually bounce a little on that first floorboard and torture her: "Eek! Eek! Eek! Eek! Eek!"

Take a diagonal, cross the living room. A big braided rug under foot keeps the floor quiet: "Hm, hm, hm." But when you step off the rug again, the old pine suddenly carps at you: "Kri-ike!"

At the old, original 1817 front door, you turn left to go up a talking staircase. Each step greets you:

Ark! Wook! Pook! (Turn.)

Wah! Frack! Gleek! Wipp! Wipperipper! (Loose board, I guess.) *Bick! Kip!* (Turn.)

The last three steps are unenthusiastic: *Kruck. Toop. Bluck.*

Now you're in Upper Monroe. Turn left, and you're in the master bedroom. I can tell where I am because the floorboards mock me: "Ooh! Ook! Yeah! Wow!" Not exactly mood-setting.

Turn away from those sardonic slats, hang a right, and head into the bathroom. Flooring: black-and-white tiles, circa 1985. What's under the tile, I have no idea, but whatever it is, it screeches when you walk on it: *Reechah! Reechick! Cheekick!* Hang a left, you're on a small wooden landing connecting 1817 back to 1797. It sounds like a grandfather: "Groak. Brrp." A couple solid 70s-era steps into Upper Adams — my office, carpeted — and only here does the house go silent. Pull a U-turn and take the stairs down to Lower Adams — these steps say *Scrake, scroik, scrake, scroik* — and you're back in the kitchen.

Simple, huh?

Now let's try it with a blindfold.

February 14th, 2013

Let It Snow, I Ain't Afraid

I looked out Friday evening at Winter Storm Nemo dropping tons of snow on my driveway and I said to myself, "Gosh, that's going to take my wife a long time to shovel."

On Saturday I came to my senses, and headed out to do the honorable thing, leaving her inside to sweep, mop, dust, wash, iron, and paint the bedroom. The bedroom did not really need painting, but it's irresistible to do those few things that the Town of Ipswich doesn't require a permit for.

Of course I was well equipped for my snow removal chores. When I moved here from the Arizona desert, where we saw exactly 16 flakes of snow in two decades (and those 16 flakes came in two separate "snowstorms"), I knew I would need the proper equipment. So I bought a snowblower. Not just any snowblower. I bought a tiny electric snowblower. Essentially a large metal mosquito. Because I have no experience with snowblowers, and I wanted one I could handle. I could imagine nothing more embarrassing than running down Linebrook Road chasing my snowblower. I have seen big snowblowers in my neighborhood. Snowblowers bigger than the facial-hairy, barrel-chested lumberjack-types who drive them. Snowblowers bigger than the sheds they're stored in. Snowblowers so big, they clear the average Linebrook driveway just by being powered up, and only need to be operated longer because their motors shake the earth and knock another ton of snow out of the trees. This kind of snowblower — the kind of snowblower the Old Testament Goliath would have owned, if he were from Gloucester instead of Gath, the gas hog snowblower, the snowblower you could pull a house trailer with — was not for me. I needed a starter-snowblower. A kindergartener's snowblower. A snowblower as delicate and sweet-tempered and unobtrusive as its owner.

When the garage door went up, Nemo's drifts remained in place, a solid wall of snow, significantly taller than my snowblower. At first I decided I would have to use my shovel. But within a minute or two, my thoracolumbar fascia muscle had conferred with my trapezius muscle and confirmed that my back had been too many weeks without anything remotely like exercise to take on something the size of Nemo.

So I took a deep breath, and pushed my little snow-sneezer into the mammoth mountain of white.

I was surprised to see how well the tiny Toro performed. It chewed up the bottom two or three inches of snow, leaving a two-and-a-half foot ledge of snow above it. I could keep pushing the machine into the snow bank, bit by bit, deeper and deeper, until the overhanging ledge got too heavy and weak, and crashed down, leaving me fresh snow to blow. In this way, a few inches at a time, I made my way from the door of my house toward Linebrook Road.

Visibility was an issue, however. I couldn't really see where I was heading. When I finally climbed up from the depths to figure out my location, there was a sign that said Topsfield Town Line.

Returning along the trail I'd blazed with my marvelous little machine, I found that my very excellent neighbor, who owns a snowblower twice the size of his boat, had graciously cleared my entire property. The driveway, the yard, the garden, everything. Everything except the igloo.

Well, it looked like an igloo. It was actually my Honda. An Ipswich tax collector was standing nearby with a clipboard.

"We don't seem to have a record of this dwelling," he said peevishly. "Your property tax will be going up."

"It's my Honda!" I replied. "Honest!"

"Well, then, it's a garage," he snorted, jotting notes. "Did you get a permit to build this?"

June 27th, 2013

You Can't Get There From Here

If you are uneasy about reading things related to "going to the bathroom," please, stop reading now. This is about "going to the bathroom."

I don't mean this biologically. I'm not talking about bodily functions. I'm just talking about walking. Starting out at the edge of your bed, which is where you're sitting when you realize you need to go to the bathroom, and then walking, from your bed, to your bathroom.

It should be a simple matter. But this is New England.

New England is the land of blocked-off doorways. In our antique houses, with our nooks and crannies and rooms added on 180 years after the house was built, we wind up with doors where we don't need them. Yet there's a certain Yankee reluctance to spend the time, energy, and money it would take to make it just a plain wall, when there's a chance that in 60 or 70 years, you'll want a doorway there again. So it's not uncommon to see a couch in front of a door, or a chair or a lamp or a table in front of a door — and the owners don't even think of it as a door anymore. It's just a wall that seems to look like a door. Yes, it was a doorway, with people actually walking through it, from James Knox Polk to Millard Fillmore, and again from Grover Cleveland to Warren G. Harding. But the whole rest of the time, basically it's just been a wall.

There's one room in our house where this becomes really serious business. After 200 years of nook-adding and cranny-shifting and space-narrowing and corridor-widening, our house has ended up with one tiny room which has not a single window, but four doors. From this little roomlet, you can get to the guest room, the laundry room, the living room, or a bent little passageway too small to be called a hall. The room is all doors. There is only one precious wall where you can put a piece of furniture without worrying about who will be entering, exiting, bumping, slamming, or otherwise ricocheting through.

What to do with such an odd little place? We are not big TV watchers, so we stuck our TV in here. There's really no other use for this space. Well, this isn't quite true. I have indeed used this odd little room for something else. A single, simple function.

I walk through it on my way to the bathroom.

I abandoned the upstairs bathroom because — I trust it's not too sexist to say — it was overrun by females. As the only guy in the household, I took ownership of the downstairs bathroom. Getting there and back was no problem at all. Until I went out of town for a couple weeks, and my wife decided to rearrange the furniture in the odd little TV room.

So now, instead of slipping downstairs and heading straight to the bathroom, with only one little sidestep along the way — well, that sidestep is now a closed door with a brown couch standing guard in front of it.

Which means, from my bed, I cross the room diagonally, out the bedroom door, hang a right on the landing, down three stairsteps, left, seven more steps, another left, last three stairs, then a right, diagonally across the living room, into the kitchen, wide arc around the table and chairs, into the bent little passageway too small to be called a hall, sharp left, one step into the accursed TV room (making a certain gesture toward the brown couch), hang a left into the laundry room hallway, and a sharp right into the bathroom.

I am planning today to go to the bathroom on Tuesday. Packing a light lunch for the trip.

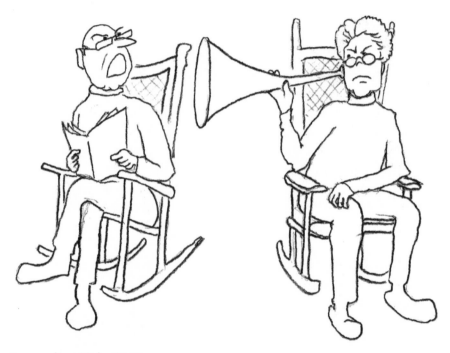

September 19th, 2013

Ipswich in September

"WHAT?"
"NOTHING."
"WHAT?"

"I DIDN'T SAY ANYTHING."

"WHAT?"

"WHAT DAY IS IT?"

"WHAT?"

"IT'S SATURDAY, ISN'T IT?"

"YEAH."

"THAT EXPLAINS IT."

"WHAT?"

"I SAID, 'THAT EXPLAINS IT.'"

"I HEARD YOU. EXPLAINS WHAT?"

"WHAT?"

"THAT EXPLAINS WHAT?"

"THE NOISE."

"THE WHAT?"

"THE LAWNMOWERS. THE CHAIN SAWS. THE WOOD CHIPPERS. THE WEED WHACKERS."

"WHAT?"

"EVERYONE WORKS IN THEIR YARDS ON SATURDAY."

"WHAT?"

(24 hours later:)

"What?"

"Nothing."

"What?"

"I didn't say anything."

"What?"

"What day is it?"

"What?"

"Will you please put down the comics and listen to me?"

"What?"

"It's Sunday, isn't it?"

"Yeah."

"That explains it."

"What?"

"I said, 'That explains it.'"

"I heard you. Explains what?"

"The quiet."

"The what?"

"Listen. It's so quiet. Not a single lawnmower. No chain saws. Not even a weed whacker."

"Mm-hm."

"It's beautiful."

"What?"

"This is why God invented football."

September 26th, 2013

Forlorn in the Corn

I'm in a certain amount of trouble.

The corn maze at Marini Farm has become a cherished annual tradition — they actually have a website just for the corn maze, at MariniCornMaze.com — and my understanding is that, if you don't try it, you're not a worthy Ipswich citizen. The Marinis carve a huge, complicated cartoon out of their cornfield — a cartoon you could only see if you're flying overhead, either by airplane, or by helicopter, or by being shot from Willowdale State Forest out of a cannon aimed toward Rowley. This year's corn maze is a huge T-rex with a pterodactyl on its back. A sinister omen, I'm afraid.

A maze of any kind is terrifying to me, because I have no sense of direction. So I have cleverly avoided trying out the Marini corn maze. I'll be out of town, sorry. I have allergies, sorry. I have a sprained tibia, sorry. Scratched cornea, itchy palms, irritable Town Meeting syndrome. Stuff like that.

But Marini doesn't help you much, if your goal is to avoid the maze, because they operate all the way from September 7 through November 2. That's 57 whole days of risk for someone trying to avoid it. Maybe you can claim workload during the work week. Maybe you can claim church attendance on Sunday, up to a point. But they will ultimately defeat you. Your kid will beg to go to Marini's corn maze, not only for the maze itself, but for all the fun, cool stuff outside the maze area, like those big bouncy things that kids love to bounce on. Your kid will also want to climb through the tunnel thing, and pump the pumps on the old-fashioned pumpy thingies.

And there's a good snack bar, with a tent and picnic tables, and friendly people behind the counter, and a wide-ranging menu — everything from corn dogs to cotton candy, and fried dough with a choice of three toppings.

Also, just before you get to the corn maze, there's a rope maze, which is like an entry-level corn maze. It's complicated like the corn maze, but you can see out the whole time you're in the maze, and everyone can see you. So of course it's humiliating to get trapped in there, but at least they can find the body.

Inside the actual corn maze, you're at significantly greater risk of becoming crop fertilizer.

Here's what I have learned in Marini's corn maze.

1. Get your fried dough before you go in, because you may never come out.

2. There are numerous stations inside the maze, with interesting clues that children can collect to solve interesting puzzles. None of these clues are intelligible to an adult.

3. They give you a flag on a long pole — it's taller than the corn — with instructions to hold it up and wave it if you get lost, so that Marini's friendly personnel can come rescue you. However, if you stop to look at one of the clue stations, and you set your flag down while you're studying it, and you forget to pick it up before you move on, your flag will be lost forever, and so will you.

4. You can start out with your family, but if they say you should go left at a fork in the path and you're sure you should go right, and they let you strike out on your own, you're doomed.

5. If you find that you have made it as far as the eye of the pterodactyl, you will have the strong sensation that this would have been the perfect location for a porta-pottie.

6. In the maze, I can hear the children out there, bouncing on the bouncy things, laughing with such sheer joy that it brings tears to my eyes. Not because the children are so precious, but because those children are so close to me. They're within earshot, but they're outside the maze, but *I can't get there.*

7. There are two high wooden footbridges standing at various points in the corn maze. If you happen to come across one, you can climb the steps and look out over the cornfield in all directions. You can see the children jumping on the jumpy things. What you can't see is the maze itself. Which means you still can't find your way out.

8. When you finally miss your third meal, you can cave in, break the rules, and pick an ear of corn. But unless you brought some gear in with you — a pot half full of water, a camp stove with fuel, and a book of matches — you'll have to eat it raw.

9. There is no WIFI in the corn maze. However, the cell signal is strong, which enables you to phone for help, unless you're too embarrassed, or your calls to your wife all go directly to voicemail. If you have GPS on your cell phone, you can also see exactly where you are, except that the maze itself is too new to appear on any online maps, so seeing exactly where you are does you no good whatsoever.

If you see my family anywhere out there, please tell them I still love them, even though they lost me in here. Assure them that I am not making any assumptions about whether they did it on purpose, and let them know that I apologize for my whining after we'd been in the maze for an hour, and my cussing beginning at the 90-minute mark. Also please let them know, even if they deliberately lost me, all is forgiven. And if they could please come find me, I would be grateful.

Sent from my iPhone.

October 31st, 2013

Silence of the Clams

I was out of town, and it broke my heart to miss Ipswich's annual Chowderfest. But the greater heartbreak was yet to come. I returned just in time to find last week's edition of the *Ipswich Chronicle* full of dreadful news on page A5. No, not the usual dreadful news. The obituaries were on Page B11. This week's really dreadful news was that a Hamilton group took the People's Choice award for best clam chowder.

Hamilton! This is so, so wrong. In about a thousand ways.

Yes, I realize that anything called a "People's Choice" award is going to involve people voting, and people are crazy. Just look at the House of Representatives. The wild-eyed whims of the unwashed masses have been a matter of concern ever since we were setting up this country, when John Adams got ulcers over the "tyranny of the majority."

Still, majority or no, what happened at this year's Chowderfest is unthinkable, like a Canadian team winning the World Series. It should not even be in the realm of possibility that any Ipswich Chowderfest award could be won by Hamilton. We are Ipswich. The clam is practically our official town mollusk.

But I am not one to cry over spilt tartar sauce. I am about solutions. So, to avoid any possibility of a repeat occurrence of this year's sickening outcome, I today suggest a couple simple but vitally important possible adjustments to our Chowderfest arrangements.

Option #1: Nobody from outside Ipswich can vote. If you're from Hamilton, Rowley, Essex, or anywhere else, you can come and spend your money and eat all you want, but you cannot vote. You proved your unreliability this year. We're only saving you from incurring additional contempt.

To keep the infidels from voting, a new Chowderfest voter-security system will be implemented. Don't worry; this will be low-cost. Our cheerful Town Constable Peter Dziadose will stand at the ballot box and determine whether you can vote or not, based on whether he knows you or not. Since he knows everyone in Ipswich, this system will be foolproof.

Option #2: Everybody can vote, but only Ipswich chowders can be entered in the competition. This seems fair to me. There's a reason it's called the Ipswich Chowderfest. Ipswich clams are world-famous, and they have been for a long, long time. As a child in Chicago, nearly half a century ago, I chose "Ipswich clams" off the menu at our local Howard Johnson's restaurant. I have never seen "Hamilton clams" on any menu. Of course not. Hamilton is landlocked. Hamilton is at its closest point more than two miles from open water, and that's in Manchester-by-the-Sea. If a clam came from Manchester-by-the-Sea — which it wouldn't, but let's just say it did — it would have to crawl all the way to Hamilton, because Manchester-by-the-Sea doesn't even have bus service, let alone clam flats.

To get to the nearest clam flat from the Hamilton town line, it's every bit of four and a half miles, as the crow flies. And if it's a crow flying, I assure you, it is not bringing you a fresh clam. Any clam a crow brings you in Hamilton is not a fresh clam. These people should not be cooking with clams. Hamilton is inland. It has stables. These people should be cooking with oats. Do we drive down from Ipswich and stuff the ballot box during their Oatfest? No, we do not. Because they don't have an Oatfest. Apparently, the time and energy they could be spending mounting their own Oatfest, they're spending on rigging our Chowderfest. Forgive me, but I'm upset.

Don't get me wrong. I like Hamilton. I have almost three really good friends in Hamilton. But this is about something bigger than friendship. This is about our own clams being used against us. It's got to stop.

Next year, we take the trophy. Until then, I say, Eat local. No, I mean *really* local.

May 8th, 2014

I Like Bike

Having lived most of my life on concrete sprawls, I never developed a great love of the outdoors. My idea of "roughing it" is stepping down to a *three*-star hotel.

But when we moved to Ipswich, not so very long ago, it was time to acquire a new lifestyle. The beach! The woods! The greenheads!

So recently, for the first time, my wife and daughter and I tried out something called Bradley Palmer. It's a 721-acre trail-laced state park that straddles Hamilton and Topsfield, and on one side comes right up to the edge of Ipswich without quite dipping its toe in.

The first trail sign we came across was a heartfelt entreaty, in alarming capital letters:

PEDESTRIANS
PLEASE
15 MPH
SPEED BUMP

I was nonplussed. I have never known a pedestrian to do anything close to 15 mph. I have also never seen a speed bump designed for pedestrians. I could only surmise that Bradley Palmer has acquired a constituency of really fast walkers. I wasn't worried, however. Since we were on our bicycles, I felt confident that we could run over any pedestrians if necessary, even the 15 mph ones.

We soon decided to leave the paved trails and take on whatever challenge Bradley Palmer could throw at us. The official contour map suggests that some of these trails are basically level. I can confirm personally that the contour map is a fantasy. The Bradley Palmer page on Wikipedia is more to be believed. It confirms that "many of the trails over the hills" were constructed "straight up and down slope instead of following the contours." Of course, someone on a horse can take these hills effortlessly, if they don't care about the horse frothing at the mouth. (But watch out for those frothing horses. According to Wikipedia, "The pedestrian is cautioned to be alert for galloping horses and not depend entirely on the alertness of the riders." On the other hand, I was comforted to see no white crosses situated alongside the trails.)

We soldiered on, and of course, it paid off. We made thrilling discoveries. For example, we found what must be the official Pothole Testing Grounds for the region. Bradley Palmer has long slopes and wide meadows pocked with rocks and nicks and notches. Descending such an incline on your bike, it's impossible to control your facial muscles. Within seconds, jowls flapping, you're making a kind of *guggity-guggity-guggity* sound. My 12-year-old, with significantly smaller jowls, was more of a *dugga-digga-dugga-digga-dugga-digga*. A fellow passed us coming the opposite way. "Bumpy road, isn't it!" he cried happily. "*Buggada-buggada-buggada!*" My daughter waited till we were a discreet distance past him before turning to me and setting the record straight. "He's wrong," she scoffed. "It's *dugga-digga-dugga-digga-dugga*."

Later, traveling alongside Bradley Palmer's mushy wetlands, we experienced the joy of encountering actual wildlife.

"Look!" I yelped. "A beaver!"

"Dad, that's a squirrel."

"There! Beaver!"

"Dad, that's a turtle."

"Beaver!"

"Dad, that's a duck's butt."

I found the wildlife to be somewhat deceptive. But perhaps this should be no surprise in a state park named after an attorney of the early 1900s who represented Sinclair Oil in the Teapot Dome Scandal.

Since I had not previously spent a lot of time on bicycles, I realize now, in retrospect, that I probably should have consulted in advance with my friend Gordon Harris, one of Ipswich's foremost bicycling enthusiasts. Gordon might have spared me the oddly uncomfortable feeling I had, most of the day, in my lower regions, which I finally realized was the result of my seat being crooked. Not a lot, just 45 degrees or so.

Still, all in all, it was a fine day with the family in the great outdoors, with only the slightest of mishaps.

"Dad! Look! A beaver!

"Dad?

"Mom! Wait up! Dad fell off his bike again."

May 15th, 2014

A Three-Hour Tour de Farce

Just sit right back and you'll hear a tale / A tale of a fateful trip / That started from this Ipswich port / Aboard a tiny ship.

My wife and daughter and I decided to rent a canoe at Foote Brothers Canoe & Kayak Rental and check out the Ipswich River from something other than Topsfield Road at 40 mph. It's a very simple process: You give a nice-looking fellow your driver's license, and sign your name to a seemingly harmless contract which makes you responsible for nothing more than bringing back the stuff that the nice-looking young man is about to entrust to your care and keeping: one canoe, three life jackets, three square orange floaty seat thingies, and three paddles. Simple enough. You're going to paddle upstream, and then, when you get tired, you turn around and let the current carry you back downstream. When you get back to Foote Brothers, which is situated at the edge of a treacherous waterfall, you simply navigate back to the Foote Brothers dock, rather than going over the treacherous waterfall, and you're home free. You get your driver's license back, pay for the time you've spent on the water, go home, and post to Facebook. No problem.

I didn't notice any poster on the wall at Foote Brothers with any information along the lines of "How to Steer a Canoe" or "What to Do If Your Canoe Turns Over." There are some nice brochures available, but they seem to be mostly about how nice Foote Brothers Canoe & Kayak Rental is, and what a lot of interesting things you'll see along the Ipswich River, assuming you stay on or above the surface of it.

I sat in the front, and soon we realized that the person in front is responsible primarily for locomotion. This was OK, because I've been training with Jen Tougas at Personal Best, the world's only fitness studio located inside a brewery (Ipswich, you rock). So I figured I would just go into my usual Jen Tougas weight-training trance, dreaming of the sound of Ipswich Ale bottling machinery, and happily pull on those paddles all afternoon.

My wife Kristina sat in the back of the canoe, and soon we realized that she was largely responsible for steering. Also OK. She has been doing this since our wedding day, and thank heaven for it.

Lydia Charlotte, our middle schooler, sat in the middle. It soon became clear that she would be responsible for photographs, and commentary.

Lydia Charlotte wisely brought a waterproof camera. I brought my iPhone. My paranoid wife said I should leave it behind, but if I refused to obey her — because God forbid I should miss a text halfway up the Ipswich River — I should at least seal it in a Zip-Loc bag. Feeling foolish, I put my iPhone in a baggie and sealed it, leaving just a little air in the bag, just in case, har har har, we would later want the baggie to float.

We were doing pretty well until that place near the Willowdale Estate where the river narrows and the current picks up and if you're not going straight into the current — let's say you've drifted off to one side or the other, and you're trying to get back out into the middle of the river — well, forget about it.

As we got sideways to the current, the canoe tipped to its left. This was my first indication that the Ipswich River, unlike the high school pool I frequented in Chicago, is unheated.

All three of us were instantly in the water, thrashing around in our life jackets, carried downstream by the current. Kristina, a strong and seasoned swimmer, shouted instructions. For a few panicky moments it was touch-and-go. I labored valiantly to save our daughter's life. I was still laboring valiantly to save our daughter's life as our daughter pulled me from the river.

We were exhausted, sopping wet and goose-bumpy, but glad to be on terra firma. Then, however, the stuff we'd abandoned started appearing from upstream. This, you understand, was stuff that would cost us dearly if we didn't turn it back in to Foote Brothers. So back into the water I went, first to grab the boat, then to grab the paddles, and then to grab the three square orange floaty seat thingies. Oh — and my sunglasses.

When I thought I had finally finished with the rescue operations, so I could begin working on my hypothermia, Lydia Charlotte cried out, pointing frantically toward the water: "Dad!"

My iPhone was floating in a baggie down the Ipswich River.

Back in I went, one more time, dog-paddling like an actual dog, and finally retrieved my precious, fragile connection with civilization.

But I quickly discovered that one cannot return to shore with one hand dog-paddling and the other hand holding a baggie up out of the water. I might have held the baggie in my teeth — like a real dog — but I was too proud. And too cold. Also, I was drowning. So by the time I got my iPhone back to the riverbank, the seal had popped, the bag was sopped, and, you might say, the call was dropped. Permanently.

As we trudged back along the path through the trees, sodden and shivering, I was stricken by the realization that I had endangered my daughter's life. I knew she had been traumatized by the ordeal, emotionally damaged, perhaps forever. Soon, I was confronted by the truth. She turned to us with one eyebrow arched, a kind of crazy gleam in her eye.

"That was awesome!" she squealed — and went skipping down the path ahead of us.

July 10th, 2014

Cover Me

You take the woman you love to the beach. This is half the reason for moving to Ipswich in the first place. (The other half is Town Meetings. Love those things. I think they should be quarterly.)

So you take your woman to the beach. Especially on a cool, cloudy day, when hardly anybody else is there.

But you do not wear shoes. And you certainly do not wear socks with your shoes. No self-respecting beachcomber wears shoes to the beach, let alone shoes and socks.

It's not easy being a nerd.

I grew up in Chicago. You don't go barefoot in Chicago. You have to protect yourself against the jagged shards of a thousand shattered wine bottles and the venomous needle points of a million discarded syringes. At least you did in my neighborhood. Not everywhere, of course. Just on the sidewalks. And on the basketball courts.

I thought my shoes were OK for the beach. I heard someone call them "deck shoes," and the boardwalks (which take you from the parking lot over the protected dunes to Crane Beach) are really just long, skinny decks. The signs actually encourage you to use "footwear" on the boardwalk, because there's a risk of splinters. Footwear! Shoes are footwear! (And don't talk to me about flip-flops. Flip-flops are an abomination. No nagging little stem of rubber is going to ride between my toes, no sir. It's unnatural. It's shoes for me. Shoes all the way.)

But shoes are meant to be worn with socks. Sophisticated people do not wear shoes without socks. I grew up painfully average, longing to be sophisticated; so I never got into the tacky habit of wearing shoes without socks. Accordingly, when I went to the beach with the woman I love, I was, I confess, wearing shoes, and yes, I confess, I was also wearing socks.

Just over the boardwalk, she deposited her sandals near the edge of the dune grass. If she expected me to leave my shoes and socks there, she had another think coming. In Chicago you don't leave your shoes anywhere. You go to a beach on Lake Michigan and leave your shoes, and they're in a pawn shop window by the time you come looking for them.

So there she was, the woman I love, sauntering along the water's edge, in her lovely bare feet, and perhaps glancing from time to time at my shoes, and my socks, and my long pants — oh, wait. Did I mention my long pants? Look, my mother raised me to be careful. You never know when a sudden squall will come up, and you'll wish you had long pants. And a hoodie. It doesn't matter that it's 70 and sunny. Things change fast in New England.

My wife did make me leave my hoodie in the car.

It was a lovely stroll. Of course, she wanted to saunter through the shallows, and I wanted to stay up where the sand was firm, and if you're holding hands, you can't have it both ways. So much for holding hands. Remove my shoes and my socks, and actually *carry* them? The thought never entered my mind.

I would have gotten away with the shoes and socks, I do believe, if it hadn't been for the tide. As the tide goes out, it often forms long rivulets, streams cutting through the sand from the upper beach to the receding bay. These rivulets form pretty quickly, and widen even more quickly, and deepen as they widen. So maybe you've walked a long way along the water's edge toward Essex, and then you turn around to head back — and you find that you've got a series of gushing channels to traverse. If you're barefoot, it's not an issue. But you don't want to get your shoes and socks wet, do you?

All the way back, as we came to each gushing tributary, I was reduced to hunting for the narrowest place, then leaping from edge to edge, like a terrified cat. It was an untidy business, as I landed each time in soft, sopping wet sand, which caked all over my nice shoes, and sometimes even got on my nice socks.

"You could take off your shoes," she suggested quietly. I was silently horrified. And I knew she would get her come-uppance when we finally got back to the base of the boardwalk. I was quite sure that by now, her sandals had been stolen.

The sun had come out, and the beach was filling up with people. She had trouble finding her sandals, among the dozens of other pairs there.

Are there no criminals in Ipswich? Does no one recognize quality merchandise?

I love it here. But I am still adjusting.

November 20, 2014

Apples to Apples, Dust to Dust

There are four apple trees at the back of our property, lined up like dutiful soldiers. Sometimes I refer to them as John, Paul, George, and Ringo. Other times I call them Groucho, Harpo, Chico, and Zeppo. Depending on the season, they can also be the Four Horsemen of the Apocalypse.

When we bought our house in Ipswich, not so very long ago, I would not have known that these four trees were apple trees, because we had no such thing as apple trees in the desert, where I spent the previous two decades. (We had mesquite trees, which are judged not by the quality of their fruit, of which there is none, but by the sharpness of their barbs, which can cut you to the bone while you're attempting to scoot under them to adjust your pool sprinkler.)

But during our Ipswich house-hunting expedition, the selling agent Ingrid Miles pointed out the four apple trees. They were planted in a prim and perfect row, almost certainly the result of a 1958 middle school science project.

Since the day we bought the house, I have learned that apple trees do not just give you apples, year after year, like mindless droids. Apple trees wax and wane. They give and they withhold. They are operating under some higher authority: maybe God, or the Ipswich Zoning Board of Appeals.

So three summers ago, our apple trees decided to go artsy. They sprouted blossoms. Wonderful! Beautiful! They were the Vincent Van Goghs of the tree world. Not a single apple, but plenty of lovely little flowers.

Summer before last, having rested up, our trees exploded with big, beautiful, juicy apples. Thousands of fabulous apples. The ground was like cobblestone, covered with fallen apples. Visiting deer made themselves sick gorging on apples — I saw a doleful doe holding a cool washcloth to the forehead of her puking fawn — and still there were apples. My daughter the apple-lover ate apples around the clock. We had apple pies, apple bread, apple cobbler. We used apples to make cake, chutney, fritters, turnovers. Apple crisp, applesauce, apple butter. Juice, cider. Candy apples. Apple-stuffed everything. I believe at one point we had creamy baked savory-sesame-bacon-onion-cheddar-caramel-mustard-chicken-apple-ginger-fennel-horseradish-slaw-sausage-crepe-sauerkraut fondue. We bought a fruit-drying contraption and learned to make apple chips. We had apple in our oatmeal. In our salads. In our meatloaf. We used apples for decorations. If we could have somehow turned them into fuel, we would have been set for the winter.

In desperation, we put out an all-call to our friends, pleading with them to come pick apples. We left a basket, a long-handled apple-picking tool, and a ladder propped outside our house, so any random stranger could come collect apples without an appointment any time of the day or night. I considered putting up a big sign on Linebrook Road: "Maybe you can't pick your neighbors, but you CAN pick your neighbors' apples. PLEASE." Only one faithful friend, dear little Vicki Hughes from Poplar Street, came to our aid. She took away a mountain of apples taller than herself. And still we were drowning in apples.

Finally, this past summer, our temperamental trees for some reason decided to go Goth. All four of them produced the creepiest crop of apples in Ipswich history: black-splotched, misshapen little reddish blobs, their skins hideously cracked to reveal the soft, fleshy domicile of a legion of worms. *Appallus domestica*. Even the deer snorted and turned away.

This year, however, we have no apple problem. Our frightful fruits are being carted off, and it isn't costing us a penny. We learned last week that our next-door neighbor's two children, a kindergartener and his even-younger accomplice of a sister, have been slipping into our yard, snagging apples by the bagful, and proudly delivering these grotesque offerings — as their own family's personal gifts — to all the homes on the street.

These children have come up with a beautifully perfect crime. They sneak, they steal, they lie — and ruin their parents' reputation for classy gift-giving. But at the same time, the meadow is blissfully clear of apples. I love these kids. I hope next year to save the $50 curbside fee by getting them to handle my compost.

January 15, 2015

Shuck the Oysters

If you grew up in the middle of the country, like I did — far from the ocean — there are certain activities in which you should never attempt to engage. They are beyond you. Operating a sailboat, for example. I have never done this. It would be crazy. Practically suicidal. Deep-sea diving. Deep-sea fishing. Deep-sea anything. No way. These are functions intrinsically restricted to natives of the coast. Landlubbers cannot acquire these skills. You can try to learn, but you will fail. In the process, you may endanger yourself and others. I know whereof I speak. Recently, I was foolish enough to engage in one of the actions well known to be off-limits to inlanders. It was my mistake. No Chicagoan should ever try what I tried.

"Shuck some oysters," my wife said.

No problem, I thought. We live in New England now. We can buy oysters, still in their shells, at the local grocery store. If we wish for a dish delish and oysterish, we don't need to pry these delightful delicacies out of a can, or unscrew the lid off a common jar, or beg a friend for help, and slide them all gooey and gray out of a Ziploc bag. We can go straight to nature. We can take the animals live, bring them home — while they still think they're invincible — then slaughter them ourselves, personally, one on one.

Not that I had ever done this myself, you understand.

But it was about time, I figured — in fact, the universe had just given me a sign that I was destined to enter the oyster-shucking season of my life. A couple days earlier, a house guest presented me with a lovely gift: an oyster knife, hand-crafted by her late father. When the oyster-shucker is ready, the oyster knife appears.

Shucking cannot be very hard, I said to myself. For starters, it has a silly-sounding name. We don't use a romantic Frenchified term like *écailler* or a euphemism like *releasing*. This is not "deliverance." We don't call it "emancipation." It's shucking. Plain and simple.

My wife made every attempt to advise me. Her own personal history, however, is as shucking-challenged as mine, so I felt no real compulsion to heed her counsel. She was suggesting babyish things like holding the oyster in a dishtowel to protect my hand, and placing the point of the knife in the hinge of the oyster the way beginners do, and twisting the knife a bit to gain leverage rather than applying intense pressure to force my way in. All nonsense, of course.

I am not a total ignoramus. I have been to Ipswich art gallery receptions attended by notable Ipswich resident Bill Sargent, an outspoken environmentalist and prolific writer well known for showing up at gala events with oysters he's harvested himself. I've watched Bill Sargent doing the oyster thing at parties. I've seen him thronged by the oyster-lovers. Don't think I haven't paid attention to his shucking technique.

So as I stood over my kitchen sink, my face reddening, my hands grappling with that first oyster of the dozen, I actually said — under my breath, smoke spurting from my ears, knowing what my wife was thinking — "No, I am *not* going to call Bill Sargent for advice!"

And at that very instant, the keepsake oyster knife lost its tentative foothold on the creature's crusty lip under the insistent pressure of my clumsy fist.

The shell splintered open, and one enormous shard came slashing through my thumb.

Let the record show, it was the shell, not the knife — it was the shuckee, not the instrument of shuckification — that severed so much of my epidermis from my musculature.

And let the record show that my adult son, who happened to be standing nearby, saved my life by running for Band-aids.

It was also my son who wisely went to his iPhone and asked, "How do you shuck an oyster?" Within seconds, Legal Seafood's head chef was offering up a YouTube video on the subject. I must report, sadly, that *le chef* was demonstrating every detail of my wife's previously ignored advice.

So today, I am older, and wiser, and bandaged.

The oysters were scrumptious.

I offer the following as a gift to future generations:

THE OUTSIDAH'S LANDLUBBER OYSTER-SHUCKING GUIDE

PREPARATION: Wear gloves.

EQUIPMENT: Oyster knife. Bandages.
Tourniquet. Oxygen optional.

BONUS NOTE: Watch the YouTube video
first.

March 26, 2015

Sit Down, Stand Up, Rah Rah Rah!

The Ipswich Zoning Board of Appeals has finally settled one of the most agonizing questions of our time: the question of how many people can sit in the dining room at the Ipswich Inn, and how many people can stand up.

The answer turns out to be quite simple, really. The Inn henceforth will be allowed to have 36 people sitting, or 52 standing. I for one am relieved. For the time being, at least, the people of Ipswich are no longer in danger of a 37th person sitting down in the dining room at the Ipswich Inn, nor a 53rd person standing up.

Of course innkeeper Ray Morley now bears the burden of compliance — or, though I hesitate to use the term, enforcement. He will have his hands full. What if there are 36 people seated at breakfast, and someone stands up to use the restroom? They're over the limit. I'm not sure of the liability question, but I believe Ray is going to have to drag that person, still in their chair, into the hallway, where they're legal to stand up.

Or maybe I have the math wrong. The numbers are intimidating. I assume if Ray can have 36 sitting or 52 standing, then he could also have half of each number: 18 sitting and 26 standing. It gets complicated. If one of the 26 sits down, I think Ray will have to haul one of the 18 to their feet. But wait — will this be OK — 27 standing, 17 sitting? I don't think so. According to the ZBA formula, a seated person is taking up 1.44 times as much space as a standing person. Every person who sits down will require 1.44 people to stand up. This is silly. It's not physically possible for 44% of a person to stand up, leaving the remaining 56% seated. I'm afraid this person will have no choice but to crouch.

Or perhaps it would be OK to round off the numbers: a ratio of 1-to-1.44 is nearly the same as a ratio of 1-to-1.50. Which is exactly the same as 2-to-3. This could work: When two people sit down, three people stand up. It's not exactly the ZBA formula, but it's pretty darn close. It will make the Inn dining room into a huge game of whack-a-mole, but at least, thank goodness, there will be compliance.

Let me warmly urge you *not* to let these new regulations frighten you into avoiding the Ipswich Inn for breakfast. I was there this past Friday; everything seemed normal. And I've urged Ray to get a slide rule. He can meet you at the door and let you know whether you'll be starting your meal sitting or standing. Also, his sidekick Becky Gayton can put an app on her iPad to track diner movements and predict how long it will be before you're asked to change positions. True, you might start in on your "McMorley special" at a pleasant table overlooking the lawn, only to finish it standing in the corner near the coat tree. But have no fear. You can lean quite comfortably against the wall. So far, the ZBA has not ruled against leaning.

April 3, 2016

If You Can Hear Me,
Tap Three Times

Please help me. Come rescue me. I'm in here, I promise.
Somewhere beyond the mudroom. If this message reaches you, please, I
beg you, come to my house, find some way, I have no idea how, to get
through the mudroom, and haul me out.

I have no idea how this happened, getting barricaded in my own
house, by my own stuff. Where I come from, we didn't have
mudrooms. In the Arizona desert, we didn't have mud. Mud, as I
understand it, is a concoction of dirt and water. Dirt, I get. Over the
course of my desert years, I became familiar with a whole range of dirt
types. We had sand, grit, gravel, dust. In the urban areas, we had grime,
filth, soot, even grunge. Plenty of what you'd call dirt. But hardly ever
did we come across dirt combined with water. Because for the most
part, the only water we ever saw was piped in from the often-dry Salt
River and carefully restricted to exquisitely profligate fountains out in
front of insanely lavish resorts.

Hence, no mud. Hence, no mudrooms.

But moving to New England and shopping for an antique house, I quickly discovered the alternate reality, the fifth-dimensional space, known as the mudroom. It is the humblest of chambers, bearing the humblest of names. The mudroom is never called the "entryway," even though it is a way of entering. God forbid a New Englander should ever call it the "foyer" — that would be way too fancy. Likewise for "reception area." And "vestibule" would be too churchy. No, this is the "mudroom." It's a wretched little cube, tacked on to an otherwise pleasant house, and named for a mixture of water and dirt.

It's also, apparently, magnetic. In my very limited experience living in New England, I find that mudrooms attract junk. Not just metal junk, like a normal magnet. No, mudroom magnetism is eclectic. In the mudrooms of New England, you're liable to find hats and coats and scarves and boots, and whatever tools don't quite fit the current season, and the carrier you take your pet to the vet in. A few valiant folks are diligent enough to keep their mudrooms from accumulating clutter, but they mostly fall into one of two unfortunate categories: they're either haggard from the continuous effort, or totally wired on caffeine, if not something stronger. And if you have school-age children — even just one of them — there is absolutely no hope for your mudroom. You're going to find yourself clambering over an ever-morphing mountain of rubber boots, forgotten schoolbooks, splintered skateboards, and the part of the sandwich they put down to get their mittens on.

I guess it's clear now that I simply couldn't keep up. Or maybe "couldn't" is the wrong word. Maybe I just made bad life choices. Maybe if I had assiduously attended to my mudroom, perhaps just removing a small percentage of the debris each day, say 50 or 60 items, I could have stayed ahead of the buildup. Maybe my priorities were misplaced. If I had spent less time making a living, if I hadn't wasted all those hours caring for my children, or eating right and getting plenty of exercise, I wouldn't find myself in the predicament I'm in today: trapped in my house behind a mass of assorted objects so intensely packed and intricately interlocked that I can hardly even get a cell signal in here anymore.

It's not as if I could simply advertise a garage sale and hope for neighbors to take this stuff away, item by item, for a dollar apiece. This is not stuff anybody else would want, under any imaginable circumstances. There's rusty barbecue equipment, and the grimy fishing hat that I always used to wear while barbecuing, before I couldn't find the barbecue equipment anymore. There's a Frisbee so warped it won't Fris anymore. There's a square of cardboard with FREE scrawled on it in huge letters, which last year advertised our bumper crop of apples on a table out by the street until someone took all the apples and the table the sign was taped to. There's a hat somebody gave to my wife which she would never wear in a million years. A random light fixture. A spool of kite string knotted beyond redemption. A haggard sweatshirt celebrating the Chicago Bears' Super Bowl victory. Mounds of various colors and textures of fabric probably constituting clothing from my daughter's fifth-, sixth-, seventh-, and early eighth-grade eras. And innumerable as-yet-unreturned empty Appleton Farms milk bottles. If the price of milk goes up out there, it will be because we have $62,418 worth of their bottle inventory in our mudroom.

So I implore you, if you're reading this, take pity on a poor fool. Bring a Bobcat. Bring a blowtorch. Possibly bring a priest. Whatever you think might help. Get me out of here. I know it won't be easy. But I'm pleading with you on humanitarian grounds. My daughter will graduate in four years, and I want to be there.

143

March 23rd, 2019

Canst Thou Hear Me Now?

We cannot be absolutely sure if there is a God (that's why they call it "faith"), and if there *is* a God, we cannot be absolutely sure what gender God is (if the concept of gender even applies to God), nor can we be absolutely sure how or whether God speaks to human beings (or whether the concept of "speaking" even applies to God), nor can we know for sure *where* God speaks *from*, nor exactly where *you* have to be *positioned* in order to *hear* from God.

So there's a lot we don't know.

However, the Episcopalians of Ipswich, Massachusetts, could not be blamed for thinking they know the answer to these questions, because of what happened in church last week.

So I'm there, at Ascension Memorial Church, in my usual spot, on the left (no political symbolism intended), in the fourth row from the back, on the aisle. It's the Lenten season, so of course we're extra-serious doing that part of the liturgy where we express penitence for our sins:

"Most merciful God, we confess that we have sinned against you in thought, word, and deed, by what we have done, and by what we have left undone...."

Then, within a few seconds, we're making our specific request of the Almighty: "Have mercy on us and forgive us...."

In the brief silence that follows, there comes a distinct, fully audible response, in a perfectly articulate female voice:

"I don't know how to help you."

In that moment, those of us who sit toward the back of the Episcopal church realize the truth — a beautiful, multi-faceted truth that human beings have sought after for thousands of years: God does indeed exist, and God actually does speak to ordinary people. And where can you hear from God? At the rear of the Episcopal church. Maybe even bigger news: God is a woman. And probably the biggest news of all: Unfortunately, She doesn't have a solution to the sin thing.

Of course, the moment we heard from God, I glanced around at my fellow parishioners, to share in this historic moment of revelation. I expected them to be jubilant, as was I. But I immediately realized I should have known better. This is a pattern: Again and again, down through history, human beings encounter the divine but misunderstand it, or flee from it, or reject it, or some combination thereof. Our modern-day Ipswich Episcopalians, sad to say, were no different. I could see in their faces that they were nothing close to jubilant over hearing the voice of God — or possibly they had a negative reaction to the fact that She was female. People are funny about traditional religious notions, I reminded myself, like "God the Father," for example.

I faced front again, and reverently returned to worship. Only after another few moments of quiet contemplation, as the Lenten liturgy continued — I think it was someplace around "we proclaim the mystery of faith" — did I begin to feel a vague sensation of doubt seeping into my faith. As I replayed my memory of God's entirely pleasant female voice, it gradually dawned on me — to my considerable puzzlement — that the voice had seemed to come from the vicinity of my butt.

And then, in the twinkling of an eye, didst mine revelation wax complete.

That wasn't God speaking. That was Siri. When I went from standing to kneeling, the iPhone in my back pocket got smushed, and the considerable bulk of my derrière pushed against the button that summons Siri. In that moment, she came down from cyber-heaven, an unseen angel of servitude; but hearing no further request from me, she felt obligated to offer an excuse:

"I don't know how to help you."

She certainly did help me, regardless of her ignorance on the subject. She taught me, through this embarrassing episode, that it isn't enough to set your iPhone on "airplane mode" if you want to guarantee that you won't be noisily interrupted. Just detaching the device from any wireless signal doesn't keep Siri from slipping in unawares and chatting you up whenever she feels like conversation is in order. It's also not enough to turn your volume all the way down. Even "mute" isn't enough to keep Siri from raising her voice to high heaven, and — as I have learned the hard way — she is obviously oblivious to the tradition of quiet in sacred spaces.

Churchgoer? Theatregoer? Moviegoer? Lecture attendee? Classroom student? Be advised: total "power off" is your only sure bet when it comes to that garrulous girl in your gadget. Trust me: This is not something you have to take on faith. There *is* a Siri, she *is* female, and she *doth* speak to human beings. And whence doth she speak? She speaks from wherever you've tucked your phone.

As for where *you* have to be positioned in order to hear from Siri — well, we know for sure that *kneeling* is on the list.

November 28th, 2019

All I Want for Christmas
(Or: 17 Ways to Make Ipswich Even Better)

Glad tidings! 'Tis the season for 'em.

The *Ipswich Local News* has brought us a great report on the value of our beloved town: If you add up all its taxable property, Ipswich is now worth more than $3.06 billion.

This is awesome. What a bargain. There is no longer any question what I want for Christmas.

I want Ipswich.

No, you don't have to buy it for me. And my wife sure won't. She is such a miser. Doesn't matter. If it's only $3.06 billion — okay, okay, a little more than $3.06 billion, but let's not split hairs — I think I can swing this purchase.

The Institution for Savings is a very generous bank; they obsessively sponsor stuff all over the North Shore — so I believe they are going to be very open to my grant application. But even if the grant doesn't work out, and I have to apply for a conventional loan, no problem. A $3.06 billion loan, at, let's say, 3.5% over, let's say, a 30-year term, means monthly loan payments of only $13.74 million a month. If IFS will give me a sweeter interest rate, this gets even easier. If I can get a few key friends to go in with me — I'm thinking Winthrop, Wasserman, Wigglesworth, a couple other names of renown (they don't all have to start with W) — I believe this is doable. (I will want my partners to take minority positions, of course.)

It's a very attractive proposition, when you think about it: By the time this loan is paid off, as I approach my 100th birthday, I will have paid significantly *less* than $5 billion in principal and interest.

And look what I get out of it! I will essentially own the finest town on the North Shore. A historical landmark. An exquisite beach. A model of civic engagement. Just look at how polite people are, in the weekly police log, and at Select Board meetings.

But life is going to become even *more* idyllic here, when I own the whole thing. Just you wait and see:

1. I'll lift the ban on free-range chickens. Because chickens clucking through your yard are charming.
2. Most of those pesky permits that you need to start a business in Ipswich? Gone. Ipswich residents won't have to go to Rowley to become successful business owners anymore. Imagine Village Pancake House on Central Street! We might get our own Winfrey's!
3. Farmers' market on the Green every weekend, with plenty of food for sale. Health inspector's approval no longer required.
4. Ipswich churchgoers will finally be free to cook their own barbecue at home and serve it at church events. This single breakthrough will improve our quality of life immeasurably.
5. Our downtown area will finally get commonsense zoning, thanks to me. We'll increase foot traffic by bringing restaurants, gift shops, and novelties to our storefronts, and steering the ho-hum low-traffic offices of realtors, lawyers, and other professionals to nearby but decidedly ho-hum low-traffic locations.
6. We'll extend the Riverwalk all the way, with no break for those annoying offices near the dam. The owners of those annoying offices will get dibs on the best of the ho-hum low-traffic spaces.
7. Marty's will be miraculously resurrected. Donuts for everybody!
8. All new construction will be outfitted for solar power. This should have happened already, but sometimes you just need a dictator to get things done. To keep costs low, solar panels will be installed by passionate Ipswich High School Environmental Club student-volunteers.

9. The two electric-vehicle charging stations on the Elm Street lot are nice; but since my car is electric, we'll be installing charging stations absolutely everywhere.
10. Five Corners? That'll be a rotary. Actually sort of a hexagon. To make space for it, we'll need to relocate the Appleton office building and the Christian Science church, and we'll scoot that cute little war memorial up the hill.

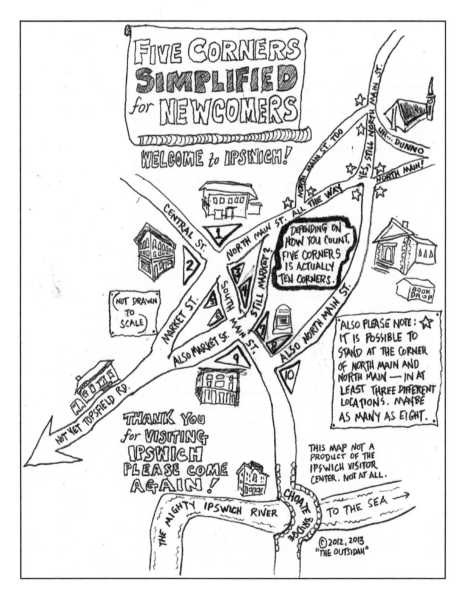

11. Lord's Square will finally get straightened out. Our traffic safety record is gonna skyrocket.

12. We'll also turn Liberty Street around, so it's one-way going *away* from Lord's Square, and the people who've been trapped there for years trying to get into traffic can finally get on with their lives.

13. The dam on the Ipswich River? Bye-bye. And when, as a result of our beloved river's damlessness, riverfront properties no longer have a river on their fronts, we'll make the Riverwalk even longer. Before long, you may be able to take the Riverwalk all the way to the Walmart in North Reading.

14. On Linebrook Road, the green line will be replaced with a white line, and the white line will be replaced with a green line. This will decrease confusion and increase safety for bicyclists, except for the color-blind ones.

15. On my first day as the owner of Ipswich, I'll place an order for a left-turn signal at Argilla Road. I won't be surprised if they rename Crane Beach in my honor out of sheer gratitude.

16. Mandatory curbside composting. Our health inspector, with nothing else to do, will come around and check your garbage for stuff that could have been composted. Slackers have to put in a week slaving at the transfer station.

17. You've seen the Galickis' fabulous Christmas light display on Linebrook Road? We'll pay them to do that in everybody's front yard.

I think you can see now why the Town of Ipswich is all I want for Christmas. Life is going to be so beautiful with me in charge.

"Hello, Institution for Savings? Loan Department, please."

November 27th, 2013

The Circle of (Ipswich) Life

The circle of life is a beautiful thing, except when it's bloody-faced lions gobbling zebra guts.

Ipswich has its own circle of life, with no gobbling of anybody's guts, fortunately. It's a five-stage circle:

Stage 1. We're driving along when suddenly a colossal *thunk* wrenches the steering wheel from our grasp, and we realize there's a major new pothole where there wasn't one before, and we'll have to remember to steer around it next time. But we don't remember, and we go *thunk* again, and we cuss. Then another pothole appears, not too far away, and then another. We learn to pick our way through the war zone, our Chrysler creeping among the land mines. Eventually, however, the plethora of potholes is so annoying that we actually pick up the phone and dial Town Hall and complain.

The Ipswich circle of life continues. Next, Stage 2. On the second floor of Town Hall, we find our intrepid Town Manager frowning into her computer screen. She has a million problems to worry about — it's like flies harassing a wildebeest. The moment she shoos one with her tail, another lands on her nose. You just get FinCom settled down, and the Rec Committee is on you. Now, on top of all this, there's the nagging little buzzing sound of citizens calling to complain about a certain passel of potholes.

Finally, the buzzing reaches critical mass. The Town Manager grabs her phone. She barks into the handset: "Get me the pothole guys." Soon, the pothole SWAT team descends on the much-maligned stretch of street. The hot black glop oozes, the smoothing specialists do their smoothing, and the plague is finally over. You can glide on this street now. You could land a small plane. You can rollerblade in your sleep. You can *speed*.

Stage 3. We're walking along on our nice new level road when a Harley roars past, doing 55. Soccer mom in an SUV whooshes past like a shark. Delivery truck roars. Old guy in an antique convertible: *Raaaaaarrr!*

This is the stage where drivers, freed from the menacing moonscape, put the pedal to the metal. It's such a joy to sail over level blacktop, you can't stop yourself. You speed.

The Ipswich circle of life continues. On Elm Street, at a massive multi-paneled console, a diligent young man in an Ipswich Police Department uniform is trying to answer all the phone calls. The young man finally rips the headset off and lunges into Chief Nikas's office.

"Everyone's complaining about the speeders!"

Chief Nikas is a calm soul. Like the wise gorilla father overseeing his troop of little gorillas in the jungle, he knows what to get exercised about, and what not to.

"Well done, grasshopper," he says to the boy. "Keep treating them nicely."

He waves the boy out. Not enough cruisers, not enough cops. Resources must be expended wisely. Stop a speeder on School Street on Saturday, miss a murder on Mitchell on Monday.

Still, the cries of the citizens are not without effect. Someone else hears them. Someone higher up than the wildebeest, or the gorilla.

Stage 4. Mother Nature, sitting in an ancient La-Z-Boy on her celestial screen porch, finishes her last gulp of gin, picks up a pack of Winstons and knocks one out. Lighting it, she rasps out of the side of her mouth: "Bring me another, will ya, honey?" Her husband grunts from the kitchen.

Soon St. Peter ambles out of the house in his undershirt. Most people don't realize that Mother Nature is married to St. Peter. He hands her another gin on the rocks, drops himself into the rocking chair next to her, takes a glug of his Corona. It would be a good life up here, except for the almost constant array of noises coming up from below — sort of a buzzing, whining, clicking, ticking, clucking — the sound of human grievance.

"They're making me crazy," St. Peter mumbles.

"It's the speeders," Mother Nature replies, her voice scratching like steel wool. She sighs heavily, smoke streaming from her nostrils. She groans as she leans forward to pull herself out of the lounger. She stubs out her butt, shuffles to the door, steps down to her front yard — which is basically a cloud. She stretches her arms wide. The cloud-yard turns gray, then smoky black. She returns to the screen porch, drops into the La-Z-Boy.

"Whadja do to 'em?" St. Peter asks.

"Winterized the jerks," she snorts. "Snow, ice, sleet, hail. Standard New England winter. Can't speed in that stuff." She picks up her glass. "Aw, heck. Get me another one, will ya, honey?"

Stage 5. Down on the street, winter falls. Snow howls out of the sky. Hail hails and sleet sleets. Ice stretches over the asphalt like deadly cellophane.

None of which slows the New England drivers a bit. They race through town, engines roaring, their death-machines flying over the slippery glare, doing 40 where the signs say 25. The complaining continues.

And under the snow and ice, things are not well. The black semisolid bituminous road-surfacing blacktop, which began life happily in a sizzling construction company vat at solar-storm temperatures, is now shivering pathetically under its frigid bedspread. The moisture trickles into every wrinkle, the freezing painfully presses every vein, the asphalt cracks and crumbles, its strength slipping, its spirit broken.

And in the spring, as the speeders dash over the fragments, the corpse begins hollowing out. A flaw opens into a gap. A crack becomes a cavity. Until soon, once again, we have potholes.

Another unexpected *thunk* of that right front tire. Another unanticipated cussword. And the Ipswich circle of life is complete. Or rather, it begins anew.

Thank God for the Winthrops

The Winthrops started Ipswich.

They live here to this day.

Thank God they let the rest of us

Stay.

Credit Due

Thanks to **Dan MacAlpine** (lovingly depicted at right), longtime editor of the *Ipswich Chronicle* (now the *Chronicle & Transcript*), who invited me to write a column, and then couldn't get rid of me. He still can't.

Thanks to my wife **Kristina Brendel** (badly depicted at left), who serves as "first reader" for every column I produce. She is truly insightful and wise, and her feedback hardly ever makes me cry.

And thanks to my ever-faithful, ever-excellent, ever-patient proofreader, **Sarah Christine Jones** (not depicted here, as a kindness), of Wadsworth, Ohio. She graciously edited all the previous books in the series. (Please don't hold her responsible for this one.)

Let Us Connect

- Doug's contact info is at **DougBrendel.com**.
- His New England humor blog is **Outsidah.com**.
- His even snarkier blog is **EnglishIsAComplicatedLanguage.com**.
- His most important stuff is at **NewThing.net**.
- Look for Doug on Facebook, Twitter, Instagram, and everywhere fine writers are sold.

NEW THING
A Response of the Heart for Belarus

Ipswich in Stitches was conceived as a fundraiser for **New Thing**, the humanitarian-aid charity based in Belarus, in the former USSR, founded and led by Doug and Kristina Brendel.

A team of Belarusian workers devote themselves to bringing hundreds of tons — millions of dollars' worth — of donated food and goods into Belarus each year, sharing this aid face-to-face with people in need from all walks of life:

- ✓ Orphans and foster families
- ✓ Abused and abandoned children
- ✓ Children and adults with disabilities
- ✓ The homeless and poor
- ✓ Hospital patients, sick kids in other institutions

And the list goes on.

This work of compassion, officially and gratefully recognized by the government of Belarus, is **all-volunteer** in the U.S., so every penny you donate goes into Belarus. We're happy to advise you that any donation you make to New Thing is eligible for U.S. income-tax deduction to the full extent of the law.

You can visit the former USSR without ever leaving home!

To receive photo reports and updates on New Thing's work in Belarus, simply visit NewThing.net and provide your name and email address.

We'll be happy to hear from you! Thank you!

And we'd be grateful to have your help. To donate, visit our donation page at NewThing.net. Thanks again!

Please visit us, follow us, like us!
Web: **NewThing.net**
Facebook: **New Thing, Inc.**
Instagram: **NewThingNet**
Thank you!

The Plural of *Proviso*, Whatever It Is

1. The material in this book is just Doug Brendel's. He wrote it all as a volunteer, so anything in this book that also appeared elsewhere is Doug's responsibility. Don't blame the newspaper, the website, or that gossip in the Shaving Needs aisle at Market Basket who insists on telling you all about the Outsidah's most recent outrage.

2. The legendary John Updike might not actually sit in a cloud in heaven and inspire the Outsidah. But just try to prove he doesn't.

3. No clams were fried in the printing of this book.

www.DougBrendel.com